D0962113

Achieving Optimal Enrollments and Tuition Revenues

A Guide to Modern Methods
of Market Research, Student Recruitment,
and Institutional Pricing

William Ihlanfeldt

Achieving Optimal Enrollments and Tuition Revenues

Jossey-Bass Publishers

San Francisco • Washington • London • 1980

ACHIEVING OPTIMAL ENROLLMENTS AND TUITION REVENUES
A Guide to Modern Methods of Market Research,
Student Recruitment, and Institutional Pricing
by William Ihlanfeldt

Copyright © 1980 by: Jossey-Bass Inc., Publishers
433 California Street
San Francisco, California 94104
&
Jossey-Bass Limited
28 Banner Street
London EC1Y 8QE

Library of Congress Cataloging in Publication Data

Ihlanfeldt, William.
    Achieving optimal enrollments and tuition
revenues.

    Bibliography: p. 251
    Includes index.
    1. Universities and colleges—United States—
Admission. 2. College costs—United States.
3. Marketing research. I. Title.
LB2351.2.I35   378'.105'0973   79-92463
ISBN 0-87589-452-6

Manufactured in the United States of America

JACKET DESIGN BY WILLI BAUM

FIRST EDITION

Code 8013

The Jossey-Bass
Series in Higher Education

Preface

~~~~~~

My first experience as an admission counselor for a relatively unknown small college led me to conclude that the admission profession consisted essentially of spending a great deal of time in an automobile, visiting three or four secondary schools during the day to talk with counselors and prospective students, and making phone calls in the evening to local prospects whom I had missed during the day.

This experience forced me to think that there should be a more efficient and professional way to inform prospective students and secondary school counselors about the pluses and minuses of a given college. Over the years, however, I found that the process did not change: the secondary school visit continued to be considered the most effective as well as the most commonly accepted form of contact. The responsibilities of different admission offices varied little from year to year, and their planning processes were basically nonexistent.

The ideas and information in this book have evolved during the past twenty years of experience and stem from my desire to seek alternative processes of contacting prospective students. During these years I have come to believe that the primary difference between a successful and a nonsuccessful admission operation is the degree to which the director of admission views his or her role as affecting the environment as a manager, in contrast to responding to the environment as a counselor. Managing and counseling are not mutually exclusive roles, of course, but the principal role that the admission director must play is that of manager: one who is responsible not only for orchestrating an extensive communication process between prospective students and those who participate in the learning process on a daily basis—undergraduate students and members of the faculty— but also for planning and assessing this process.

For admission directors to approach these tasks as managers requires, in many cases, new information and techniques that permit systematic planning, programming, and assessment. The application of marketing concepts to enrollment planning and student recruitment provides the necessary generic ideas and methodology. The language of marketing was introduced into higher education admissions no more than a decade ago, but colleges and universities have applied basic marketing techniques throughout their history to curricular planning and assessment. They have periodically upgraded course offerings to accommodate student interests; they have updated program requirements to appeal to anticipated interests. Such programmatic change in relation to consumer demand is the foundation of marketing theory. The conceptual framework for the application of this theory involves (1) better market research and institutional assessment (2) to permit better planning (3) to facilitate better communication with potential markets. This book applies this theory and conceptual framework to enrollment planning and student recruitment. It seeks to help administrators improve their effectiveness in achieving their enrollment objectives by managing cost-effective recruitment and admission strategies.

In other words, this is a how-to-do-it book. For the president or admission officer who is seeking a simple or a single answer to enrollment shortfalls, it does not contain one such answer, but the information it does contain should provide a systematic means of attacking the problem more effectively. To achieve this goal, the book is divided into four sections following the introductory chapter: one on research; a second on planning; a third on implementing institutional and communication strategies; and a fourth on pertinent resource materials. The specific examples stem from my own institution, Northwestern University, but the concepts apply to all types of institutions, both public and private. For example, the material about the pricing of higher education should be useful at public institutions as well as private. The previous literature on pricing as applied to higher education is quite limited and the tuition revenue produced by a pricing policy increasingly affects the budget and operations of public institutions, while in the majority of independent institutions such revenue supplies the very foundation for the institution's continued existence.

The text covers everything from the current state of higher education as reflected by potential demand to the competitive position of similar institutions in relation to their market, with major attention to student decision making, the identification, development, and segmentation of markets, and alternative program and communication strategies as well as pricing. From it, I hope readers will grasp how directors of admission can become directors of marketing and, as marketing experts, can see their task as an attempt to improve the product that their institution offers. Because of their concern for marketing, they can be catalysts for institutional improvement.

Many educators still mistakenly believe that marketing simply means sales, promotion, and hucksterism. On the contrary, the application of marketing principles to higher education goes far beyond promotional activities to address the core of the educational process. By asking "To what extent are students satisfied with their experience at our institution?" and "Are there markets for our educational offerings beyond our traditional pool of applicants?" as well as "Can we expand our educational services to tap new markets?," a marketing orientation may be the most appropriate and responsible response to the problems of "fair practice" identified by the Carnegie Council on Policy Studies in Higher Education in its recent report (1979) and to the problems of "the integrity of higher education" discussed by the American Assembly in its meeting on that topic (1979).

In developing my thinking on this subject, I am grateful to members of my staff who have been unwilling to accept standard answers or excuses to pressing questions. Special recognition is due

Roger Campbell, Grier Davis, Daniel Hall,and Donald Gwinn, who contributed uniquely by providing the research methodology, and Gaye Abbott, who lent her support by typing the manuscript.

Evanston, Illinois   WILLIAM IHLANFELDT
January 1980

Contents

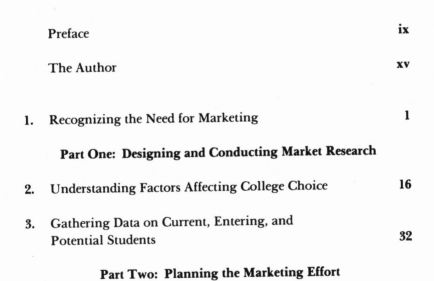

The Author

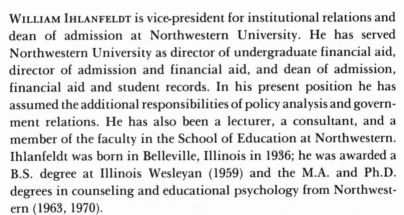

WILLIAM IHLANFELDT is vice-president for institutional relations and dean of admission at Northwestern University. He has served Northwestern University as director of undergraduate financial aid, director of admission and financial aid, and dean of admission, financial aid and student records. In his present position he has assumed the additional responsibilities of policy analysis and government relations. He has also been a lecturer, a consultant, and a member of the faculty in the School of Education at Northwestern. Ihlanfeldt was born in Belleville, Illinois in 1936; he was awarded a B.S. degree at Illinois Wesleyan (1959) and the M.A. and Ph.D. degrees in counseling and educational psychology from Northwestern (1963, 1970).

　　　During his tenure at Northwestern he acquired funding from the Wieboldt Foundation for the education of minorities; this program, which he directed in the mid 1960s, has substantially changed the demography of the student body. Other noteworthy accomplishments include the implementation of an integrated admission and financial aid operation; the development of an alumni-admission council that has become a model for other institutions; the application of marketing principles to student recruitment; and the design of the University's pricing and loan strategies. Since 1968, Ihlanfeldt has been involved in writing numerous proposals for federal and state student aid legislation, an interest nourished by his membership on the board of directors of the Student Loan Marketing Association, the policy committee of the Consortium on Financing Higher Education, and the executive committee of the Federation of Independent Illinois Colleges and Universities. His articles have been published in *College Board Review*, *Change Magazine*, *Case Currents*, *Liberal Education*, and *NACAC Journal*.

To my Mother
Olivia Ihlanfeldt Fatsis
whose energies and dedication appear to be boundless

Achieving Optimal Enrollments and Tuition Revenues

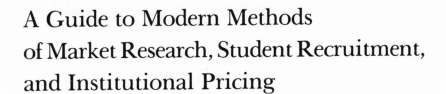

A Guide to Modern Methods
of Market Research, Student Recruitment,
and Institutional Pricing

1

Recognizing the Need for Marketing

Our colleges are not filled because we do not furnish
the education desired by the people. . . . We have produced
an article for which the demand is diminishing. We sell it at
less than cost, and the deficiency is made up by charity. We
give it away, and still the demand diminishes. Is it not time to
inquire whether we cannot furnish an article for which the
demand will be, at least, somewhat more remunerative?
[Francis Wayland, 1850, p. 34].

Since these words were expressed more than a hundred years ago by
President Francis Wayland of Brown University in his prescient
report to Brown's trustees, higher education in the United States has
become one of the largest service industries in the world, aspiring to
meet not only educational needs of individual students and of the
society but its own needs as well. For the past twenty-five years, higher
education has been experiencing unprecedented growth. Without
any real national or regional plans, for example, its expenditures

1

increased from under $5 billion in 1958 to over $47 billion in 1978 (Andersen, 1976, p. 62; Golladay and Noel, 1978, p. 212), and enrollments rose from 3 million students to 11.5 million (Andersen, 1976, p. 80; Pepin, 1978).

However, the end of this era of growth may be near. Echoes of Francis Wayland's concern are being heard, and forecasts of zero growth or decreases in enrollment during the 1980s are common, based on the accelerating decrease in the number of high-school-age youth. College and university policy analysts, planners, and administrators may be able to insulate their institutions from the vagaries of the marketplace, but to do so they must understand this marketplace and become demand-sensitive in responding to the developing interests and needs of new student markets as well as the changing interests and needs of their traditional market. For those willing and able to respond, the decrease in the number of high school graduates may lead to a new period of opportunity; but for others whose institutions are too embedded in tradition and structure, this decrease may bring about not only a period of decline but the possibility of collapse. Whether this new era represents a new morning or a late afternoon and evening for institutions depends on individual and institutional recognition of higher education as a service industry.

Growth of the Education Industry

As a service industry, higher education faces the question "Who wants to be educated under what conditions?" rather than deciding unilaterally "Whom will we decide to educate under our prescribed conditions?" (Vermilye, 1974). It may seem unnecessary to emphasize that higher education is a service industry, but, historically, few faculty members and administrators have perceived their role as that of meeting consumer needs. This is not to say that many of them have not been responsive to student needs. The continued demand for institutional programs is significant testimony that people derive benefits from them. However, the industry of higher education evolved with little or no direct input from consumers, and, in many large universities, faculty members have often created programs that responded to no other demand than their own research interests and the availability of research support. Not until 1964, when Mario Savio and other students challenged the establishment at the University of California at Berkeley, did the reality of higher education as a major service industry become evident in America (University of California, Berkeley, Academic Senate, 1966). Since that time, a change has emerged, marked by student strikes, boycotts, and, more recently, participation in the institutional decision-making process by students and recently graduated alumni. If for no other reason than the threat of economic insolvency, institutions have become more responsive to student needs and interests. One example is the growth in career-related and developmental education programs since 1970 in liberal arts colleges and community colleges despite the initial resistance of many of their faculty members to such programs as not adequately "academic."

To understand the emergence of this changed concept of higher education and the role that marketing should play in its future, compare several highlights from the expansion of American higher education over the past thirty years with conditions today. Three landmark legislative efforts contributed to the rapid growth of higher education in the 1950s and 1960s—the Servicemen's Readjustment Act of 1944 (the "GI Bill"), the National Science Foundation Act of 1950, and the National Defense Education Act of 1958. Together, they provided the impetus for future legislation in three key areas of campus operation: educational programming, research scholarship, and student aid. The GI Bill created educational opportunities for millions of Americans through the concept of educational entitlement—the cornerstone of the present Basic Educational Opportunity Grant Program. The National Science Foundation Act created the National Science Foundation—a principal funding source for scientific research on college and university campuses. And the National Defense Education Act, passed as a reaction to Sputnik, not only provided financial incentives for secondary schools to improve educational programming and for secondary school teachers to pursue graduate education but also, in the area of undergraduate student aid, established the concept of borrowing as a means of financing one's education. Its creation of the National Defense Student Loan Program, known today as the National Direct Student Loan Program, laid the foundation for the development of present public policy whereby educational loans have become a primary financial aid resource—as through the Guaranteed Student Loan Program, under which students, particularly at the graduate level, are now borrowing more than $3 billion a year.

The resulting rapid growth in educational opportunity brought calls for more personal and professional guidance of students. Special funds through the National Defense Education Act served as the impetus for the enhancement of secondary school counseling as a profession by granting a significant number of college graduates fellowships to pursue college counseling as a career. The development of this profession of counseling in secondary schools to assist students in college planning further stimulated the growth of higher education—growth that many came to believe would be a never-ending process.

Meanwhile, the creation of the National Merit Scholarship Corporation in 1955 and the beginning of state scholarship programs in 1957 had helped create a positive attitude toward academic achievement at the secondary school level. Until 1960 or so, many of the best high school students suppressed their intellectual ability because of peer-group pressure (Lavin, 1965, pp. 134–138). Students were not considered to be "in" if they appeared too smart or conscientious in the classroom. These new scholarship programs provided for a long-overdue recognition of the high school scholar.

Then, in the 1960s, a further series of congressional acts accentuated this growth process. The Higher Education Facilities Act of 1963 provided funds for the physical expansion of higher education at very low interest rates. The Educational Opportunity Act of 1964 served as a stimulus for public focus on creating access to higher education for the economically disadvantaged. And the Higher Education Act of 1965 and its amendments, which followed in 1968, 1972, and 1976, reinforced and expanded the concept of educational opportunity, boosting the Basic Educational Opportunity Grant Program from expenditures of $111 million in fiscal 1973 to an estimated $2.6 billion in fiscal 1978.

The physical expansion of higher education and the political endorsement of universal access to higher education as desired public policies created new opportunities not only for millions of students but also for numerous faculty members and administrators. For example, in 1966 there were 445,000 full- and part-time faculty members in American colleges and universities teaching resident courses. Faculty positions will likely peak at about 855,000 in 1981 and then decrease throughout the rest of the decade (Golladay and Noel, 1978, p. 184).

A Period of Uncertainty Ahead

Today, in large part because of its recent rapid growth, higher education is perceived by Congress and the general public more critically than in the expansionist climate of the 1950s and early 1960s. In contrast to the legislative largess of those years, the fiscal uncertainties of the 1970s have led to increased demands for efficiency and accountability. As a labor-intensive industry, higher education finds it hard to identify ways to increase productivity while reducing costs (O'Neill, 1971), and hence coordinating boards and legislatures are trying to increase productivity, and theoretically accountability, by introducing complex systems of planning. In Illinois, for example, the public sector of higher education is now guided by a Resource Allocation and Management Plan (RAMP) that aims to assess present and future needs of the total system as well as those of individual institutions and to assign resources accordingly (Illinois Board of Higher Education, 1978).

At the same time, the value of a college degree relative to its rising cost is being questioned, and families confronted with high tuition bills are expecting not only personal attention for their children in the classroom, in the residence hall, and in extracurricular activities but also the development of career-related or at least advanced technical skills. Institutions that do not meet these expectations will find little interest in the product they have to offer.

Although there is considerable speculation about likely changes in participation rates among the eighteen- to twenty-four-year-old group ("The 1980s: New Challenges, New Responsibilities," 1979), there appears to be no evidence that would suggest that these rates are likely to increase. In fact, the opposite appears to be true, because some of the reasons for attending college no longer exist or are depreciating in value. Peer-group pressures and the promise of greater employment options and more income have diminished as enrollment stimulants among recent high school graduates. The draft, at least for the present, is no longer an incentive, and the number of veterans utilizing their educational benefits is rapidly decreasing. Another way of assessing the situation is to recognize that historically the demand for education has been more a function of external stimuli not generated by the industry itself.

Hence, even without a declining market of high school graduates, higher education would find itself faced with the problem of how to manage its operation more effectively and efficiently. But the demographic facts suggest that colleges and universities are likely to undergo major difficulties during the 1980s, despite the views of some presidents (as in one sample of 135 independent institutions) that their campuses will be unaffected by decreases in the college-age population in the near future (Minter and Bowen, 1978, p. 109). As one reviews the data available from the National Center for Education Statistics and elsewhere, troubling trends are quite obvious (Centra, 1978; Eddy, 1978; Golladay and Noel, 1978; Henderson and Plummer, 1978).

1. The number of eighteen-year-olds, who represent 75 percent of first-time college freshmen, peaked at 4,292,000 in 1979 and will decrease 20 percent by 1990. It is unlikely that we will observe a comparable number during this century. On the basis of current births, in 1994 there will be 3,199,000 eighteen-year-olds; and only if the birth rate during 1980 were to reach 2.7 or higher per woman during childbearing years, instead of the more likely 1.7 to 2.1 of recent years, would the number of eighteen-year-olds in 1998 exceed the 1979 peak (U.S. Bureau of the Census, 1977, pp. 38–61). Thus, the pool of traditional college-age youth from which higher education has long drawn will shrink significantly and is not likely to expand in this century.

2. In 1976, 45 percent of the eighteen-year-old population were enrolled in first-time degree-credit college programs. If this participation rate of eighteen-year-olds in college increased to 56 percent by 1990, the number of eighteen-year-olds enrolled in higher education would remain relatively constant despite the smaller overall pool (Cartter, 1976, p. 50). This would mean that higher education would suffer little or no erosion in traditional college-age enrollments. But if this participation rate is to increase, it will have to grow primarily among students who graduate in the lower half of their secondary

school classes and who come from families of limited financial means. The percentage of students who perform well in secondary school and who elect not to attend institutions of higher education is already quite low. Therefore, colleges would have to attract many more academically low-achieving and financially needy students for any substantial growth in participation rates.

3. The percentage of high school graduates who attend college but defer their college enrollment from one to three years is increasing and now represents more than 22 percent of first-time college enrollments. Without greater incentives to attend college immediately after high school, this percentage may continue to grow, with scattered effects not only on enrollments but on curriculums, housing, and student services.

4. In contrast to the 20 percent decrease in the eighteen-year-old population during the next decade and a 15 percent decrease in the age cohort of eighteen- to twenty-four-year-olds, the twenty-five to forty-four age group will increase 26 percent (U.S. Bureau of the Census, 1977, pp. 40–50). Since over 30 percent of this age group will have had some form of higher education, a significant percentage of the group should be interested in additional formal learning. Studies suggest that some twenty-four million adults expect to return to some form of education (Arbeiter and others, 1978) and that eighty million adults report at least some interest in further learning (Gould and Cross, 1972, p. 42). Their interest stems from a number of factors, including professional development within their current careers and a desire for new skills in order to change careers. However, their needs will not be met by the traditional format of most college programs operated on a full-time enrollment and a daytime attendance schedule.

5. Accordingly, college students of the 1980s are likely to be considerably older, on the average, than the traditional eighteen- to twenty-four-year-old cohort. Already in the fall of 1977, 36 percent of the nation's college students were over age twenty-five, compared with 28 percent in 1972.

6. As a result, the proportion and number of students enrolling part-time—currently 40 percent of all students—are likely to continue to increase. What we have learned in the past ten years about adult enrollments is that people over twenty-five who enter college

for the first time or re-enter do so either part-time or for a very brief period. Not only do they not enroll as full-time students, except in programs of a specific nature offered in a limited time frame, they do not see themselves as students. Taking one or two courses is to them just another part of a busy workday.

7. As more and more older people enter higher education, the demand for non-degree-credit courses will continue to increase. Between 1970 and 1975, the number of non-degree students grew 17.1 percent, compared with only 4.2 percent for degree candidates (Golladay, 1976, p. 225). So far, private institutions and four-year public institutions have not been the beneficiaries of this non-degree growth, compared with public two-year colleges. For example, in 1975, nearly 1.4 million non-degree students—92 percent of all such students—were enrolled in community colleges, in contrast to only 45,000 in private institutions and only 70,000 in public four-year institutions. These numbers essentially reflect the traditional structure and mission of these latter institutions, but they also point out the demand for non-degree courses at institutions that offer them (Grant and Lind, 1977, p. 87).

8. Already, the number of women enrolling as first-time students exceeds the number of men—a fact that is likely to continue into the 1980s. The number of blacks and people of Hispanic origin entering higher education is likely to increase, whereas the number of Caucasian male students has begun to decrease. Wherever the educational interests and needs of women and minorities differ from those of white young men, both these trends will affect institutional programs and support services.

9. Another factor will be unemployment. A substantial number of institutions have found that their enrollments are inversely related to the rate of unemployment. This indicates that for a large number of people higher education is still a lesser alternative to work. It should suggest that programs integrating work and study would meet a consumer need.

10. Population trends differ among states. An analysis of the decrease in the eighteen-year-old population and the migration patterns of first-time college freshmen indicates that eleven states are likely to suffer the most serious decreases in freshman enrollments— at least a 10 percent drop by 1985 from their 1975 totals: Arkansas,

Connecticut, Illinois, Iowa, Kentucky, Minnesota, New Jersey, New York, North Dakota, Ohio, and Pennsylvania (Henderson, 1977, p. 19). Thirty-two states may observe little change—that is, 10 percent or less in either direction. And only seven states—together representing a small percentage of total freshman enrollments—are likely to observe a 10 percent growth in enrollments, based on current rates of participation.

These trends will prove troublesome for many institutions. If the ultimate prevailing force that affects college enrollments is likely to be people's need to learn in order to work, the curriculum of many institutions will require change. Interest in traditional liberal arts education is likely to subside while demand grows for career, developmental, and continuing professional education. Residential institutions that once attracted large numbers of college-age students of modest ability either because of peer pressure or because of their hope for greater employment opportunities will find that neither of these reasons is of much significance to tomorrow's students. By itself, a B.A. degree will not necessarily mean more employment opportunities or more income, given present employment alternatives.

Particularly hard hit may be institutions in rural settings whose location does not permit them to attract significant numbers of part-time older students readily. State legislatures and state officials responsible for higher education may decide to retain most rural public colleges because local economies depend on the continued existence of these institutions. But private colleges are less secure. Forecasts by several organizations indicate that among the approximately 1,500 private institutions now in existence, as many as 400 may no longer exist by 1990. One particularly severe projection in the magazine *Futuristic*, based on the least-price theory (that consumers buy those products that cost less if all other benefits are considered equal), predicts that only 170 of the present 1,500 private institutions may remain in operation by the year 2007 (Pyke, 1977).

Approaching the Future

The changing demographics of the college population, a fear of considerable excess capacity, and the present and likely enduring recession in higher education have stimulated a significant management interest in reassessing institutions' missions, their practices, and their historic markets. Although many institutions have just begun this investigation, other such efforts have already revealed numerous deficiencies in such areas as program offerings; student services; intra-institutional communication; staffing within the admission department; understanding the institution's markets and how the student consumer makes decisions about college choice; and the communication system between the institution and prospective students, alumni, and the media. The following subsections highlight these deficiencies.

Demand for Program Offerings. Many educational institutions have found that the demand for various types of programs has decreased over the last five years. As students have become increasingly career-oriented, their interest in the humanities and the social sciences has waned. Part of the problem is that higher education has made little effort to define the value of the humanities and the social sciences. In other words, there has been no effort to stimulate demand, and most colleges and universities that have not made readjustments in these areas—or have failed to anticipate the decrease in demand—are finding that they do not have the financial resources to respond to new market interests or else that in an effort to do so they have not been able to develop programs of substance to satisfy the student consumer. Often programs for which there is a demand and which have not reached their potential in attracting additional students suffer from the lack of either program flexibility or scheduling flexibility. Other deficiencies include a lack of price sensitivity to demand and simply a bad location for the type of program offered.

Student Services. Throughout the 1970s, the principal failing in the area of student services has been inadequate support services for a changing student community. A student services office organized to meet the needs of the middle- and upper-middle-class eighteen- to twenty-four-year-old white population is simply out of touch. Yet, this appears to be the modal staff organization. Moreover, the partnership between student affairs and academic affairs has been a reluctant one at many colleges and universities. Faculty members have often divorced themselves from the extracurricular lives of students or have been unwilling participants. This attitude and the related behavior must be re-examined at all institutions where they remain prevalent. If attrition is to be reduced, then the student services area must be the concern of faculty members and administrators alike, and institutions must be prepared to meet diverse needs, including many unrelated to the ascribed educational mission of the institution.

Intra-institutional Communication. The admission office has often not received adequate support from other departments and offices within the institution. At many institutions there is little or no public-relations staff, and the admission staff does not have the skill to develop the appropriate communication pieces. Subcontractors are used, but they generally do not have the capability to satisfactorily express what it is like to be a student at the institution. Commonly, communication problems exist between the admission and financial aid offices, and most financial aid staffs do not understand the relationship between market demand, pricing, and financial aid practice. These problems have led to conflicts between the admission and financial aid staffs that generally are not easily resolved if the respective department heads are reporting to different segments of the institution.

Another deficiency in communication is found between the admission staff and the faculty. Many admission offices do not have the benefit of faculty committees to assist them in policy and decision making. The admission staff's effectiveness in keeping the faculty abreast of changes in market interests is thereby limited. However, the main administrative failing is the lack of communication between the president and the dean or director of admission. Many presidents are just beginning to recognize that tuition is the principal source of revenue and that shortfalls in this area have a devastating effect on the institution. But even under the leadership of a president who does recognize it, one often finds the director of admission reporting to someone other than the president who views his or her primary responsibilities as being in an area other than admission. It is unusual to find a vice-president for academic affairs or student affairs professionally interested in either admission or the financial aid process. These are organizational deficiencies that must be corrected if an institution wishes to achieve its revenue objectives related to enrollment.

Admission Staffing. Most admission offices have not had the resources or the management to seek complementary and requisite skills among their staffs. The principal role model has been either salesman or counselor, and there has been a void in such professional skills as communication, group dynamics, research, and computer. Salaries generally have been low, and the admission staff has had little access to the institutional decision-making process. After World War II, when many admission offices were established, they began with a desk, a chair, and a person who seemed likable. More and more nice people entered this profession who had a basic "people" orientation but limited technical expertise. Currently, the admission office which encompasses the technical skills that the 1980s will require is rare.

Understanding Market Behavior. For years most colleges and universities have had a shotgun approach to student recruitment. Secondary schools are often visited on a random basis with little interest in or knowledge of whether those schools have produced students for the college in the past. Moreover, little effort is made to systematically segment the market to determine which submarkets are more likely to be attracted to the institution. Understanding the student recruitment process requires an investigation into the process of choosing a college and how the institution is viewed by the typical student interested in the institution. In other words, little or no market research has taken place, and as a result decisions that make up planning are far more intuitive than they should be.

Promotional Literature. Preparation of attractive materials sent on a timely basis remains the immediate management problem facing most offices of admission. Information pieces created for prospective students and their families appear to be given little thought; many are written by people unrelated to the admission enterprise, and many are issued at the wrong time. Once an institution begins to do some survey market research, it is common to find that prospective students do not receive the information that they requested or, when they do, their interest has waned. Timely receipt of the information is as important as quality of the message presented. Whether an item is attractively presented, easy to read, and sent on a timely basis should be one of the primary concerns of those responsible for managing the admission office.

As one assesses the problems that colleges and universities are having in achieving their enrollment objectives, one frequently finds that those with serious problems are plagued by all of the above deficiencies. Even colleges whose present market position is relatively strong suffer from poor intra-institutional communication and have a limited understanding of why their students enroll. In search of answers to resolve these deficiencies, an increasing number of college presidents are turning for assistance to the concepts and principles of marketing as they have been developed in both the private and the public sectors.

Marketing in Higher Education

To some people outside marketing, including some faculty members and administrators, the idea of "marketing" higher education connotes pure hucksterism. To others, it implies promotional activities to improve an institution's fund-raising and student recruitment efforts. To a few, it means merely the application of new words and phrases to well-established management procedures and operations.

Marketing is a methodology that permits decision makers in any organization to think systematically and sequentially about the mission of the organization, the services or products it offers, the markets it currently serves, and the extent to which these same markets and possibly new ones may demand its products or services in the future. It allows managers to view the operation of the organization as a whole by assessing what has become known as the "marketing mix"—the interaction of the product, its price, its place, and its distribution—and asking whether the right product is being delivered at the right price at the right place and under the proper conditions to increase consumer demand. Succinctly, the concept of marketing provides a means by which management can assess the degree to which the mission of the institution is in harmony with market interests.

In its simplest form, marketing is a series of exchange relationships and, as such, can easily be confused with selling, promotion, recruitment, or image formation. But these are only components of marketing. For example, to some extent, in higher education we are all involved in marketing. This becomes more evident as one assumes more responsiblity and thus acquires more authority and visibility.

Every time administrators greet someone, they are building an impression of themselves as well as of their institutions. However, a complete definition of marketing includes the application of such concepts as research, planning, and various strategies related to program assessment and development, to packaging, and to the communication process of image building and name recognition.

For example, applying these concepts to the development and modification of an academic program requires, in the *research* phase, an understanding of market demand, of the program's interrelationships with other programs at the institution, of similar programs at competing institutions, and of projected development and recurring operating costs of the program. Once such questions are answered, the necessary *planning* can proceed: revising the curriculum, preparing faculty members, and deciding among alternative *strategies* for marketing the program. Questions that need to be resolved here include whether it is possible to focus on a specific market in promoting the program, whether the program should be promoted as an integrated part of the total curriculum or whether a specific effort should be made to differentiate it among current institutional offerings, and how it can be differentiated from offerings of competing institutions. In marketing annals the consideration and resolution of these questions are called "portfolio planning" and "positioning."

After resolving such questions, *communication* strategies can be implemented that employ effective styles, formats, frequencies, and sources of contact. With regard to this last, if the program is to be marketed as a separate entity, then additional questions must be asked: Who or what department should assume the responsibility for explaining the nature, the content, and the purpose of the program to different audiences? And should a faculty member in the program be designated to respond to inquiries about it, or should this be a public-relations or an admission office function? This promotional effort usually requires a coordinated plan between the academic department, the office of public relations, and the office of admission. In each of these units, a particular person should be assigned the task of following through, but the admission staff will need to orchestrate the various forms of communication with different audiences. Thus, although it may not be the admission office's responsibility to generate press releases announcing a new academic program, it is its

responsibility to make sure that such press releases are generated by the appropriate office—for example, that of public relations. As the communication process becomes more specific and focuses on individual potential students, the academic department in cooperation with the office of admission can become the primary contact source.

The application of these three phases of marketing—research, planning, and the implementation of strategies—to the process of promoting institutions of higher education is essentially the purpose of the remainder of this book. The best possible product cannot maximize its demand potential without a commitment to the marketing process, and as educators we must recognize that education is a service that is packaged and purchased in various ways. The chapters that follow will provide a format for an institution to use in developing a sophisticated marketing plan. Although the content tends to focus on marketing from an admission perspective, what is said can be generalized for developing a marketing philosophy for the entire institution. Applying the marketing concept is no easy or quick solution: it requires assessment, planning, sophisticated implementation, and introspection. Those colleges and universities that adopt a marketing approach not only will strengthen their process of communication but will improve the product they offer. As we look toward the future, those institutions that wish to thrive must be willing to look at themselves. The result will be a restoration or a reaffirmation, depending on one's view of the credibility and integrity of higher education.

2

Understanding Factors Affecting College Choice

To develop a marketing plan, a college needs to determine how and to what extent the experience it has to offer affects its students in a more beneficial manner than its main competition. The impact of the college experience on personal and intellectual development has been well documented by Trent and Medsker (1968), by Feldman and Newcomb (1969), and more recently by Astin (1977). Moreover, different types of institutions tend to affect students quite differently. One reason is that students of various abilities and interests select particular types of institutions; a community college attracts a different type of student than a four-year private college does. But that is not the only reason; the type of college is important too. The experience offered by a small liberal arts college tends to differ from the experience offered by a community college or a large university. Summarily, Astin states, "Students change in many ways after they enter college. These changes can be affected by a number of factors, including the student's characteristics at the time of college entry, the type of

college attended, and the extent of the student's involvement in the college environment" (1977, p. 211).

Knowledge of how a college affects its students permits the college to differentiate its product in relation to its competition. However, product positioning (differentiation) is but one part of marketing. Once the product's position is determined, the process by which a college communicates its position becomes of primary importance. This communication process, too, should be differentiated from those of competing institutions to the extent of the available creative skills. Because the research generally has not been done, a problem for many institutions is inability to differentiate themselves, on the basis of both product and process, within given institutional typologies, such as small liberal arts colleges, community colleges, or medium-sized universities.

Gathering the Marketing Data

New and updated information on the institution and student markets passes over the desks of most admission officers daily. Too often the information is either not read or, if read, is not interpreted in relation to similar ideas or as possible responses to a given problem. In other words, the sources of data are readily available. What is needed is to develop the personal capability to assimilate and interpret data to facilitate problem solving.

The following sources are the principal references for developing an orientation for marketing research: The American Council on Education provides a series of factbooks containing data related to demographics, potential student populations, growth in per capita disposable income, cost of higher education, faculty salaries, and so forth. By using the Student Search Service program of the College Entrance Examination Board, one can assess the potential yield from primary and secondary markets (see Chapter Five). Summary reports from the Admissions Testing Program of the College Entrance Examination Board and from the American College Testing Program can be helpful in identifying national, regional, and institutional market trends. Further, some state scholarship commissions and state higher education assistance authorities provide student demographics and family economic data by ZIP code within a state.

Sales and Marketing Management magazine provides semiannual data on potential markets based on effective buying power (after-tax income) by region, state, county, and community. The Cooperative Institutional Research Program's annual survey of entering freshmen (Astin and others, 1977, 1978) provides normative data on entering students at up to 500 institutions subdivided by sex and type of institution. These data are particularly helpful in providing the information at the beginning of this chapter if the institution participates in the survey. However, all these sources provide data that can help the admission office to use its resources more effectively and to expand an institution's market in desired areas.

An institutional analysis of the college's market position should include the following:

- Program offerings in relation to the competition.
- The quality of the facilities, such as the library, laboratories, recreational facilities, and residential facilities.
- The nature of the student body; its demographic characteristics and its academic interests.
- The nature of the faculty; the extent to which it is student-oriented, pursues research, is interested in teaching, and is available to the typical undergraduate.
- The retention rate, or, to reinforce the negative, the attrition rate. If attrition is high, is it because of misrepresentation before students enter the institution, or is the faculty unresponsive to students' needs (Astin, 1977; Noel, 1978)?
- Location. How does it relate to the interests of principal markets? For example, a college located in a rural area of Iowa may not meet the personal needs of students from large metropolitan areas. Yet, a number of students living in large metropolitan areas may at one time have lived in smaller communities and may desire to attend college in such a community. Students without such a prior experience may find the adjustment difficult.
- Community attitude of a college. Is the college positive, interested, aware of the outside world; what is the ambiance? Defining the ambiance is most typically achieved through questionnaires, such as the College and University Environment and Experiences Scales (Pace, 1977), the Institutional Functioning Inventory (Beck and

Park, 1978), and other self-study instruments developed by the institution or by external agencies like the American College Testing Program and the Educational Testing Service.
• The economics of the institution. Is the institution suffering from deficit financing, deferred maintenance, and faculty overloads, or has the school prospered in rather difficult times?

Responsible answers to these questions should provide an admission staff with a competitive advantage over its counterparts at other schools. Few admission officers—or, for that matter, administrators in general—systematically investigate their school's market position in relation to other institutions. An honest assessment of the market position can identify the institution's strengths and weaknesses and permit the offices of admission, alumni, development, and public relations to project a more enlightened image of the institution. In fact, if these offices can act in harmony, the goals of each become easier to achieve. Conversely, offices operating on the boundaries of an institution and projecting different messages make it that much harder to achieve the objectives of a single office.

Interpreting the Data

Chapter One summarized some broad market trends: the decrease in the eighteen-year-old population, migration patterns, the increase in participation rates of women and minorities, and the enrollment potential of an older student market. I now focus on what is known about the present student market, based on various research efforts and the interpretation of available data.

The Application Process and Student Mobility. Data collected by the Cooperative Institutional Research Program (Astin and others, 1977, pp. 47–61) show that 40 percent of entering freshmen apply only to the colleges they plan to attend and 92 percent attend colleges within 500 miles of their homes. Moreover, an additional 18 percent apply to only one other college, and over 50 percent attend colleges within 50 miles of their homes.

For market planning, these data should be interpreted in relation to the type of institution. As one might guess, students who attend private universities and colleges are the most mobile, as gauged by the number of colleges to which they apply and the distances from their homes to the colleges they plan to attend. Only 8 percent of freshmen enrolling in private universities apply to one institution, and only 14 percent of freshmen enrolling in private colleges apply to one institution. Further, up to 30 percent of these students will attend an institution in excess of 500 miles from their homes, compared with only 8 percent of the students attending all colleges.

Mobility appears to be greatly influenced by economic background and the number of colleges located in a particular region of the country. The greater the number of colleges in a given geographic region, the less likely it is that students from the region will travel considerable distances to college (Astin and others, 1977, p. 96). Students from the East and the Midwest are less likely to travel considerable distances to college than students from the South. In the West, students travel either very few miles or a considerable distance. This reflects the extensive community college system in the state of California as well as the market position of Midwest and East Coast schools. Regardless of region, however, students from more affluent backgrounds are more mobile.

The one exception to the above conclusion is the black student. Black students are among the most mobile. One can only suggest a number of possible reasons: heavy recruitment of black students by private institutions outside their states, the concentration of predominantly black colleges in the South, the current emphasis within the black community on education as a means of socioeconomic advancement, and the possibility that a relatively loose family structure encourages mobility.

Students of Hispanic origin are among the least mobile, regardless of social class. These students generally come from a well-defined family structure and are reluctant to go too far away to school. The strong affiliation with the Catholic Church may be the dominant factor. The question of student mobility is addressed in greater detail in the next chapter. For an additional analysis, see Tierney (1978).

Academic Ability and the Ability to Pay. It is not uncommon for an admission office of a private college to be given the assignment of increasing the quality of the freshman class as well as the number of full-paying students. How realistic is such a request? The data suggest that this goal is impractical. First of all, over the last ten years the standardized-test scores of college-bound high school seniors have eroded considerably. In 1967 verbal scores on the Scholastic Aptitude Test (SAT) averaged 466, mathematical scores 492. By 1978 these scores had dropped to 429 and 468, respectively (College Entrance Examination Board, 1978, p. 6). From a market position it should be recognized that in some states and in some regions the decline has not been so drastic; nonetheless, scores have dropped in all areas of the country.

How many students combine high academic ability and ability to pay for higher education? In 1978 only 73,000 of the 1,000,000+ students who took the SAT had a verbal score of 500 or above and parents able to contribute $5,000 or more annually to their education (College Entrance Examination Board, 1978). Moreover, without regard to academic ability, about one quarter of all families could meet the full cost of education in a public four-year college or university. The average annual per student charges at such institutions were $3,054. Only 16 percent of all families were estimated to be able to contribute the whole cost of private four-year institutions, which had average student budgets of $5,110. (These percentages are probably high, because the population of students that takes the SAT is, in general, more affluent than the total college-bound population.)

Doermann (1976, p. 44) estimated that of 3,183,000 high school graduates in 1978, 116,000, or 3.6 percent, would achieve a verbal score of 500 on the SAT and would have parents who could contribute $6,000 or more to their education.

Thus, both these analyses indicate that the pool of relatively high-ability students from rather affluent families is quite small. A rough estimate suggests that at least 70 percent of college students are receiving some form of financial assistance and that without this assistance a high percentage of students would be severely restricted in college choice. One reason that the vast majority of public and private institutions have remained solvent is the massive infusion of government student-grant assistance.

Noncognitive Factors in College Choice. Numerous studies have attempted to isolate the effects of noncognitive factors on college choice, with limited success (Corwin and Kent, 1978). Yet, it does seem clear that such factors as the secondary school attended, the education of the parents, the family's economic status, colleges attended by older brothers and sisters, extracurricular interests, and religious preference may significantly affect college choice. The extent to which any one factor dominates college choice is difficult to quantify, but a number of observations can be made from experience and from a review of the literature on student demographics.

The significance of the *secondary school* attended with regard to college choice may, at first, appear obvious because of the percentage of graduates from a given secondary school who enroll in college the following fall. Often a market judgment is made that secondary schools that have a substantial number of their graduates enroll in college are better schools than those with a much lower percentage. However, the literature in sociology suggests that whether a student attends college is more a reflection of family background and peer-group interests than of the secondary school attended. From a marketing position, the fact that a high percentage of graduates of a given secondary school attend college is of little value. The interest should not be in the percentage of students who choose to go to college upon graduation from high school, but in what type of college these students attend. For example, if 90 percent of the graduates of a given secondary school attend public four-year and community colleges, that school may not be a good market for a private college. More typically, however, one will find that the students who attend such a secondary school come from relatively affluent backgrounds and are quite mobile geographically with regard to college choice. Consequently, before determining whether a particular secondary school may be a productive market, a college must first know from what type of schools its current students graduated. It is quite likely that for many colleges, secondary schools located in less sophisticated and less affluent areas will generate more applications. The primary market for a state college may be secondary schools that serve marginal white-collar and blue-collar neighborhoods; whereas the primary market for a denominational college may be high schools in small cities where many people are affiliated with that denomination. (The church or temple may serve as the main source of market contact for such a college.) Thus, in assessing a secondary school as a potential market, one should have in mind the general characteristics of the community the school serves and the type of students who have found a particular college attractive in the past.

Quite obviously, the *career aspirations* of prospective students will determine their course of study and thus influence college choice. A student interested in the fine arts is likely to consider a different set of colleges than a student of equal intellectual ability from the same secondary school who is interested in the allied health sciences.

Career interests, to a great extent, appear to be a function of family background. For example, students interested in engineering tend to come from less affluent families than students interested in the humanities and the theater arts. Moreover, there appear to be differences in socioeconomic background between students interested in similar fields. As an example, students in the theater arts tend to come from more affluent backgrounds than students interested in pursuing music as a career. Research at Northwestern University indicates that students interested in the traditional liberal arts and the theater arts come from more affluent families than students interested in any other area. It follows that they will need less financial aid. Consequently, a desired expansion or contraction in enrollment in any area of study has cost implications. The cost of recruiting and of maintaining given levels of enrollment in different areas of study will vary.

In recognition of this variation, development of a market plan should include consideration of the size of the potential market by interest area and the related recruitment and financial aid costs. A similar analysis should be applied to the development of new programs; unfortunately, some colleges, in an effort to respond to anticipated demand, have not taken into consideration the requisite costs of financial aid to achieve desired enrollment goals. The result has been that the annual recurring costs are greater than the development costs. Consequently, unless such costs are considered, it may be more prudent to maintain or reduce enrollments than to expand enrollments in some areas. The variation in the number of students interested in different fields and the related financial aid costs can be interpreted from information provided by the College Entrance Examination Board, the American College Testing Program, and the National Merit Scholarship Corporation. Within the institution, financial aid costs (average and per capita) can be easily calculated by segmenting financial aid recipients by interest area.

Another influence on college choice is *parental education*. The task here is to determine the educational backgrounds of the parents of currently enrolled students. Does the college tend to attract students whose parents have never attended college, have had some college, and so forth? Parents who have had a considerable amount of higher education are more likely to encourage their children to apply to colleges with a high level of market visibility. Parents with little or no higher education may be more concerned about such factors as the denominational affiliation of a private college or the job opportunities that their child will have on completing college. The significance of recognizing the educational background of the parents is related to the type of communication or contact that may be the most appropriate. A marketing plan should consider the variety of concerns that parents with different educational experiences are likely to have, and their interests should be anticipated in the communication process.

Family economic status to a great extent reflects the educational background of the parents; yet, as one assesses relative affluence, it is often the degree of wealth that affects college choice. As is true of educational background, the more wealth parents have, the more likely they are to encourage their children to consider high-visibility colleges. However, this appears to be more true of families who have inherited their wealth and the related social position than of families who have achieved a degree of affluence within their lifetime. Although these latter families are often status oriented, they may not be secure enough to be willing to lower their standard of living to send their children to high-priced institutions. However, all the following factors tend to interact to influence college choice: degree of affluence; a family's concern about social status; the value they place on education; and whether they live in a corporate, urban environment. The more these factors are dominant, the more likely it is that families will consider only a small number of highly visible colleges. Conversely, the less these factors are dominant, the less prestige is likely to be a factor. When a given college considers prospective students, these kinds of information should be interpreted as they relate to the type of college one represents.

Older brothers and sisters who have attended college can be quite influential in college choice, especially if the parents have not attended college. A brother or sister who has had a good college experience is likely to encourage younger siblings to consider the same college. Accordingly, as prospective students apply, an appropriate question to ask on the application is the names and ages of other children in the family. These siblings' names should enter the prospective-student file and be contacted at the appropriate time— generally no earlier than the end of their sophomore year in high school. A small college, because it has fewer potential students, should be able to cultivate such students' interest by maintaining personal contact over a period of time and by considering the family as producers of additional students.

Whether *extracurricular interests* affect college choice depends on the degree to which a student excelled in a given activity in secondary school. Many students with considerable academic ability who have excelled in the arts or in athletics give priority to their activity interests in selecting a college. If a college offers a good program in such areas, the market plan should include focusing on prospects with such interests. This is simply a process of attempting to match prospects and programs.

Religious preference may affect college choice. Each year many students select colleges with strong denominational ties. The fact that a college has such an affiliation may be the main reason for choosing the college. More often, however, a combination of factors influences the decision. Denominational affiliation alone, without a history of academic credibility, is not likely to attract many students. Yet, a college that has maintained a reasonably distinguished academic reputation with strong denominational ties should be in a strong market position. For many families, the religious experience is as important as the academic experience, and for those families the two should not be separated.

There are many able students who, along with encouragement from their families, will consider only those colleges that reinforce their religious beliefs. A college that attracts such students should include in its market plan the churches from which it draws most of its students. Frequent contact with these churches should be a part of a systematic communication effort. In a number of denominational colleges the principal marketing strategy is to maintain contact with the youth directors of the respective churches.

This section has identified some of the noncognitive factors affecting college choice. A marketing plan should take into consideration the cognitive and the noncognitive factors. Summarily, college choice is affected by grades received in secondary school, career aspirations, education of parents, family economic status, college experience of siblings, religious background, and the concentration of colleges within a given geographic region. Students with higher grades, better-educated parents, and greater family income are more likely to apply to more than one college and to attend private institutions (Corwin and Kent, 1978, pp. 19–25; Tierney, 1978). In terms of market analysis it does not appear that these factors are completely interdependent. In other words, high grades alone may be enough of an inducement for a student to consider institutions that represent a particular type of academic environment; the same can be said for any of the other factors mentioned above. The data suggest that the more any one of these traits is dominant—high socioeconomic background, well-educated parents, religious interests, high intellectual ability—the greater the chances a student will attend a private institution: the probability that a student will attend a private institution tends to increase as the various factors are added to describe a given student. Once a market is analyzed using these factors, then the type of institution can be isolated. Students with high grades, strong religious preferences, and well-educated parents are likely to consider a different set of colleges than students with high grades, strong religious preferences, and less-educated parents. Well-educated, affluent parents who also have a strong religious preference will generally not let their religious preference influence their children's college choice, particularly if the children have considerable intellectual ability.

Clark and others (1972) is recommended as a source that focuses on noncognitive factors.

Other Factors Affecting College Choice. Astin (1965) and Nichols (1966) argued that colleges having good students attract good students irrespective of the cost of tuition. Anderson (1975, 1976) reported that given two colleges both with distinguished faculties, a scholarly (research) orientation, and fiscal strength, a student is likely to select the institution with the lower tuition. Anderson tends to overlook the consequences of financial assistance; in my judgment, what is critical is not gross tuition differences between institutions but net tuition differences. However, high-priced institutions must realize that unless a concerted effort is made to explain net price in terms of the amount of financial assistance available and the eligibility criteria for financial aid, a substantial number of students will be discouraged by the listed tuition and will not investigate further. Accordingly, one measure of the effectiveness of the communication process is the economic distribution of the applicant pool.

Spies (1973, 1978) concluded that high tuition was not in itself a deterrent in the application process among high-ability students as defined by composite SAT scores. His studies focused primarily on a selected group of private institutions with well-defined market positions. Generally, one might conclude that price was not a consideration in the application process because the market positions of these schools were so strong. However, his results showed some variation by region of the country, apparently reflecting competition with low-cost public universities in the same region. Another factor that must be considered in Spies' conclusion is the relation between economic background and high test scores. Since test scores are strongly related to affluence and to cultural interest, one might conclude that the main reasons students applied to these institutions were the affluence of the family, the educational interests of the parents, and the perceived market positions of the institutions. The interaction effects are obvious, and the dominance of any single variable is difficult to segregate. High-ability students may apply to an identifiable group of institutions, not because they tend to have high tuitions but rather because of such factors as those mentioned above, as well as because—as Astin and Nichols concluded—high-ability students attract other high-ability students. The one lesson to be learned from Spies' studies is that perceived quality is more important in attracting high-ability students than is price. Nonetheless, the number of such students is quite small, as indicated earlier in this chapter, and consequently their behavior with regard to college choice will not affect the future of most colleges.

College Choice and Student Mobility

As indicated in preceding sections, where students go to college is affected by a number of factors. Certain facts, such as a student's prior academic performance and family financial strength, either inhibit or facilitate geographic mobility with regard to college choice. An assessment of the interaction of ability and family financial strength should enhance understanding of the process of choosing a college and should suggest a method by which admission staffs can evaluate their markets to estimate yields. A yield may be defined in various ways: as the response rate to a general or a restricted mailing to a pool of prospects; as the percentage of students who enroll who were initially contacted through a mailing or another form of contact; or as the percentage of students who enroll of the number accepted. No matter which definition is used, a yield can be more precisely defined, as well as projected, if the market is subdivided by intellectual ability and family financial strength. The following discussion will act as a foundation for an analysis of the identifiable primary, secondary, and tertiary markets (which are defined in Chapter Five).

Although numerous quantitative and qualitative factors affect college choice, the main ones are family background, career aspirations, prior educational performance, and family financial strength. Accordingly, we expect a student with considerable ability and with no financial need to be more mobile geographically with regard to college choice than another student with limited ability and high financial need. Although such a hypothesis could be justified on the basis of common sense, the paradigm presented in Figure 1 is an attempt to graphically describe the degree of mobility based on intellectual ability (or academic performance) and financial need. Ability is arbitrarily subdivided along a continuum 1 through 4, with 4 representing the highest quartile. Ability could be interpreted as standardized-test scores or high school grades. Financial need is also defined along a continuum: high need, moderate need, low need, and no need. Prospects who fall into the no-need category may or may not apply for financial assistance.

One assumption that can be made, based on empirical evidence, is that students who fall into cell H1 (high need, low ability) are the least mobile geographically and students who fall into cell N4 (no need, high ability) are the most mobile. In fact, students who fall into cell H1 are also the least likely to attend college immediately after secondary school. If they do pursue postsecondary education, it is likely to be either at a community college or at a proprietary school, assuming that one or the other is near their homes. Generally, this pattern holds for all students who fall into cells located in the first quadrant: cells H1, H2, M1, and M2. However, because of the relative

Figure 1. Student Mobility Paradigm

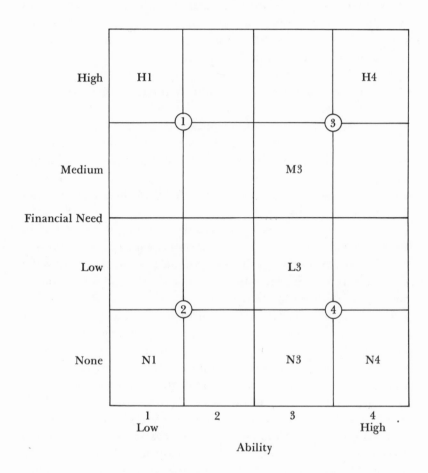

nature of a continuum, the behavior is less predictable in these other cells in quadrant 1. In contrast, students who fall into any cell in quadrant 4—cells L3, L4, N3, and N4—are quite mobile. Students in N4 are the most mobile and, in fact, apply to more than four colleges and are accepted by almost as many.

As one moves along the ability continuum from H1 to H4, the likelihood of a student's attending college increases considerably. It also increases along the need continuum from H1 to N1. Students who fall along the continuum from H4 to N4 will be increasingly more mobile geographically with regard to college choice. One could come to a similar conclusion for students in the cells along the continuum N1 through N4, but students in cells N1 and N2 will not have as many choices available to them; hence, they are not likely to apply to as many colleges.

Summarily, the student mobility paradigm suggests that participation rates are a function of ability and family wealth. To an extent, participation rates at the lower end of the ability continuum have been inflated by the infusion of government student assistance, but these funds do not compensate for lack of ability or for lack of interest in education. An institution that attracts a high percentage of students who would be categorized as falling within quadrants 1 and 2 should expect a high attrition rate.

These conclusions are derived by reviewing the literature in sociology related to family background and by interpreting information from such sources as the Admissions Testing Program of the College Entrance Examination Board and the Annual Survey of American Freshmen by the Cooperative Institutional Research Program. The conclusions result from an analysis of data on the distribution of family income by type of institution, average grades received in high school by type of institution, and distance from home to college by type of institution. Empirical data in support of these conclusions are provided in the next chapter. However, for almost any conclusion, there is an exception. For example, black students who fall into cell H4 appear to be far more mobile than students of other ethnic groups. Although students who fall into cell N4 are quite mobile geographically, students from Hispanic backgrounds are the least mobile within that cell because of the nature of the family unit. The available evidence suggests that a student with considerable ability is likely to select a college within commuting distance if his family ties are quite strong and his parents have no more than a high school education and limited financial resources. The interaction effects of parents' education, family ties, and limited income appear to be quite restrictive of college choice and student mobility.

The student mobility paradigm, in addition to permitting a segmented market analysis of behavior with regard to college choice, can be used to assess the educational needs of all prospective students within a given market area and to determine whether those needs are being met by the educational institutions within that region. In other words, an admission staff should evaluate the potential of a given geographic market by determining the number of prospective students who fall within the various cells and comparing that distribution with students who are currently attending college within the region. This, again, is a matching process but provides some guidance regarding the amount of resources required to attract and to serve students who fall within any one of the cells within a given market segment. For example, a college that would tend to attract a significant number of students who fell within the first quadrant should be prepared to provide a variety of academic support services. Such services would not be required for a college that was able to attract many students from either quadrant 3 or quadrant 4. Of course, the more students a college attracts from quadrants 1 and 2, compared with quadrants 3 and 4, the greater the cost of financial aid. One must therefore ask how much diversity any one college can afford, keeping in mind not only the cost of providing financial assistance but also the cost of the necessary support services.

Finally, most research that has been done at Northwestern and elsewhere indicates four threshold reasons for selecting a given college: special programs, academic reputation, financial factors, and location. Once students decide that a certain set of colleges will meet their criteria on these four factors, the final choice is likely to be determined by noncognitive reasons—for example, the religious history of the family, the college affiliation of the parents, prior educational experiences of older siblings or friends, or interests in extracurricular activities.

As a matter of information for those of us in admission and secondary school counseling who may be suffering from some delusions of grandeur, the data suggest that the personal influence of the secondary school counselor and the admission representative has little effect on college choice (Astin and others, 1978). Our influence results more from how we manage the communication process. There appears to be some relation between the degree of sophistication of a community and the personal influence of the secondary school counselor: the greater the intellectual sophistication of the community, the less the influence.

3

*Gathering Data
on Current, Entering,
and Potential Students*

An effective marketing plan requires an understanding of an institution's traditional markets and present competition. This requires an interest in data analysis and an orientation toward research. Within the office of admission, members of the staff should approach the implementation of new projects systematically, thus permitting the subsequent evaluation of outcomes. This chapter raises some fundamental questions to serve as a guide for the development of an orientation toward research, identifies market trends for which data are readily available through other sources, and suggests questions to be asked and procedures to be followed in developing research methods.

A continuous research effort should seek to measure the effectiveness of particular strategies among different markets and to stimulate interest in additional hypotheses. However, because institutional marketing involves interpersonal relationships and lacks laboratory controls, explicit cause-and-effect relations are hard to establish. Questions are often raised about the effectiveness of direct mail, different forms of advertising, various types of school visits, campus visits, and other marketing tactics. Such questions are important to raise, but the continuation of a particular tactic should not be based simply on quantitative assessment. In considering the available data, personal impressions and common sense should prevail. Once a decision is made to implement a particular plan, results will be hard to assess in less than three to five years. A plan should be modified as situations change and additional information is acquired, but the basic plan should remain intact. In fact, before a plan is modified, a new strategy and the related communication tactics should first be applied systematically to a small segment of the market. If the strategy is effective, then it may be prudent to modify the total plan as it applies to the entire market. For example, if the communication strategy includes a direct-mail approach, off-campus programs, structured campus visits, and faculty and undergraduate contacts, each tactic may be modified or eliminated within a given market segment before changing the time dimension of that tactic. The phrase *time dimension* refers to the frequency and quality of contact and the point in the recruitment cycle in which the various communication tactics are most effective. Only by varying the several contacts in relation to time can the proper tactic mix be determined. In addition, if it appears to be wise to add radio advertising and alumni/ prospect contact to the strategy, these should be introduced gradually and restricted to a given market segment. Such an approach will permit continued modification on a limited basis until the adoption of a new tactic has been sufficiently refined.

In an effort to continue to improve the market plan and the efficient use of resources (which include money, time, and people), five questions should be investigated. One, what do you want to know? This question relates to the specific function or responsibility, such as fulfilling individual assignments on a timely basis, or to the effectiveness of some component of the marketing effort, such as a direct-mail piece. Obviously, as a good manager, you want to know because you want to be able to feel somewhat confident that resources are being used efficiently. Two, how will you proceed to know? This question is related to collecting data, analyzing the data, and determining what statistical methodology will be applied in assessment. Three, now that you know, how will you proceed? The information gathered may help redefine the way individual tasks are approached. It may or may not validate the significance of a given task or the application of a given tactic; but above all, the information should permit you to make better decisions rather than operating on a trial-and-error basis. Four, who should know besides you? To a great extent this depends on the magnitude of the project. Was the assessment of the project or task significant only to the primary function of the admission office, or did it extend beyond the boundaries of the admission office to the faculty, other offices, or the student body? What is the likely impact of the analysis on better use of resources? Five, how will you communicate what has been learned? A most common method is to write a report and circulate it among the parties likely to be interested. For an administrator interested in constructive action, this may not be the most effective way of communicating the results of a given study. To achieve a quicker response, a more desirable approach may be to write a two-page memorandum to the people with whom you would like to share the information and who might be able to assist in some form of follow-through. The memorandum should be followed by a small group meeting or by meeting individually with the desired parties. Another effective method of communication is to advocate a particular position on the basis of the information acquired. This should be done in a memorandum of no more than three pages that explains the position and why. If a proposal requires a reallocation of resources, this information should be included in the memorandum. Such a position of advocacy is often a call for action, particularly if the reasons for the position are persuasively stated.

Too often research is undertaken and positions are advocated without adequate explanation. Being succinct is important, but understanding the biases of one's audiences and appealing to those biases in order to stimulate the required action is often critical. I am reminded of a story about a college president who saw little or no reason to make an effort to create access to his institution for minorities. When the position was stated in different terms—that the power structure of the community in which the college was located would undoubtedly be shared by a significant number of minorities within the next twenty years—he understood and became quite supportive of the proposed efforts of the admission office. In this instance, pragmatism prevailed where idealism had failed. Although this example is not directly related to research, it does serve to indicate the significance of understanding one's audiences before communicating what has been learned. As will be clarified in a later chapter, the process of communication is as important as the method of communication.

To lack an understanding of your competition comparable to your understanding of your own institution is to place constraints on the information you have obtained and to limit whatever advantage you may have in competing with similar institutions for the same students. Knowledge of your competition should include student demographics, the number of admission overlaps, specific (noncompetitive) program differences, comparisons of relative program differences, and financial position. The question is how the institution you represent differs from the competition individually or collectively: how can you differentiate your product in the marketplace? In marketing, this process of differentiation is called "positioning."

Although new research may be required on the students attending a given institution, a significant amount of data is available about the marketplace in general, including family financial data. General family demographics can be acquired from reports issued by the American Council on Education, the Bureau of Labor Statistics, the Bureau of the Census, and the National Center for Education Statistics. For example, the growth in family after-tax income for different age brackets in different market segments should be considered before increasing tuition. An overpriced institution will decrease the size of its potential market unless there are compensating increases in student assistance from either institutional or governmental sources. An underpriced institution is not maximizing its revenues and, therefore, may be forfeiting the opportunity to improve the quality of its product unless it has substantial reserves. More is said about this topic in Chapter Six.

Developing Data on Applicants and Entering Students

To develop a marketing plan, data must be gathered through common sources, and certain institutional questions should be answered. The following questions are thought to be of interest to every college administration, particularly to the president and to the director of admission: What is the institution's current principal market? How do its students make decisions related to the application process? Why do its students select the institution? How do families of applicants expect to pay for higher education? How does information related to financing higher education affect college choice?

Other questions of equal significance for attracting students but not specifically related to the application process are these: What is the expected market demand for the programs the college offers? To what extent are present undergraduates satisfied with the academic and social programs offered by the institution? What career and further education opportunities will be available to current undergraduates at the time of graduation?

The area of decision analysis, defined as how prospective students determine where they will go to college, is most difficult to quantify. The questionnaires presented in this chapter are examples of how a single institution can begin to study the decision question.

Surveying Nonapplicants. A questionnaire, either abbreviated or extensive, should be sent to nonapplicants as well as to applicants. The purpose of canvassing the nonapplicant group is to determine why students who at one time expressed an interest in the institution did not follow through with an application. Information about the nonapplicant pool should be of greater value than information about applicants and should permit an institution to broaden its potential market. Nonapplicants may be defined along an interest continuum from those students who expressed an interest in the college through a single mailing restricted to only those who visited the campus and had an interview. If a questionnaire is restricted to the latter, the response rate is likely to be greater. The response rate will be even greater if such a survey is restricted to nonapplicants from a given market segment who expressed considerable interest in the college. To verify the validity of the responses received, a random group of nonrespondents should be contacted by telephone and asked the same questions that were mailed to them.

The nonapplicant questionnaire used at Northwestern University is shown in Exhibit 1. It has six objectives: to determine what precipitated the student's interest in the university; to determine the degree of contact with the university; to evaluate the competition; to compare the profiles of nonapplicants with those of applicants; and to identify the explicit reasons for not applying to Northwestern.

Exhibit 1. Nonapplicant Questionnaire

The information from this questionnaire will be used to analyze the quality of information provided by Northwestern to potential applicants. The information will be used for research purposes only and will be kept strictly confidential.

1. Did you visit the campus? _____ 1 Yes _____ 2 No
   If yes, what was the occasion?
   _____ 1 Open House (which? _____)
   _____ 2 Overnight stay in dorm
   _____ 3 Interview
   _____ 4 Visit a friend
   _____ 5 Casual stop
   _____ 6 Other _____

2. Did you receive an invitation to an on-campus program?
   _____ 1 Yes _____ 2 No
   If yes, did you attend the program? _____ 1 Yes _____ 2 No
   If you received an invitation and did not attend the program, why not?

   If you did not receive an invitation, would you have attended a program if invited (barring time conflict)?   _____ 1 Yes _____ 2 No

3. What specifically led to your inquiry into Northwestern as a potential college choice?

4. Did you receive any information about a specific program that you found particularly useful? If so, what was it?

5. Did you have any personal contact with Northwestern in your home town? If so, what was it?

   Was it useful? In what way?

6. To how many colleges did you apply? _____
   To how many were you admitted? _____

   Please list the colleges to which you applied in order of choice, first choice at the top. If you applied to more than 8, please list your top 8 choices.

Exhibit 1 (continued)

	A	B	C	D
		Out-of-	Estimated	Financial
	Private	State?	Total Cost	Aid?
1.	_____	____	____	____
2.	_____	____	____	____
3.	_____	____	____	____
4.	_____	____	____	____
5.	_____	____	____	____
6.	_____	____	____	____
7.	_____	____	____	____
8.	_____	____	____	____

Please indicate with a check mark in columns A and B whether each school is private (vs. state) and whether it is located out of your home state.

In columns C and D, please give the estimated total cost of attending each institution and indicate whether you received financial aid to attend that institution.

7. What college will you be attending next fall? _____
   Why did you choose it?

8. Did you or your parents complete the Financial Aid Form?
   _____ 1 Yes _____ 2 No
   If yes, did you receive the *Report of Filers* from the College Scholarship Service? _____ 1 Yes _____ 2 No
   If yes, what was its effect? Please explain.

9. Did you receive an offer of any type of scholarship *not* based on need? Please explain below.

10. What was your rank in your high school class?

    _____ 1   Upper 5%   _____ 4   Upper 20%
    _____ 2   Upper 10%   _____ 5   Upper 25%
    _____ 3   Upper 15%   _____ 6   Below upper quarter

11. How large was your graduating class? _____

12. What were your ACT or SAT scores?

    SAT Verbal   _____
    SAT Math   _____
    ACT Composite   _____

13. What is your proposed college major? _____

14. What is your proposed career? _____

Exhibit 1 (continued)

15. Please enter your home ZIP code. _____

16. What is your total family income?
    _____ $0–$25,000
    _____ $25,000–$50,000
    _____ Over $50,000

17. Why didn't you apply to Northwestern? Please explain below.

In response to these questions and in contrast to findings reported by Spies (1973, 1978), nonapplicants, who presented similar profiles to applicants, indicated that price was indeed the main reason for not applying to Northwestern. They also appeared to have little knowledge of the financial aid possibilities. However, 50 percent did elect to attend private institutions, albeit those with a much lower price; the others attended public four-year institutions. The response pattern indicated that religious affiliation may have had some influence for those nonapplicants who applied to private institutions. Nonetheless, this study does appear to show that the published price discourages a substantial number of prospects regardless of the amount of financial aid available.

Surveying Accepted Students. The more typical type of survey is one in which a questionnaire is sent to only those students who are accepted. The purposes are to acquire some understanding of the demographic profile of students interested in the institution and to obtain information about factors that influenced the application-decision process. As an example, Northwestern University annually surveys all students who have been accepted, whether they intend to enroll or go elsewhere. They fill out the admitted-student questionnaire shown in Exhibit 2 (developed by Donald Gwinn, registrar, Northwestern University), and the respondents are divided into three groups, depending on whether Northwestern was their first choice, was never their first choice, or was equally considered with other schools. Each category is further divided into matriculants and non-matriculants, and the following assessments are made:

• General characteristics of the three different respondent groups: such as personal, social, and academic characteristics.

- Market position: students were asked to rate Northwestern on ten items in relation to other colleges to which the student applied.
- Recruiting contacts: students were asked to rate each of eighteen contacts in terms of their reaction to the contact along a Likert-type scale.
- Competing colleges: students were asked to identify other colleges to which they applied and to impressionistically compare Northwestern with each of the colleges as to whether they were considered to be virtually identical, very similar, somewhat similar, slightly similar but mostly dissimilar, and extremely dissimilar.
- Financial aid comparisons: students were asked to identify the amount and kind of financial aid that they were offered by those colleges to which they were admitted. (A more complete analysis is presented under "Testing Market Perceptions" later in this chapter.)

A less complex questionnaire is used in alternate years, but in each instance new questionnaires are pretested by asking prospective students who are visiting the campus to read and complete the questionnaires. This is a field test to determine whether the questions are understood by the typical candidate for admission.

Other Data-Gathering Methods. Other techniques that may serve the uniqueness of a particular effort are panel discussions, discussions of a general nature, small groups that focus on a particular question or problem, and interviewing students on a structured basis. Often the aggregated information received is sufficient to provide better planning, but the use of statistical designs, such as regression analysis or probit analysis, adds statistical validity to the results. However, in order to begin, one must return to the fundamental questions of what you want to know and how to proceed to know. Possible answers can easily be generated by reading studies related to market analysis in the admission field or by reading the College Guide of the Admissions Testing Program of the College Entrance Examination Board. This monograph is an excellent tool for initiating institutional market research.

Although the information collected in any one year has some value, its usefulness for market analysis and planning improves as the information is collected and analyzed over a number of years. As with

Exhibit 2. Admitted-Student Questionnaire

The information collected from this questionnaire will be used only for research and will be kept strictly confidential. Your I.D. number as shown on this form will be used to match this information with information in your application folder. You may omit any question you feel is too personal.

1. Which best describes the location of your home?

_____ 1. Open countryside
_____ 2. Small town under 20,000
_____ 3. Town 20,000-150,000
_____ 4. City 150,000-500,000
_____ 5. Large city over 500,000

Is your town a suburb of a larger city?

_____ 1. Yes   _____ 2. No

2. In which grade did you first consider applying to North-western?
_____ 1. 12th   _____ 4. 9th
_____ 2. 11th   _____ 5. Earlier
_____ 3. 10th

3. How far from your home is the college you plan to attend?
_____ 1. Under 100 miles
_____ 2. 100-199 miles
_____ 3. 200-299 miles
_____ 4. 300-399 miles
_____ 5. 400-499 miles
_____ 6. Over 500 miles

4. To how many colleges did you apply? _____

To how many were you accepted? _____

5. During your senior year, was N.U.
_____ 1. Always first choice
_____ 2. Considered equally with other colleges
_____ 3. Never first choice

Will you be attending your first-choice college in the fall?
_____ 1. Yes   _____ 2. No

6. Were you enrolled in any College Board Advanced Placement courses in high school?
_____ 1. Yes   _____ 2. No

If yes, how many? _____

7. How many dependent children are in your family? _____

How many will be attending college next year? _____

8. What is your religious preference?
_____ 1. Catholic _____ 3. Protestant
_____ 2. Jewish _____ 4. Other

9. Place the letter F in the blank corresponding to the level of your father's education and an M in the blank corresponding to the level of your mother's education.
_____ 1. Grade school
_____ 2. Some high school
_____ 3. Finished high school
_____ 4. Some college
_____ 5. Finished college
_____ 6. Advanced degree

10. What is your parents' income before taxes? (Use total if both work.)
_____ 1. $ 0-$ 4,999
_____ 2.   5,000- 9,999
_____ 3.   10,000- 14,999
_____ 4.   15,000- 19,999
_____ 5.   20,000- 24,999
_____ 6.   25,000- 29,999
_____ 7.   30,000- 34,999
_____ 8.   35,000- 39,999
_____ 9.   40,000+

Exhibit 2 (continued)

11. Were you selected by the National Merit Scholarship Corporation as a

_____ 1. Natl. Merit Finalist
_____ 2. Natl. Merit Commended Student
_____ 3. Natl. Achievement Finalist
_____ 4. Natl. Achievement Commended Student
_____ 5. None of the above

12. Place the letter *F* in the blank which best describes your father's occupation and an *M* in the blank which best describes your mother's occupation. If either parent is retired or deceased, please indicate the former occupation.

_____ 1. Household worker, laborer, farm worker
_____ 2. Semiskilled worker, operator, waiter
_____ 3. Foreman, craftsman, technician, skilled worker
_____ 4. Homemaker
_____ 5. Salesperson
_____ 6. Farm or ranch owner
_____ 7. Owner or manager of business
_____ 8. Executive in large corporation
_____ 9. Teacher, educator
_____ 10. Physician, dentist, lawyer
_____ 11. Other _____

13. In which area is your ultimate career goal?

_____ 1. Business, industry
_____ 2. Science, math, engineering
_____ 3. Journalism, writing
_____ 4. Entertainment, theater
_____ 5. Medicine, dentistry
_____ 6. Education
_____ 7. Law, government
_____ 8. Other _____

When did you begin anticipating this goal?

_____ 1. Before 9th grade
_____ 2. 9th–10th grade
_____ 3. After 10th grade

How definite is your commitment to this career?

_____ 1. Very definite
_____ 2. Fairly definite
_____ 3. Subject to change
_____ 4. Not at all definite

14. Did you apply for financial aid from any college other than Northwestern?

_____ 1. Yes   _____ 2. No

If no, did you receive any type of scholarship not based on need?

_____ 1. Yes (for which college? _____)
_____ 2. No

15. Please list below the colleges to which you applied and indicate your admission status at each school. If you applied to more than 8, please list your top 8 choices.

College	Admitted?	
	Yes	No
1. Northwestern Univ.	①	2
2. _____	1	2
3. _____	1	2
4. _____	1	2
5. _____	1	2
6. _____	1	2
7. _____	1	2
8. _____	1	2

Which college will you attend, if not Northwestern?

_____

16. How did you first hear about Northwestern? Please comment below.

Exhibit 2 (continued)

17. Did you or will you receive college credit for any courses taken while in high school *other than during the summer?* (This does *not* include courses taken at the high school under the College Board Advanced Placement program for which credit is granted based on your score on the AP examination.)

_____ 1. Yes   _____ 2. No

If yes, please answer the following:

a. Who taught the course(s)?

_____ 1. High school teacher
_____ 2. College professor coming to the high school
_____ 3. College professor at the college

b. Did you pay tuition to the college for the course(s)?

_____ 1. Yes   _____ 2. No   How much per course? _____

c. What college offered the course(s)? _____

Is this a _____ two-year _____ four-year college?

d. Were you taking high school courses simultaneously with the college course(s)?

_____ 1. Yes   _____ 2. No

e. Will these courses be used for high school graduation?

_____ 1. Yes   _____ 2. No

f. How many college courses did you take? _____

g. Will the college you are planning to attend in the fall accept credit for these courses?

_____ 1. Yes   _____ 2. No

18. The following list consists of informational contacts with Northwestern. Please rate each item according to its usefulness to you in making the decision whether to attend Northwestern. Please circle the ratings in the blanks according to the following scale:

1. Especially useful
2. Somewhat useful
3. Interesting, but not particularly useful
4. Not at all useful
5. No opportunity to observe

1	2	3	4	5	1. Article in magazine, newspaper, popular press
1	2	3	4	5	2. Interview with admissions representative
1	2	3	4	5	3. Financial aid information regarding availability of federal, state, or university assistance

Exhibit 2 (continued)

1	2	3	4	5	4. Catalogue
1	2	3	4	5	5. Visit to campus
1	2	3	4	5	6. Contact with NU alumni
1	2	3	4	5	7. Evening program in home town
1	2	3	4	5	8. "Northwestern University Now" booklet
1	2	3	4	5	9. On-campus weekend, open house
1	2	3	4	5	10. Day at Northwestern (April 27, 1978)
1	2	3	4	5	11. Talk with local friends
1	2	3	4	5	12. Contact with NU faculty
1	2	3	4	5	13. Contact with NU students
1	2	3	4	5	14. Contact with NU representative in high school
1	2	3	4	5	15. Letters, brochures, and so on, from NU regarding specific programs
1	2	3	4	5	16. Responsiveness of admission and/or financial aid personnel
1	2	3	4	5	17. Your financial aid award
1	2	3	4	5	18. Overnight stay in dorm

19. Why did you apply to Northwestern?

20a. If you are planning to attend Northwestern, why did you choose NU over your primary alternate?

20b. If you are planning to attend another college, why did you choose that college rather than Northwestern?

The next three questions deal with the colleges to which you applied. Please enter the college names in the same order as you listed them in question 15.

21. Please list the colleges to which you applied in the spaces below. If you applied to more than 8, please list your top 8 choices. Then for each of the statements below, please indicate the degree to which you *believe* the opinion expressed is true for each institution. Write the number of your response to each statement in the space provided, using the following scale:

1. Strongly agree
2. Agree slightly
3. No opinion
4. Disagree slightly
5. Strongly disagree

Exhibit 2 (continued)

Colleges applied to

	Northwestern Univ. 1.	2.	3.	4.	5.	6.	7.	8.

1. The curriculum of this institution is excellent in most areas.

2. The national reputation of this institution is very impressive.

3. The quality of the faculty is very high.

4. The social environment of this institution is conducive to personal growth.

5. Graduates of this institution are likely to have greater potential for academic and professional advancement than graduates of many other colleges.

6. The physical facilities of this institution are very attractive.

7. The student body of this institution is very diverse.

8. This institution is very innovative.

9. This institution places as much or more emphasis on undergraduate education as on graduate education.

10. The information available from the admission office of this institution is well prepared and helpful.

22. Please list the colleges to which you applied in the numbered blanks (as listed in question 15). Each box now represents a pair of colleges. In each box write the number according to the scale below which represents the degree to which you believe the colleges are similar. Please be sure to rate *every* pair of colleges.

Exhibit 2 (continued)

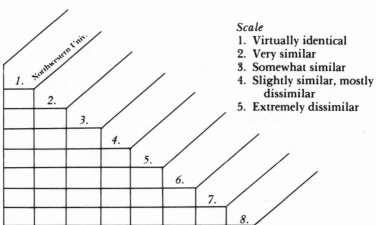

Scale
1. Virtually identical
2. Very similar
3. Somewhat similar
4. Slightly similar, mostly dissimilar
5. Extremely dissimilar

23. Please complete the table below for only those colleges to which you were *admitted* (as listed in question 15); omit those to which you were not admitted. If you did not apply for financial aid from a particular college, please so indicate.

Financial Aid Award (please enter amounts)

College	Estimated Total Cost	Did Not Apply for FA	Outside Award[a]	Grant from College[b]	Loan	Work	Other
1. Northwestern Univ.							
2.							
3.							
4.							
5.							
6.							
7.							
8.							

[a]National Merit, State Scholarship, local corporation, and so on.
[b]Please indicate if college declared you "no need" as a result of your aid applications.

any type of survey research, differences that are likely to occur are more observable if viewed over a longer period. Responses over time tend to eliminate variations from one year to the next unless trends clearly are in a specific direction.

Analyzing Market Behavior

An analysis of data on candidates for admission to Northwestern University provides support for the assumptions related to the student mobility paradigm discussed in Chapter Two. The rather simple formats are presented as a method for analyzing enrollment behavior by market area. The information presented includes only those students who were accepted and who applied for financial aid.

Table 1 shows how many students who were offered financial aid by Northwestern University enrolled there and how many enrolled in other institutions, for each level of parental financial contribution. The table indicates that as financial need decreases, the

Table 1. Enrollment Decisions of Accepted Applicants Offered Grant Assistance by Northwestern University, 1974, 1975, and 1976, by Level of Parental Contribution

Parents' Contribution ($)	Number Enrolling at Northwestern	Number Enrolling Elsewhere	Percent Enrolling at Northwestern	Percent Enrolling Elsewhere
0	160	67	70.4	29.6
1–499	225	116	65.9	34.1
500–999	260	150	63.4	36.6
1000–1499	402	201	66.6	33.4
1500–1999	388	248	61.0	39.0
2000–2499	345	239	59.0	41.0
2500–2999	270	221	54.9	45.1
3000–3499	232	165	58.4	41.6
3500–3999	195	165	54.1	45.9
4000–4499	124	144	46.2	53.8
4500–4999	92	129	41.6	58.4
5000–5499	100	144	40.9	59.1
5500–5999	56	58	49.1	50.9
6000–6499	9	15	37.5	62.5
Total	2858	2059	58.1	41.9

percentage enrolling at Northwestern decreases. The two exceptions to this relationship are intervals $3,000–3,499 and $5,500–5,999. An analysis of individual records showed that a number of these students had been accepted into special programs within the university—an example of special programs having a stronger market position than the university.

Table 2 lists some characteristics of these students. As indicated by the level of parental contribution and geographic origin, students with the greatest amount of financial need came from the Midwest. If the student mobility paradigm is applied to the data in Table 2, the columns $0-3,499, $3,500-4,999, and $5,000+ would represent cells H4, M4, and L4 respectively. Students who fell within cell N4 were not included. However, the farther candidates lived from the university, the less likely they were to apply for financial assistance, with the exception of black students.

From the data presented in Table 2 the following conclusions can be reached:

1. As mean aptitude scores increased, the yield (number enrolling) decreased. This is a function of the relation among test scores, family background, and student mobility.
2. In each category, among those applicants from Illinois, a greater percentage enrolled than did not. This is also true for students from the Midwest in general; however, as aptitude increases, yield decreases both for students from Illinois and for students from other parts of the Midwest.
3. Students from the East are less likely to enroll, irrespective of financial need and intellectual ability. As a reaffirmation of the conclusions drawn previously with regard to student mobility and financial need, it is interesting to note that substantially more students enrolled whose parents were expected to contribute less than $3,500 than students in either of the other two need categories, in which the parental contribution was greater.
4. There appears to be a relation among parental contribution, standardized-test scores, and the number of colleges to which a student applies. The differences may be marginal, but one might conclude that their existence reflects the relation between the family's financial circumstances and student mobility.

Table 2. Characteristics of Freshmen Offered Grant Assistance by Northwestern University, 1974, 1975, and 1976, by Level of Parental Contribution and Enrollment Decision

| | Level of Parental Contribution | | | | | |
| | $0–3499 | | $3500–4999 | | $5000+ | |
Characteristic	Enrolling at Northwestern	Enrolling Elsewhere	Enrolling at Northwestern	Enrolling Elsewhere	Enrolling at Northwestern	Enrolling Elsewhere
Number	2282	1407	319	309	165	217
Percent male	58	64	65	64	64	62
SAT verbal	610	621	615	631	613	620
SAT mathematical	635	678	667	690	678	693
ACT composite	29	30	29	30	29	29
High school rank (percentile)	96	97	96	98	96	97
Geographic origin (percent)						
Illinois	36	26	14	7	34	19
Midwest	35	31	52	41	29	30
East	13	25	17	31	14	34
Other	16	19	17	20	19	16
Colleges applied to	3.01	4.42	3.16	4.36	3.13	5.28
Colleges admitted to	2.65	3.85	2.74	3.81	2.47	4.25
Enrolling public (percent)	0	15	0	27	0	17
Enrolling private other than Northwestern (percent)	0	85	0	73	0	83

5. The vast majority of those students who decided not to attend Northwestern did choose to attend a private university.

As stated previously, this information is helpful in determining the university's primary markets and the potential yield from those markets with regard to students with specific levels of financial need. Clearly, Illinois and the immediate Midwest would be viewed as a primary market and the East Coast as a secondary market. The geographical area identified as Other is also a secondary market, but this category needs to be further subdivided in order to determine why the yield was relatively high for students whose parental contribution was under $3,500. It is likely that some secondary schools within the geographical area identified as Other are primary markets. The Other category for this level of parental contribution also would reflect black students, who had been extensively recruited by the university. These data support the following research findings reported in the literature: (1) that students with relatively high ability and financial need are more likely to attend a college or university near their homes; (2) that as family income increases, student mobility increases; and (3) that students of high ability are more likely to enroll in private colleges and universities than in public institutions, once they have elected to apply to at least one independent institution.

Data on Institutional Market Position

The market position of a college or university, its standing relative to its competition, depends on a number of variables. As indicated previously, perceptions of market position include such criteria as program offerings, quality of facilities, nature of the student body, nature of the faculty, location, ambiance, and economics. What is significant is the realization that each college or university does have a particular market position that is determined by a number of quantifiable variables. Therefore, the administrator, particularly on the admission staff, should be able to compare the market position of the college or a program with that of its main competitors. For the purpose of developing a positioning strategy Geltzer and Ries (1976, p. 85) emphasized three questions: "First, what position, if any, do you already own in the prospect's mind? Second, what position do you want to own? Third, what institutions should be outgunned if you are to establish that position?" To a great extent these three questions should govern the planning process.

Factors in Market Position. What factors permit a college or university to establish a unique market position? Certainly offering students a quality experience is one of them, but often quality alone is not enough. Sixteen hundred private four-year institutions and another 900 four-year public institutions is reason enough for an institution to seek to differentiate its offerings in its various markets from its main competition. (Of course, every institution competes with a rather small number of schools, often restricted by geography and/or similar market positions, not with the total universe of colleges and universities. For one institution the competition may be local; for another, regional; for another, national. However, since even among private institutions 70 percent of the students attend colleges within 500 miles of their homes, the main competition is more regional than national for any institution.) Factors that may contribute to an institution's market position include its price compared with those of other institutions within the region, the desirability and breadth of its program offerings, the interests and diversity of the students attending the institution, the facilities provided, and the opportunities upon graduation.

Most institutions must seek to create a market position by meeting the needs of their present students as well as anticipating the future needs of similar students. Most colleges that lack definition with regard to uniqueness are likely to find the future quite grim. The community college that recognizes a market interest in career and developmental education is likely to thrive, in contrast to the community college that continues to push its transfer program. Sectarian liberal arts colleges that relate their historical pasts to their present constituencies will find a sustaining market, and well-established private and public institutions with fiscal strength will continue to attract their fair share of the market. Institutions that lack definition of role as well as fiscal strength will continue to struggle, and some will close their doors. After studying the environment at some forty institutions that "were single sex and/or religious in the middle 1960s," Anderson (1977) concluded that the general decline in the distinctiveness of those colleges that became coeducational or more secular may in the long term make student recruitment especially difficult. He states, "The loss of unique characteristics is likely to make recruiting students in the future especially difficult. Similar to colleges that supplement their budget by using endowed principal, these 'change' colleges may be considered to have expended educational capital" (Anderson, 1977, p. 85).

Testing Market Perceptions. To develop a fuller appreciation of the need to understand the market perception of an institution, some discussion of the rationale for including certain questions in a questionnaire should be helpful. Question 21 on the admitted-student questionnaire earlier in this chapter exemplifies the kind of question to ask to determine how various institutions are perceived. The question presents a series of statements in such a way as to force an opinion if the respondent has thoughtfully considered the various colleges to which he or she has applied. However, since almost 60 percent of first-time freshmen have applied to only one or two colleges, the question would gather information about perceptions of more colleges if restated to ask applicants or nonapplicants to evaluate colleges they seriously *considered.* Further, the type of statements included in the question should vary with the type of college, the mission of the college, and whether the product or the process is to be evaluated.

As a preliminary question, to broaden the understanding of the market position of a given institution as perceived by a particular market segment, respondents should be asked to identify those colleges they consider the best in their region. These responses should be compared against the responses to the question about colleges that the student applied to or carefully considered. The degree that responses to the two questions vary will provide information about the mobility and the intellectual sophistication of the market. If a college finds that its market does not consider it to be among the best institutions in its region and it has no difficulty in meeting its enrollment goals, then either the institution is meeting a need not being met by the institutions perceived as better or it is attracting students who do not consider themselves to have strong enough records to be admitted to the better institutions. This is a realistic type of self-analysis. Similarly, a Cadillac may be considered a better car than a Ford, but there are more people who can afford Fords. However, another group of consumers who can afford Cadillacs but who buy Fords may believe that the marginal difference in perceived quality does not justify the great difference in price. In both situations, the consumer is making a choice based on expected value in relation to perceived needs.

Question 22 on the admitted-student questionnaire provides for a general but direct comparison between any two institutions or a number of institutions. The reason for including such a question is to determine whether prospects apply to what they consider to be similar institutions or to a variety of different institutions. The responses to this question should be segregated by type of respondent, based on biographical data and geographic area. Such an analysis will determine the level of knowledge about various colleges among various market segments. This analysis should provide rather precise market-segment information and, as a result, should facilitate the planning and communication processes.

Question 23 is an example of an effort to determine the price-discounting practices of competing institutions. Responses to this question should provide information about the following: To what extent do candidates interested in receiving financial aid apply to a different set of colleges than candidates in general? To what extent is the amount of grant assistance awarded by competing colleges determined by financial need? To what extent do competing institutions attempt to improve their market positions by discounting price irrespective of financial need? To what extent do the financial aid packaging practices of the main competitors vary? To what extent is self-help (loan and work) allocated as a fixed amount and as a percentage of the total financial need? To what extent do the academic credentials presented by candidates affect the awarding of grant aid? To what extent are minority candidates treated differently from nonminority candidates in the awarding of financial assistance?

Accepted candidates' reports are likely to be a more valid source of this information than the announced policies of colleges and universities. Once an institution has derived this information, it may wish to vary its policies and practices.

The responses to these three questions should permit a college to identify the following: its principal competition among financial aid candidates as well as other applicants, how the college is perceived by its various markets, the effectiveness of the communication process in selling the college's strengths, the degree to which the perceptions of the college among the various markets are consistent with the perceptions among faculty and staff, and the actual financial aid practices of competing colleges.

National Data on Potential Students

The Carnegie Foundation for the Advancement of Teaching (1975, p. 44) has identified six categories of students with potential growth: part-time students, non-degree students, students aged twenty-two and older, graduate and first-degree professional students, women students, and minority students. The growth among these categories of students has been facilitated by expansion of the Basic Educational Opportunity Grant Program—the foundation of federal student assistance—and by creation of the State Student Incentive Program to encourage states to develop grant programs. The former is considered a program for providing access to higher education, and the latter is related more to choice of college. The substantial increase in part-time enrollments may be partly accounted for by the fact that half-time students recently became eligible for federal assistance programs. As the country approaches universal access to postsecondary education, it is likely that a saturation point will be reached in the categories of students named above, except graduate and first-degree professional students. How much elasticity there is among these groups has yet to be determined. Some colleges will be able to develop programs to attract students in several of these categories, whereas others may only be able to meet the needs of students in a single category. As more people receive baccalaureate degrees, the professional-adult continuing education market should continue to expand, as long as program offerings are short-term and do not conflict with these potential students' day-to-day responsibilities.

Clearly, the greatest growth in enrollments has occurred in the non-degree-credit areas. From 1970 to 1975, degree-credit enrollments increased 4.2 percent and non-degree enrollments 17.1 percent (Golladay, 1976, p. 225). Since most of these non-degree enrollments were in community colleges, it would appear that they fall into the category of general continuing education that is not part of a professional-adult continuing education program. The latter is defined as offering a special series of courses to members of a given profession in a specified period of time. Examples of such students would include electrical engineers, orthopedic surgeons, and life-insurance underwriters. If there is to be growth, it may well be in the professional-adult area. Arbeiter and others (1978) found that individuals who had previously achieved success in an educational setting were more likely to want to acquire additional education at another time. Additional evidence for this finding is provided by the education demands placed on professional employees in industry. In 1977, 4,300,000 employees of larger corporations took courses offered by their companies at a cost of $2 billion (Luxenberg, 1978/79). However, the American Society for Training and Development estimates that the world of business is spending $40 billion annually for the education, re-education, and training of employees; much of this training occurs outside the walls of higher education ("Why Business Takes Education into Their Own Hands," 1979, p. 70). Obviously, this suggests a demand that is not being met by higher education. Conversely, opportunities for four-year colleges and universities in the non-degree, nontechnical continuing education market appear to be limited. Secondary schools (through adult education programs) and community colleges will continue to meet the demand of this market because these consumers do not have the time for courses that require substantial intellectual commitment.

The relation between size of institution and ability to accommodate various consumer needs remains to be determined. Although the Carnegie Council conjectured that the larger institutions should have more flexibility to accommodate the changing needs in the marketplace, size often spells bureaucracy. Minter and Bowen's (1978) report on private higher education suggests that the small college and the comprehensive university are showing considerable tenacity in surviving. If survival requires responding to the needs of a new and an older market, then small private colleges, especially those in major metropolitan areas, may be able to accommodate change more willingly and with less stress than larger institutions.

The traditional liberal arts college located in a rural area faces a difficult future unless it has strong sectarian support. Whom will such colleges serve as the number of eighteen- to twenty-four-year-olds begins to decline? Many such colleges have sought to develop good relations with community colleges, but two-year colleges are enrolling an increasing number of non-degree candidates and students interested in two-year career programs. As evidence that the two-year college attracts a different type of student, in Illinois the typical student enrolled is over age twenty-five and is working part-time, if not full-time. Hence, two-year institutions do not appear to be a substantial source of students for traditional programs in four-year institutions.

At least temporarily, the foreign student market is expanding. In 1976–77, for the first time, more than 200,000 students from foreign countries enrolled in American colleges. By 1977–78, the number of foreign students exceeded 235,000—double their number ten years earlier. A high percentage of these students are from oil-producing countries. Factors that may accelerate the number of foreign nationals are the continued decrease in the value of the dollar in relation to foreign currency and the increased interest in learning and applying Western technology. The number of students from foreign countries will very likely continue to increase. Thus, this is another market that could be cultivated by some colleges (Institute of International Education, 1978b).

Interestingly—and maybe a sad commentary—at a time when higher education at the undergraduate level is preparing for a substantial decrease in the numbers of students, the demand for a trade school diploma appears to be increasing. In fact, an article in the *Chicago Tribune* ("Trade Schools May Be 'Bargain,' " 1979) reports that there are now more than 7,000 proprietary schools with revenues of $3 billion a year. A closer look at this booming demand for proprietary education shows that many of the students could attend a community college and enroll in a similar program at substantial savings. The question is why these students have elected to attend more-costly schools. My best guess is that these are students who previously did not find their formal learning experience in public education to be very satisfying but who realize the need to develop better technical skills. Another reason may well be the interest many proprietary schools show in seeking satisfactory employment for their graduates. In each instance there is a lesson to be learned by higher education. Obviously, these schools are meeting a market need—ironically, one that may have been created by a poor experience previously in either secondary or higher education.

Student Satisfaction and Attrition

As a catalyst for institutional change, the staff in the admission office should assume an attitude of continued institutional evaluation. This effort not only requires assessing its own role and how successfully each staff member is performing it but also includes keeping in touch with undergraduates to determine their degree of satisfaction. Such a program will require using various research techniques to assess the degree of satisfaction, such as interviews, questionnaires, and focus groups. (In a focus group, faculty members, students, and administrators are brought together to discuss a particular topic.)

If there is another office within the institution that is assigned the responsibility of institutional research, the admission office should coordinate its efforts with that unit. However, gathering information is just the first step. Communicating what one has learned to the appropriate opinion leaders is the next step; it may or may not be a call for action. The office of admission should take the initiative and provide the faculty with information on the degree to which student needs are being met. If attrition is a problem, the admission staff should find out why attrition is high and suggest ways to reduce it.

The answer to the enrollment problems of many colleges is simply to reduce attrition. Henderson and Plummer (1978, p. 31) provide information that underlines the attrition crisis in public and private higher education. In order to graduate 100 seniors, four-year public institutions must enroll from 160 to 311 freshmen, depending on type of institution. The range among four-year privates is 120 to 192. A 10 percent decrease in attrition in each class in one year is equivalent to a 30 percent increase in enrollment, assuming that the enrollment in each class is about the same. In recognition that no more than 60 percent of students at private colleges and universities graduate in four years and about 40 percent of those at public four-year institutions graduate in four years, it would appear that there is much room for improvement in this area.

Reasons for attrition tend to vary by type of institution. The recruitment practices of some institutions contribute to the attrition problem. Colleges that offer no-need scholarships to students with greater ability than students currently enrolled are likely to find that their investment transfers to another institution. Enrolling students who find it difficult to identify with upperclassmen are not likely to stay long. An example of this type of mismatch is found in colleges that try to recruit students whose religious profiles are quite different from that of the typical student enrolled. The same can be said of students who are recruited from major metropolitan areas to small rural colleges. A college may not have any choice, but the attrition is likely to be quite high .

At the same time there are areas within many colleges that require change if attrition is to be reduced. An important factor in reducing attrition is to get students involved in some area of the institution (Astin, 1975). However, the objective should be to communicate the message "Yes, we really care about our students, particularly you." Faculty members may need to become more responsive, student support services, such as advising and personal counseling, may need to be improved, and residence-hall life may require greater programming. One example is the residential college plan that requires courses or field study experiences as part of the living experience. If such improvements are made, the result is a system of early intervention before a student encounters academic difficulty or becomes dissatisfied with the college environment. Moreover, an effort should be made to stay in contact with those who drop out. They remain alumni of the institution and potential returning students.

As additional references on the subject of attrition, articles by Pantages and Creedon (1978) and by Peng and Fetter (1978) are suggested.

4

Organizing for Planning

Once the research questions discussed in Chapter Three are understood, if not answered, a plan needs to be developed that will permit the admission staff to use the new information efficiently and effectively. Historically, little planning has taken place in admission offices. Each year the same cycle is followed: brochures and catalogues are updated; prospective students are contacted either through direct mail or personally; the same secondary schools are visited; campus tours are offered, with the opportunity to stay overnight; and the same conferences are attended. Some admission personnel ask why, but either because of lack of skills and time or because representatives of other schools continue on the same beaten path, no changes in the cycle occur until faculty members or other administrators ask why. Then, before the "why" is answered, a change in personnel is made, and the cycle, with modest changes, is continued by someone else. I am not saying that all the traditional efforts are inappropriate, but their effectiveness remains in doubt because the "why" for a given college is seldom answered.

For the education of those who have never represented a typical college at a typical secondary school, let us review the scenario. The college representative makes an appointment with a secondary school counselor about a month in advance of the visit. A typical schedule for a representative will include visiting four to five schools a day, depending on the distance between schools. When the admission representative arrives, the counselors are often quite busy, and often there are no students to see—either because there is simply no interest or because the counselor failed to announce the visit. If no students appear, the representative will request a few minutes to provide the counselor with some additional information about the college. At about the time the representative begins the third or fourth sentence, another representative from another college appears, and the counselor and the second admission representative go through the same process. The first representative politely leaves and begins the drive to the next school, with a brief stop to make a call to an alumnus, a parent of an undergraduate, or a parent of a prospective student. Frequently, no one is at home, and the drive is continued to the next school.

Although there are exceptions, this process, in general, is inefficient and often professionally demeaning. It seldom leads to professional development and continued enthusiasm for the institution, and it creates a third-party dependency on secondary school personnel that is not necessary and often counterproductive—not necessary in that it is not the role of a high school counselor to direct students to a given college, and counterproductive in that both the admission officer and the secondary school counselor can use their time more effectively and efficiently working directly with students and their families. Accordingly, a recruitment plan should be developed to maximize the use of human and financial resources.

Assessing and Improving the Institutional Image

If the admission staff is fortunate, other administrators will be equally interested in developing a marketing plan for the institution as a whole. In so doing, they will want to assess the current perceived image of the institution. This requires a coordinated effort and involves top management and all the units that operate on the boundaries of a college or university. Assessment of the image requires input from undergraduates, faculty members, alumni, and friends who are opinion leaders. For the most part, images held by people both in and outside the university are outdated. Often, faculty members and students have very little understanding of what the present demographics of the student body are, who among the faculty are considered to be the most outstanding teachers by the undergraduate student body, and who among the faculty are regarded by their peers in various disciplines as having contributed significantly to scholarship. Because it is hard to quantify the effect of the educational experience at a given institution, images are often based on hearsay, misleading press, or criticisms that have been passed from one generation of students and faculty members to another.

Only through the interest of top management in institutional assessment can a plan be developed to promote the institution as it exists today. The usual procedure is for the president to name a task force of faculty members, administrators, alumni, and distinguished professionals to evaluate each segment of the institution. Kotler (1975, pp. 55–62) calls this process a "marketing audit" and defines it as "an independent examination of the entire marketing effort of an organization covering objectives, programs, implementation, organization, and control, for the purpose of determining and appraising what is being done and recommending what should be done in the future."

Many colleges and universities have observed a decrease in enrollment at a time when the quality of the experience they have to offer is at its peak. The reason is usually that top management is suffering from myopia and has not concerned itself with communicating in any systematic way with the external publics of the institution. The president of a college or university, like it or not, is not only the image maker but also the image leader. However, the director of admission cannot be content to pass on the responsibility. If an outdated image is lowering enrollment, the director of admission has no alternative but to assume the leadership by involving faculty members, students, and alumni in developing a plan to project the current image to the various external markets. Implicitly, if not explicitly, the director of admission may have little choice but to become the director of marketing.

The responsibility of the admission office is to facilitate problem solving; however, top management and distinguished members of the faculty should be involved. Participation by the dean of faculties is most critical to acquiring faculty support. To make the institution more attractive to the traditional college-age population and/or to older students in the 1980s, an enlightened dean of faculties should facilitate the following changes: (1) stimulate a concern about increasing student satisfaction with the total institutional environment; (2) encourage a greater commitment by the faculty and the administration to the instructional mission of the institution in order to improve the quality of the experience within and outside the classroom; and (3) review and recommend changes in the pricing policies and course-scheduling practices, if required to make the institution attractive to older students. Greater flexibility in both scheduling and pricing is likely to be required to accommodate the work obligations of a part-time student population.

From the perspective of the admission office, a first step in improving student satisfaction is to develop an effective communication plan that describes the mission of the institution. Students should know why they are attending a particular college. Many colleges and universities have tried to become too many things to too many people and, as a result, have undermined the quality of programs for which they had become known. Consequently, the development of new programs should be consistent with the mission of the institution and should not be a response to the capricious interests of the marketplace, which may be here today but gone tomorrow. Nonetheless, once programs have been implemented, it becomes the responsibility of the admission office in cooperation with the faculty, the department of public relations, and the various student and alumni groups to orchestrate the promotional effort.

Fundamental Concepts for Organizing the Marketing Effort

Many professional admission officers have long recognized their role in serving potential students and their families. Given the increasing competition among colleges for students, however, admission officers have the responsibility of expanding the perception of the service they are performing to other areas of their institution. Not uncommonly, the members of the admission staff perceive themselves, and are perceived, as outsiders looking in. Many faculty members have not considered the admission staff to be a part of the academic community because in many institutions the director of admission reports to someone other than the vice-president for academic affairs. In a large institution, reporting to the vice-president for academic affairs is the only line relationship that makes sense if the director of admission is to develop credibility with members of the faculty and maintain their support. It might be argued that the function of the admission office is a student service and, therefore, the line relationship should be student affairs. In theory this may appear sensible, but in practice the objectives to be achieved by the admission office must be recognized as a high budget priority directly related to student satisfaction with the academic experience. Consequently, because of the degree of authority resting with the faculty, the admission office should report either to the chief academic officer or to the president.

Regardless of the organizational structure and the line relationship, two concepts are basic if the admission office wishes to maintain integrity with its various audiences. One is "openness" and the other is "involvement." Openness in this context means that directors and their staffs should be willing to share information with faculty members, alumni, and students. Too often the admission office has had a withdrawal philosophy. Because of a lack of research capability and often just plain insecurity among members of the staff, the admission office has been unwilling to share with faculty members and alumni its overall plans and objectives. Two forms of openness apply: internal and external. This openness should be viewed as an exchange relationship not only with faculty members, students, and other administrators but also with other admission officers, alumni, and secondary school counselors and teachers.

The other concept, "involvement," is basic to improving the credibility of the admission staff. The admission staff will derive an ultimate benefit from adopting a posture that permits anyone from its various audiences to be involved in the admission process. An effective admission marketing team will include faculty members, alumni, students, and the staffs in other departments. Although many arguments are given why alumni, faculty members, and students should not formally represent an institution, they generally are without substance. For every poor representative one might find from the above-named groups, there are hundreds of excellent representatives. The risk of having faculty members and alumni provide bad information or create a poor impression is well worth taking if the admission office can adequately support the information needs of a diversified marketing team. Alumni and faculty members will be only as responsive as the staff of the admission office is. Kotler (1975, p. 43) suggests that for an organization to be fully responsive it must formally and regularly audit constituent needs, encourage active communication and participation, and accept the consensus of its constituents. If the concepts of openness and involvement can be operationalized, they will form the foundation of a highly responsive marketing organization.

Basic Functions of the Admission Staff

Along with the development, alumni, governmental-affairs, and public-relations offices, the admission office operates on the boundaries of the institution. This position provides the office of admission with the opportunity to keep the faculty in touch with the needs of the marketplace and to assess how effectively the institution is responding to those needs, as well as to the needs of the current students. The office of admission should not only gather information from outside but disseminate information to the faculty and to various external audiences. This flow of information from the admission office to different audiences requires that a well-orchestrated plan be developed. Effective communication is a part of the overall marketing strategy. How well this communication among the faculty, students, and external audiences is orchestrated depends on the staff in the admission office.

The admission office should be responsible for monitoring the overall recruitment effort. Accepting such a concept is quite different from assuming that it is the admission staff's responsibility to recruit a particular number of students. The admission staff should create the communication structure, but the primary communication should take place between faculty members, students, and alumni and prospective students, their families, and secondary school personnel. Thus, through implementing the concepts of openness and involvement, the staff in the admission office can facilitate fluid communication by means of the structure it creates and monitors. If the admission staff perceives its role as being a catalyst and a facilitator, both the external and internal audiences should have a good sense of what each has to offer the other. Providing the community inside the institution with information about the programs presently in demand in the marketplace and the extent to which the institution is meeting these demands is critical to the institution's future.

People who have influence are all around us. Their involvement is significant in achieving institutional objectives. Nevertheless, unusual sensitivity is required in order for an admission staff to identify those people who are opinion leaders as demonstrated by their capability to influence other people as well as community organizations. Opinion leaders exist throughout the internal framework of the institution. A director of admission is responsible for maintaining continued contact with those faculty and staff members who can influence others and who hold opinions generally representing a consensus of their colleagues.

The same analysis can be made of people in communities external to the university. Opinion leaders are in every occupation, whether it be education, banking, law, or labor. A marketing plan should include communicating directly with opinion leaders who live in communities near the institution and who either currently or at one time have expressed an interest in the institution. We are all in the business of making friends, and those friends who influence others are extremely important to fulfilling the overall mission of the institution.

Admission Planning

Effective planning is more likely to result in good management, and developing a marketing-oriented admission office will encourage more-effective planning. The intent in this section is to provide the rationale for changing prior practices and to recommend an organizational structure.

The marketing plan must be flexible so that it can be modified from time to time. There ought to be two plans: one that is short-term, related to achieving immediate enrollment objectives, and the other of a longer term, from three to five years. The latter will provide for continued modification through experience, research, and intuition.

A number of reasons can be given that the admission officers of even the most selective colleges and universities should be more systematic in their planning and should be willing to think in marketing terms. Every institution faces one or more of the following objectives: increasing enrollments despite national trends, stabilizing enrollments through the 1980s, changing the socioeconomic mix of the student body, improving the quality of the student body, achieving a better distribution of student academic interests across programs, publicizing newly developed programs to various audiences, and projecting a realistic image of the institution.

The planning effort should consider what is known about the institution, its competition, and the various market segments. From this information a plan should evolve that includes a number of strategies, depending on the demographics of a particular market. Different markets perceive the institution differently and therefore require a modification of the basic plan. The various forms of communication should vary, at least to a degree, by geographic location, socioeconomic background, racial dominance, and a given market's orientation toward higher education.

To provide a frame of reference, a basic marketing plan is presented below. This plan provides a foundation for creating a comprehensive marketing strategy and is expanded on throughout the remainder of the text. The basic outline can be applied to the admission activities of any college or university.

i. Two committees should be created consisting of faculty members, alumni, and students. One committee will be responsible for establishing admission policy, and the other for developing a marketing plan. The latter committee will have broader responsibility for creating a market-oriented institution but will work closely with the admission director. The two committees should work together to assess the character of the institution and how it is perceived. Through this assessment each committee will be

able to establish reasonable policies and to acquire an understanding of the type of student who has elected to attend the institution.

2. The student body should be subdivided into market segments
based on geography, academic fields of interest, financial need,
and ethnic and racial background. Each subdivision should be
reclassified into primary, secondary, and tertiary markets (see
Chapter Five).

3. A comprehensive prospect list should be developed by market
area, fifteen months before the desired date of enrollment, that
matches the demographics of the current student body. A secondary list can be created to accommodate the enrollment needs of a
new program or a desired change in the nature of the student
body, but this should be viewed as a pilot effort.

4. A quality first-contact piece should be created with a postage-paid
reply card.

5. The capability should exist to keep track of which prospects have
been contacted, how frequently, and who has responded. This
may be done by hand or at small expense through the use of a key-
punch machine, a card sorter, and a printer. A computer software
package permits greater tracking ability but is not necessary.

6. The replies to anticipated inquiries should be prepared.

7. The second and third contact pieces for nonrespondents by
market area should be created. Students from different markets
will require different types of communication.

8. A recruitment strategy by market area should be planned. Campus and noncampus events should be considered separately for
different market areas.

9. An alumni admission program on a pilot basis should be developed and restricted to a specific geographic area.

10. In institutions that enroll dependent students, an ancillary communication plan directed toward the interests of parents should
be implemented.

11. A series of information programs for counselors and secondary
school teachers should be planned. It may consist of newsletters
and campus and off-campus programs of an instructional and
social nature.

12. A contingency recruitment plan should be developed to accommodate a forecasted shortfall in enrollment based upon a market analysis of the candidate pool.
13. An evaluation program that includes surveying applicants and nonapplicants should be developed to measure the effects of the marketing strategy.

The order of items in this list is not meant to imply a sequence. Clearly, a number of tasks would have to precede others, and several projects would have to be developed simultaneously. For example, the creation of the committees should precede the development of admission policies and institutional assessment, but it is not necessary to create the two committees in order to proceed with the other activities.

Organization of the Admission Staff

In admission offices no one organizational model for function, staffing, general and specific responsibilities, and reporting relationships appears dominant. The personalities and the sophistication of the leadership of the admission staff and the immediate supervisor have often determined the organizational format. Organization is affected by other factors, such as size of the institution, its nature (public or private), and societal pressures. Commonly, during an era of growth, the larger public institutions have been more concerned with processing problems than with interpersonal relationships. Conversely, the admission staffs of smaller private institutions have been so informal and personal that records often have not been maintained. These, of course, represent the extremes, but, in fact, such operations still exist.

More recently, the larger impersonal processing centers have been modified by the demands placed on them by minority groups and by either real or anticipated erosion in enrollments. Increasingly, those who have been responsible for the computer-software approach to admission have begun to realize that the computer is only a support tool and that the processing of paper cannot be perceived as the principal responsibility of the admission office. Consequently, these institutions are beginning to emphasize the importance of developing strong interpersonal relationships with their various constituencies. In contrast, the smaller private institutions that have operated their admission offices on an ad hoc basis are recognizing the need for more-sophisticated methods, including software packages to support their recruitment efforts. The result is that both types of institutions are becoming more marketing-oriented in their approaches to recruitment. Both now realize the need to develop a good data base and to cultivate, in a personal way, the interests of present constituencies and potential new markets.

Yet, since the admission responsibilities across institutions are somewhat uniform, a number of objectives should be achieved through the organizational structure. If the director of admission perceives his or her role as orchestrating the marketing effort, then the admission office must be structured in such a way as to include and monitor the activities of alumni, faculty members, current students, friends, and secondary school personnel as members of the marketing team. Such a structure will lead to an evaluation of both personnel and management objectives.

Personnel. Regrettably, the professional staff of most admission offices is unqualified to meet the management task at hand. Until recently, top management's attitude toward the admission office has been one of neglect. The admission staff is generally thought to be unskilled but loyal—expendable and cheap but necessary as long as it does not get involved in educational programming. Too often admission staffs consist of recent graduates who are enthusiastic but who know little or nothing about management processes and who have not developed the necessary skills to achieve the objectives of management.

Limited skills, low salaries, and a lack of input into the decision-making process have resulted in high turnover among admission staff members. Too often those who have the skills become dissatisfied and leave. Those who remain, unfortunately, assume more and more responsibility and often become intransigent in their views. There are certain skills that the staff of every admission office should have. A lexicon of basic skills would include communication, analytical, statistical, computer, counseling, and interpersonal. These skills do not have to be finely tuned, but the staff collectively should demonstrate interest in these areas.

Developing the proper mix of complementary personalities and skills may be difficult. To the extent possible, the personal backgrounds of the staff members should be as diversified as those of the community they represent. One source of such talent may be the faculty itself. In this era of tenure quotas there is a surplus of faculty talent seeking administrative positions. Almost every campus has young faculty members who know that their teaching days are numbered because they will not receive tenure. Such personnel provide the office of admission with the opportunity to add complementary skills and at the same time acquire greater credibility among the faculty members it represents. To employ one or two former members of the faculty who offer the kinds of skills mentioned above and to permit them to teach one course a year is an attractive option that assists in bridging the gap between the admission office and the faculty, in addition to enhancing the director's credibility.

In setting salaries the objective should be to attract and retain competent people. Members of the admission staff should consider their positions as careers, rather than temporary employment, and accordingly should be paid on a scale comparable to that of the faculty. As a model, salary ranges would parallel those of assistant, associate, and full professors. An assistant director of admission should be paid as well as an assistant professor, an associate director as well as an associate professor, and a director as well as a full professor. Indeed, in the future, as the role of the admission office is increasingly recognized for the revenue it generates, an admission staff that produces is likely to be among the highest-paid personnel in the administration. To the skeptic, I would add that it is cheaper to be able to retain competent staff members than to contract with a consulting firm, a common practice among many colleges.

In such an environment the director should not be at all hesitant to release staff members who are not performing effectively. The kind of organization and accountability that is effective and individually gratifying is one in which each member of the staff fully understands his or her responsibilities as a specialist within the department and as a program manager. Further, as specialists all members should understand how their skills complement one another's and how their performances relate to achieving the department's overall goal. Clearly, at times, each person must be a generalist, which includes such repetitive activities as visiting high schools, reading folders, and interviewing candidates. At the same time, a structure must exist that defines specific roles for each member of the staff. As a specialist with a given skill related to a given responsibility, each member of the staff should be made to feel that there is considerable flexibility. The intradepartmental organization should be horizontal, as contrasted with the more traditional vertical structure that exists within departments in the corporate world or within the institution's administration. Through a horizontal structure the free flow of ideas is more likely, territories are not likely to be protected, and the environment is likely to be one that stimulates personal growth.

Creation of such an environment, representing various personalities and skills, will result in greater use of resources, whether they be dollars or people. A staff that finds that it has plenty of flexibility will generate ideas to implement new programs and will seek out significant publics in order to share ideas, proposals, and accomplishments. A staff of people with different talents and convictions will extend the boundaries of the admission office through the natural process of identifying with other people similar to themselves and outside the department. People with common interests and hobbies will seek one another out, independent of departmental boundaries.

Management. The management function in the admission office is usually assigned to the director or the associate director and requires unique personal traits. It is an extremely visible position, entailing contact with as many audiences as the presidency of the institution, if not more. At the same time, it requires a personality that is goal-oriented and not easily threatened. Successes and failures of the director are measured on an annual basis. To have more successes than failures requires stability among a staff with varied skills, an environment that stimulates personal growth, and input by the director into the institutional decision-making process.

As a good manager, the director should select staff members with complementary skills, not skills that mirror his or her own. The assignment of responsibilities should capitalize on the available skills of the staff. In football, a good coach will adapt his system to take advantage of his players' skills as he encourages his players to develop new skills. If no one on the staff has a requisite skill, someone on the staff with interest in acquiring the skill should be given the opportunity to attend workshops and to take courses in order to develop it. For example, a person with two years of college math could quickly acquire "cookbook" statistical skills.

In relation to staff skills and the assignment of responsibilities, the manager is responsible for creating an environment that encourages development of individual professional interests and use of personal skills. A person who has literary skills should be assigned the responsibility of either writing various publications or working with the department that is assigned this task, such as public relations. For every resource required by the admission office but within the province of another unit, a member of the staff with the related skill or interest should be given the assignment to cooperate with the other unit. It should not be necessary for each admission office to write all its own publications, establish its own computer support system, and do its own research. However, an understanding of such skills as writing, computer programming, or applied mathematics is necessary if the admission staff is to communicate effectively with the units, either inside or outside the institution, that are responsible for such support activities. A systems analyst can be of greater assistance if she is able to speak her language to someone on the professional staff in the admission office. The same is true of publications and of research. Another skill, that of humanness, is one that we all try to achieve—some with greater success than others. To have someone on the staff who sets an example in interpersonal relationships tends to embellish and enhance this trait in other members of the staff. Summarily, the director of admission should seek people who have skills that complement his or her own and who either independently or collectively improve the effectiveness of the department.

Humane and experiential skills that cannot be quantified are absolutely necessary if the admission department is to have credibility. On every staff, some people relate best to students, others to faculty members, and still others to alumni and parents. The sensitive manager will make these differentiations in the assignment of people-to-people responsibilities. Certainly, all members of the staff must be able to relate to prospective students, but to match members of the staff with prospects of common interests is far more productive, particularly in one-on-one situations.

Whether a manager has input into the institutional decision-making process depends largely on his or her ability to meet institutional enrollment objectives. A director will have input at the time he or she accepts the position, but the honeymoon will be over within a year unless progress is shown. A director can reduce the risks by developing a staff with the requisite skills, by creating an environment of growth, and by involving faculty members, students, and alumni in the planning process. It is prudent for a director to request that an admission committee be formed if one does not exist. The function of such a committee should be to act as a sounding board and to recommend admission policies based on information from internal and external sources. It should not be the responsibility of the admission committee to make decisions on applications except on a selected basis. An involved and active committee of faculty members, administrators, and students can help the admission staff develop institutional credibility. An informed committee also can act as a buffer during a crisis or if other institutional officers try to influence admission policies in undesirable ways.

An Organizational Model. Kotler (1979) suggests a number of approaches to developing a marketing-oriented college or university. They range from such modest proposals as appointing a marketing committee and task force to conduct institutional audits to more dramatic and institutionalized recommendations, such as creating a position of vice-president for marketing. Obviously, other titles can be suggested, such as "vice-president for institutional advancement" or "vice-president for institutional relations." More important is the desirability of creating an environment that will permit the director of admission to begin to think like a director of marketing. Therefore, the time to reflect so that one can direct research and plan is critical. Most directors of admission are involved too much in day-to-day operations to be able to reflect and to introduce new plans based on empirical data—although by definition these are the functions of a director of marketing. To create such an environment, a director of admission should remove himself or herself from the daily operation and assign the related responsibilities to an associate director. The objective should be to create an organizational structure that will permit the free flow of ideas within the admission office and between the admission staff and audiences external to the admission office.

Although there may not be one best organizational plan and staffing pattern for all institutions, there are some common needs that should be fulfilled by any admission staff. The acquisition of the skills described under "Personnel" earlier in this chapter provides for an organization that will be able to respond to the information and participation interests of various audiences, as well as to the goals established by the institution for the admission office. However, the management of those skills as defined by the organizational structure will determine the extent to which the skills are fully utilized. The organizational model that enhances the development of various skills and appears to best accommodate a marketing approach is one that integrates the admission and financial aid processes. In this period of increasing costs and substantial amounts of financial aid, the admission staff should be well informed about the various financial aid options available to families, and the financial aid staff should be cognizant of the market problems facing the admission office. Unfortunately, it is frequently found that the admission and financial aid offices report to different vice-presidents having different budget priorities. A likely consequence of such an organizational plan is to further separate the functions of the two offices. A director of financial aid who is responsible for administering freshman financial aid but who does not work closely with the admission office can undermine the marketing efforts of the admission staff. Moreover, a complete separation of functions of the two offices as defined by the organizational structure does not lend itself to meeting the financial aid information needs of the admission staff or of potential students.

The desirable model is one that encourages a flow of information between the two offices and sensitizes the financial aid staff to the informational needs of students and their families. The organizational model presented in Figure 2 separates the administration of entering-student and returning-student financial aid but permits the director of financial aid to monitor the administration of new-student assistance. Since the directors of admission and financial aid report to the same vice-provost, this model provides for greater individual opportunity through the maximization of available skills. Staff members in the office of financial aid should assume some recruiting responsibilities, and interested staff members in the admission office

Figure 2. Organizational Plan and Staffing Pattern

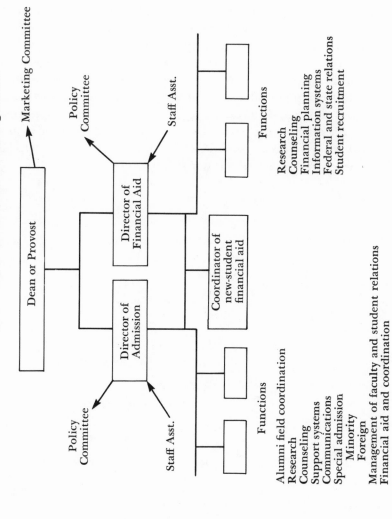

Marketing Committee

Dean or Provost

Policy Committee

Director of Financial Aid

Staff Asst.

Director of Admission

Policy Committee

Staff Asst.

Coordinator of new-student financial aid

Functions

Research
Counseling
Financial planning
Information systems
Federal and state relations
Student recruitment

Functions

Alumni field coordination
Research
Counseling
Support systems
Communications
Special admission
Minority
Foreign
Management of faculty and student relations
Financial aid and coordination

should assist the financial aid office in the renewal of returning student aid.

This organizational model also identifies a policy committee assigned to each office, but under the integrated model only one committee is necessary. A separate marketing committee would report to the vice-provost but would work closely with the admission and financial aid policy committee. The responsibilities identified on the chart may vary to some extent by institution, but under an integrated plan, a person with computer or research skills can serve the interests of both offices; duplication of personnel is not required. The same can be said of other necessary skills. However, special attention should be given to the responsibility of federal and state relations in the office of financial aid. An understanding of the complexities of federal and state financial aid programs and the related application processes and regulations has become a highly technical and required skill. This is a premium skill, and no institution can afford to have someone in this area who is not well informed.

5

Identifying and Segmenting the Markets

The preceding chapters provided information within a general marketing context, with marketing defined as applying to both product and process. Three components were identified: research, planning, and developing strategies involving both programs and the communication process.

This chapter will expand the discussion of market segmentation begun with the presentation of the student mobility paradigm in Chapter Two. The focus will be on interpreting and developing an institution's primary and secondary markets and on a suggested methodology for penetrating these markets. A forecasting model will be developed to project enrollments on the basis of the size and characteristics of the prospect pool. The last section will address the nontraditional market.

The Primary Market

The primary market is defined as a high-yield market in terms of the number of applications received over time from a single

secondary school, a number of secondary schools, or a given geographic area. Typically, a high percentage of primary-market candidates who submit applications are accepted and elect to attend the
institution. Arbitrarily, one might define a single primary market as
generating an enrollment yield of at least 40 percent of the students
accepted over a period of three to five years. Implicitly, there are
numerous primary markets. A primary market should be easily identified if simple records have been preserved showing the number of
students submitting applications, the number accepted, and the
number enrolling by secondary school within a geographic area. It is
not uncommon for a secondary school, or for that matter a church, to
be a primary market for a college as far as 1,000 miles away. This
would be true for a secondary school that has a national reputation
and sends a high percentage of its graduates on to four-year colleges
or a church that has developed a strong relationship between its youth
groups and a given institution. Many high schools located in or near
major metropolitan areas have a large percentage of students who
attend four-year institutions and who are quite mobile with regard to
college choice. The same can be said of a number of independent
preparatory schools throughout the country. Generally speaking,
though, the primary market is within 300 miles of the institution.

However, even within the primary-market geographic area,
there will be many secondary schools that are not primary markets.
Proximity simply increases the likelihood that a given secondary
school will be a primary market. Moreover, within a primary-market
secondary school a matching process will occur between the market
position of the institution or of a program offered by the institution
and the interests and abilities of a given student. The key to a successful recruitment effort is to be able to identify a large number of
prospects within the primary market with interests and abilities
similar to the profile of students currently in attendance. For many
colleges it is a waste of effort to try to attract students from secondary
schools serving sophisticated populations. A college must acknowledge the type of institution that it is, unless it is prepared for the long
and difficult task of radical change. If it generally draws students
from middle-class and less sophisticated backgrounds, then the
admission staff should focus its efforts on that market. Secondary
schools that send only 30 to 40 percent of their students on to college
may be the best market for some institutions.

One way to assess the impact of geography is to draw a series of concentric circles around the location of the institution with radii of multiples of fifty miles. The percentage yield should be substantially higher in the first fifty miles than in the last fifty, which may be as far as 1,000 miles from the institution. The yield will decrease as distance increases. One exception to this rule is that the initial distance may be more than 50 miles for colleges located in areas with low population density. Often the primary market is the closest major metropolitan area, since density of population is certainly critical to this analysis. Another exception would be colleges located in metropolitan areas with predominantly commuter populations. In this instance, the market should be analyzed by ZIP-code area or by neighborhood to determine the primary market. For such colleges the primary market may be the area within a radius of no more than five miles. Moreover, for such colleges to expand their enrollment, it may be necessary to establish branch campuses beyond the primary market area.

Although it seems inconceivable that a college would not have a primary market, institutions both well known and almost unknown have been unable to define their primary market; or, if one exists, the college has not been able to forecast the productivity of that market. This situation has resulted because no records have been kept and, therefore, no plan existed. From year to year the same "shotgun" procedures have been followed without any questions being asked. For example, a major private university in the Midwest was drawing more students from the East Coast than from the city in which it was located, although that city and the surrounding suburban areas have a population of at least two million. The result was a rather high attrition rate because too many students enrolled from a secondary rather than a primary market.

Smaller colleges located in cities away from major metropolitan areas often do not have primary markets because they have not developed their market plan on the basis of the demography of their student bodies. A common plan for such schools has been to locate admission representatives in large metropolitan areas without ever assessing the rate of return on the investment. Typically, small independent institutions in nonmetropolitan areas in the Midwest have full-time representatives living in the Chicago or New York areas or both. This type of assignment is generally unproductive for the greatest number of schools. Before such an assignment is made, some questions should be asked: Is a representative living in the area several hundred miles from the college the reason for whatever success the school has achieved? Could the representative's time be better spent if he or she were based on the campus? These are not only questions of time utilization but ones of personal identification and morale. The admission representative who lives in the community where the college he or she represents is located has a different sense of identification with and interest in the institution than does the admission representative who lives 300 or 1,000 miles away. No matter how successful its present techniques, an admission office should consider the potential of other management alternatives, which may be far more effective for converting potential candidates into applicants and ultimately into matriculants than present practices.

There are numerous examples of poor marketing and institutional decision making, but one should be sufficient. In an effort to become more cosmopolitan, a once-distinguished college in the Midwest expanded its recruiting activities nationally during the late 1960s but failed to maintain its efforts in its primary market. This college had formerly attracted some of the most able students from the Chicago and St. Louis metropolitan areas. For some reason, this institution decided to divert an increasing percentage of its resources to an attempt to attract students from the East, the West, and the Rocky Mountain areas. There was nothing wrong with this idea, except that the institution either simply overlooked its primary markets or assumed that since it was well known in these areas, it would not have to maintain its past effort in order to achieve the same results. Today this college is having serious enrollment problems, and these difficulties date from its adoption of an imprudent marketing strategy. This is not an isolated example, for the story can be generalized to other institutions. The moral of this story is quite simple: Once an institution has developed a primary market, if that market is within a reasonable distance of the institution, the admission staff should make sure the primary market is protected and continually cultivated. An additional investment in a primary market will always bring about a greater return than a similar investment in a secondary market. This is not to deny that a point of diminishing return exists, but few colleges ever reach that point in their primary markets.

The Secondary Market

In contrast to a primary market, a secondary market is defined as basically a low-yield market. From such a market, a college typically would have received a steady flow of applications over a period of three to five years but would have matriculated few of the students accepted. For example, a director of admission might find that from secondary schools that normally send 80 to 90 percent of their students to college, his or her college has always received applications but has seldom obtained matriculations. Evidently that college is perceived as a second or third choice among the students attending those secondary schools. Since the primary market even for a residential institution generally does not exceed a radius of 300 to 400 miles, the secondary market is substantially larger than the primary market. Because of this size difference between the primary and secondary markets and because of a lack of data analysis, it is common for an institution to divert more of its resources to the secondary market than to the primary market. The apparent hope is that the circle will widen and that more secondary schools will become a part of a given institution's primary market. This result will occur only if the institution's reputation becomes more prestigious or if new programs are offered that are more responsive to the market needs. Even with program modification and new-program development, effective methods of communication will be required to expand a primary market. However, regardless of the reputation of the institution, which is generally created by the quality of its faculty and its student body, many institutions, both public and private, may find their paths very difficult in the 1980s unless they understand the components of marketing and the means of cultivating and sustaining various markets.

As indicated, a secondary market can be defined by assessing trends of applications from various high schools either independent of geography or within a given geographic area. Generally, beyond the radius of 300 to 400 miles, an institution will find a large secondary market, and to convert applications into matriculations will come at excessive cost. This fact does not imply that a segment of the secondary market should not be identified and cultivated, for it is absolutely necessary to do so. The question is by what means and with what resources the cultivation of the secondary market can best be achieved. This question will be covered in the next chapter.

The Test, or Tertiary, Market

In contrast to the primary and secondary markets, the tertiary market is an unknown. In the 1960s, for many colleges and universities, the test market was the inner-city high schools, and for many institutions these high schools still remain tertiary markets. Other tertiary markets may be defined by geography or, again, by secondary school: a college may not have received any applications from secondary schools in a given geographic area within a reasonable radius of the institution. For a small college, the tertiary market may be larger than the primary and secondary markets combined. For a larger institution with a national reputation, the tertiary market may be quite small. The question that must be raised is to what extent a college should invest its rather scarce resources in a tertiary market. A college or university with considerable resources and a national reputation has a moral and institutional obligation to try to recruit students from every part of the country. For an institution with limited resources and limited prestige, it may be totally inappropriate to invest in a tertiary market. If such a college makes a commitment to develop a tertiary market, it should be done only on a pilot basis and evaluated accordingly. The decision to expand the recruitment effort in a tertiary market should be made only after a pilot program has operated for at least three years, and then only after systematic assessment of the results as related to the investment.

Development of the Primary and Secondary Markets

Recently, I had the privilege of being a member of the faculty of an institute to discuss the marketing of higher education. After my presentation, a representative of one college stated that his institution did not have a primary market because of high turnover in the admission office, lack of recordkeeping, and an unfavorable location. Although one could sympathize with the position he expressed, it would be extremely unlikely for this college or any other institution not to have a primary market. If he had said that he was unable to identify the primary market, his statement would be plausible, since many institutions find themselves in similar circumstances because they know very little about the demography of their student bodies.

If a college or university is unable to identify its primary market, the easiest way to begin is to canvass the present undergraduate students for general demographics: their ages, academic ability, home towns, high schools, parents' education, religious affiliations, and families' estimated income. Once this data collection has been accomplished, some trends ought to become apparent. In the worst case, when the demographics appear to be completely random, a primary market must be developed. Since the primary market falls within a given geographical radius of an institution, a beginning is to identify the nearby high schools that serve students with socioeconomic backgrounds and career interests similar to those of the students on campus. By placing current students in the cells of the student mobility paradigm (SMP), a college should be able to determine the ability, mobility, and financial capability of its student body once the primary and secondary markets have been identified. The costs of expanding the enrollment from the different markets can then be estimated. For example, a college where most of the students fall into quadrant 2 of the SMP should be providing different services, as well as possibly a different educational experience, than a college that finds that most of its students fall into quadrant 3. Thus, any market can be assessed in relation to the SMP, and this assessment should tell a college a great deal about the intellectual and personal needs of the students it is attracting.

For many colleges, secondary schools serving highly affluent areas and sending as many as 90 percent of their students on to four-year institutions may not be at all appropriate as a primary market. This is particularly likely for a small private college that historically has attracted students from entirely different socioeconomic backgrounds. Matching profiles between the present undergraduates and the potential student market is the only way to begin to identify the primary market.

Once such secondary schools have been identified within a reasonable geographic distance from the institution, a series of programmatic efforts should be developed. Information about students currently in attendance should be sent back to local high schools and churches, if appropriate, and to the newspapers serving areas in which these secondary schools are located. Advertisements can be bought in high school newspapers and church bulletins. Special on-campus programs can be offered for prospective students, parents, and teachers from such high schools. The president of the college, through the alumni, should seek as much exposure as possible in communities that produce students similar to the ones currently in attendance. The more a college is dependent on tuition as the primary source of revenue, the more the president becomes the principal marketing agent of the admission program.

If it is not possible to identify the primary markets, then the following procedures should be implemented:

1. Identify the secondary schools of those students who entered during the past four years, including those who have dropped out.
2. Query the present undergraduates, through interviews, questionnaires, and/or focus groups, to determine why they elected to attend your college.
3. Follow the same investigatory procedures with all students admitted to the next entering class.
4. Identify high-density population areas within a 300-mile radius of the college and ask what marketing efforts have been undertaken in these areas in the last several years and what the results have been.
5. If prospect lists have been used in direct-mail activities, select the names of prospects with an academic and interest profile similar to that of the undergraduates currently in attendance. Focus the marketing effort on those prospects who fall within a defined geographic area of the college. This emphasis does not preclude a separate effort on another set of prospects with different profiles either within the same geographic radius or beyond it, but such an effort should clearly be differentiated in recordkeeping, and resources should be separately allocated to it.
6. Maintain an ongoing press service to provide home-town newspapers with information about entering students and the activities of current undergraduates.
7. Invite a select number of secondary school counselors and teachers from a limited geographic area to the campus for special programs.

8. Involve alumni on a pilot basis. If at least two alumni are involved from one city, a sense of teamwork and a sense of accountability are created.
9. Identify friends of the college who live within a desired primary market and keep them informed of the activities of the admission office through a newsletter.
10. Make sure the parents of current undergraduates and prospects are invited to alumni-sponsored events, such as those that bring the president or members of the faculty to a local area.
11. Encourage the college's public relations staff to get to know members of the media within the primary market. These contacts will eventually increase the public exposure of the college.
12. Keep in mind that such a systematic effort as is outlined above does not occur overnight, but it is absolutely necessary to the development of a primary market.

When considering development of a secondary market, remember that the return on the investment is always greater in the primary market. Therefore, developing the secondary market should be achieved with the least amount of investment. For development of a secondary market to be cost-effective, the alumni should be the main resource used. This principle does not imply that professional staff members should not visit geographic areas identified as secondary markets, only that the amount of professional time spent should be directly related to the expected return. If the alumni are successful in significantly increasing the number of applications in an area and eventually the number of matriculations, then the amount of staff time devoted to that area should increase proportionately.

Alumni who live in secondary market areas as well as undergraduate students from these areas should become key resources in the continued development of the areas. From time to time management may wish to spend more money in one secondary market than another simply to test potential. If the return increases upon additional investment of time, personnel, and capital, then programmed activity should increase in that area. However, this change should not occur at the expense of the primary market. A good index is the degree of alumni support. At Northwestern, in order to increase a commitment to a secondary market without considerable additional expense, we expand the alumni admission team in a defined area, try to publicize the accomplishments of present undergraduates more frequently in local newspapers, and commit more professional staff time during summer to the secondary market activity.

Forecasting the Size of the Freshman Class in Relation to Market Segments

If the proper research and planning have been done, it should be possible to determine how many students are presently on campus from the primary, secondary, and tertiary markets, how many were accepted, and how many enrolled. The gathering of these data should be an integrated part of the management function. In assessing the transformation from prospects to alumni from the three market segments, one can identify six subgroups: prospects, candidates, applicants, admitted applicants, matriculants, and alumni (Ihlanfeldt, 1975). An appropriate paradigm would be a funnel, with the prospects near the larger opening and the alumni at the smaller opening, as shown in Figure 3.

Figure 3. Prospect-Alumni Paradigm

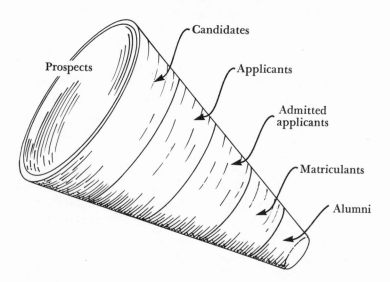

A *candidate* is a prospective student who has initiated some interest in the institution within a year prior to the desired date of entry, whereas a *prospect* is defined—based upon demographics—as a student who may be interested if contact is initiated by the college or university. Generally, the demographics of a prospect pool should be similar to those of students currently enrolled. An exception to this would be an effort to identify and recruit a new group of students, such as minority or older students. However, the cultivation of a new market will require time and additional resources not only in the area of student recruitment but also for support services once the students are enrolled. Once a prospect responds to an institutional contact, he or she is considered a candidate.

Prospects may be identified in numerous ways. The two most likely are that the student initiated contact earlier than a year before the desired date of entry through written inquiry, campus visits, or attendance at secondary school meetings with college representatives and that the student's name appears on a list of secondary school juniors and seniors purchased by the college from any number of agencies involved in identifying potential students. Ways to increase the size of the prospect pool include encouraging undergraduates and alumni to forward the names of high school students from their local areas, acquiring names from church youth groups, and obtaining various lists offered by the National Merit Scholarship Corporation. Generally, the prospect pool or file can be adequately developed through individual student inquiries, alumni referrals, and the use of the Student Search Service and the Educational Opportunity Service programs.

Of particular importance in using the Student Search Service is to be conscious of which search offered during the year is likely to include the largest percentage of prospects who have profiles similar to those of students attending one's institution. Unfortunately, during the first several years of the Student Search Service program, many colleges and universities requested the names of students with personal demographics and academic credentials that were not similar to those of most students who were interested in those institutions. This type of incongruence, even if successful in attracting a more capable freshman class, may result in a higher attrition rate. Some colleges and universities are not prepared to meet the intellectual needs of highly talented students from rather sophisticated backgrounds. This is not to imply a value judgment; it is just a matter of fact. Concomitantly, the needs of many able young people from less sophisticated backgrounds can best be met in less sophisticated environments.

The percentage of names in the prospect file that is from the primary market is critical in determining the required size of the prospect pool. The optimum size of the prospect pool will vary for each college but it should not need to exceed twenty times the desired size of the freshman class, and at least 50 percent of the prospect pool should be from the primary market. These percentages can be statistically derived for a given college if enough is known about the demographics of the current undergraduate student body and the conversion ratios from prospects to candidates to applicants.

If an evaluation of the prospect file indicates that the vast majority of the prospects are from secondary markets, then clearly the present plan should be modified. Efforts should be made immediately to increase the number of prospects from the primary market. If a high percentage of the admitted students are from a secondary market, the number enrolling is likely to be lower than expected; by definition a secondary market is a low-yield market. Should this analysis not be done and the composition of the prospect file remain unknown, it will be very hard to meet the required enrollment objectives. Even if more students apply, the fact that they are from secondary markets will result in a lower enrollment yield should they be accepted. The surprise comes in September, when fewer students than expected enroll.

If the anomaly should occur that *more* students from a secondary market enroll than expected, then one must ask the next question: Is it likely that more students than usual will withdraw at the end of the freshman year? Generally, the answer is yes. The secondary market is not only a low-yield market in terms of the ratio of number matriculating to number admitted, it is a high-attrition market. To make the point, as one travels through Texas it is quite common to find a decal on the rear window of a car with the words *The University*. It is also quite common for students from Texas to attend rather distinguished colleges and universities outside the state for the first year or two and to return to "The University" at the beginning of their sophomore or junior years. For most out-of-state institutions

Texas is a secondary or tertiary market. If this kind of provincialism prevailed throughout the country, the primary markets would be very restrictive. Nonetheless, the example is a lesson to be kept in mind as one plans.

By developing a prospect pool fourteen to eighteen months before the desired enrollment date and by segmenting the prospects into primary, secondary, and tertiary market pools, it is possible to forecast the size of the freshman class nine months in advance. Through such an analysis a director of admission should be able either to tell the president of the college that it appears the enrollment objectives will be met or to initiate the action necessary to correct the projected shortfall. To segment the various markets within the prospect and candidate files, all that is necessary is to have a card sorter, as long as the information is on computer cards. More sophisticated forecasting can be achieved through probit analysis if the demographics of the prospect and candidate files are known. Thus, having the appropriate information keypunched onto computer cards and having these cards periodically updated and sorted should permit an admission office to reassess its objectives at any time in the recruitment cycle.

The more sophisticated the information about students from the various markets, such as academic interests, socioeconomic status, ethnicity, and religious background, the more accurate the assessment of probable yield from each of the three markets. For example, a prospect from the primary market who is interested in programs that a school does not offer is not likely to become a candidate. Socioeconomic, ethnic, and religious data should be compared with the demographics of the students currently attending the college.

As stated previously, as an estimate the prospect file should be twenty times as large as the desired freshman class, and at least 50 percent of the students in the file should be from the primary market. As the percentage from primary markets decreases, the size of the prospect pool must increase. However, these estimates change with the prestige of the institution. If an institution has a high desirability quotient, as determined by high ratios of number of applications to number accepted and of number accepted to number who eventually matriculate, then the prospect pool can be somewhat smaller. For example, a college that accepts only one out of four applicants has a rather high desirability quotient and may not need to create a large prospect pool. Conversely, a college that has been receiving an insufficient number of applications needs to increase the size of its contact pool dramatically. Through trend analyses such information can be derived to forecast the size of the entering class.

Although what has been presented implies a correlation between the market segments of the prospect pool and the number of students who eventually matriculate, it may be in the best interest of a college or university to expand the prospect pool beyond the number derived empirically. A marketing plan should have two components: one directed toward attracting students for the following fall or in the near future and another designed to expose the university to the prospective parents of another generation of students twenty or thirty years hence. A potential student who learns something about a given institution today is likely to know a great deal more when he or she becomes a parent. Direct mail is an effective form of advertising and can publicize the college so that it will have a broader primary market when today's prospects become tomorrow's parents. The Student Search Service program provides the opportunity to contact students in secondary markets who may know very little about the college and who have no intention of applying. Nevertheless, it would appear to be beneficial to promote the institution as widely as possible among such students in order to protect or improve the institution's market position a few decades from now. Therefore, as part of the overall promotional effort, the prospect file should be purposely inflated to increase awareness of the institution as it exists today. The hope is that future generations will know that much more about the college because of such market-sensitive planning.

Segmenting and Developing Nontraditional Markets

A commuter institution that attracts a large number of students who either delay entering college immediately after high school or elect to re-enter college after a long absence has some special marketing problems that have not been addressed earlier. This type of institution cannot readily obtain lists of prospective students from the typical sources because there currently is no way to create a data base of a broad age range of potential students with particular interests and abilities. Most of these students work full-time and may only wish to take a course or two periodically to update their skills. However, the fact remains that each college or university does have primary and secondary markets and must understand the demographics of its current students to develop a market plan.

To determine the present interests of its current market and to develop a plan, the institution should periodically obtain the following data:

- A frequency distribution of ZIP codes or telephone prefixes of currently enrolled students, whichever provides the smallest area of concentration.
- A frequency interval distribution of ages by sex.
- A frequency distribution showing how many courses students are taking, to determine how many students are enrolled at least half-time.
- The type of courses for which there is greatest demand.
- The students' interest in achieving a degree or their interest in noncredit courses.
- Their employment status and career interest.
- Their employer and type of corporation.
- Their community interests and avocational interests.
- Their principal mode of transportation.
- Their radio habits and the stations they listen to most frequently.
- Their reading interests.
- Their religious interests.

By collecting and storing this information, an institution can begin to determine whether it is meeting the needs of its current students and what the demographics of its primary markets are and to plan a promotional campaign that focuses on people whose profiles resemble its current students'. For example, most likely a college located in a large metropolitan area should be able to identify why people enroll, in what part of the city they live, their dominant occupation patterns, how they travel to and from work, and their religious and political preferences. This information permits the creation of a promotional plan, which might include any or all of the following:

- If currently enrolled students tend to live in a concentrated area, a blanket mailing might be considered; however, if it can be determined that students from different age groups tend to live in different areas, then mailings should be developed to appeal specifically to their interests. Replies to mailings form the basis of the candidate pool. Following the traditional-student paradigm, the recipients of the initial mailing would be identified as part of the prospect pool.

- If enrolled students tend to be employed by certain corporations, advertisements in the union or management newsletter or bulletin may be appropriate. These can be particularly helpful if returning to school is endorsed by either the union or management. In fact, a premium may be offered, such as a modest price discount. As a result, the advertising space may be made available at no charge.

- If public transportation is most frequently used to go to and from work, then poster advertising is most appropriate. If the automobile is used, radio advertising is desirable.

Once the demographics of current students are known, there are many alternatives to stimulate additional demand. In fact, once a name and address is acquired, it can be maintained in the data files far longer than can that of a secondary school senior. Eventually, a forecasting model can be developed similar to the one described earlier in this chapter. As trends are studied, the educational habits of almost any population can be projected.

Alternatively, should a school believe that it has exhausted the potential of its present markets, then it will be interested in tapping new markets and probably new interests. Exhausting the potential of present markets is likely to happen only if the mission of the institution is narrowly defined, the competition is most severe, or both. Developing new markets is possible only if previous promotional efforts have been rather restricted or new programs are being introduced. The fact remains that colleges and universities in urban areas have unlimited demand potential as long as they offer attractive programs that are provided at times that will maximize demand. Moreover, since so many older people today are eligible for government and corporate grant assistance, price is not likely to be a factor affecting demand; program quality and the process by which programs are distributed will continue to be the primary factors.

The preceding paragraphs have tried to shed some light on how a commuter institution serving mostly nontraditional students can identify its primary markets and how it might increase demand. The following analysis serves as an example of how a residential institution serving traditional students might begin to assess the potential demand from nontraditional students, particularly older women, by utilizing the skills and interests of its faculty.

Historically, Northwestern University has not been interested in attracting older students to its undergraduate programs on the Evanston campus. However, within the past five years, a faculty planning report and the Program on Women at the university have urged the admission office to begin to recruit older students to add to the diversity of the university environment. Although a token effort was made by advertising in an alumni magazine, the admission staff was presented with two problems: to determine the size of the potential market who could do the work at the university and to develop a promotional campaign to create awareness. Both these problems were presented to the Program on Women. After some study, the faculty members in the Program on Women indicated that they thought they knew how to proceed, and the office of admission commissioned a study to determine the potential size of the market.

Karen Fox, a member of the faculty in the School of Education at Northwestern, was the principal investigator and used what is known as the chain-ratio method to estimate the market size. What follows is extracted from the report she prepared (Fox, 1979, pp. 18–20). It is shared as an example of a unique and thoughtful analysis.

> [The] exhibit presents an estimate based on the chain-ratio method. The segmentation was first done by geographical and socioeconomic-status factors. Census tracts in Evanston, Glencoe, Kenilworth, Wilmette, and Winnetka which had 1970 median household incomes over $15,000 were selected. The number of women between twenty-five and forty-five was extrapolated from the 1970 data and multiplied by the estimated percentage that are in the top quartile of the population on apparent aptitude.
>
> But census data do not provide the most crucial information: the prevalence of college noncompletion by upper-SES, high-aptitude women. Fortunately, these data are avail-

able from Project TALENT, a longitudinal study of a probability sample of the entire United States secondary school
population in the spring of 1960. (Those who graduated from
high school in 1960 would be in the midrange of the 25-to-44
age cohort.) The 400,000 respondents were mailed follow-up
questionnaires five years after graduation. The college completion probability of .71 for females in the upper quartile of
SES and academic aptitude is based on the weighted responses
from the five-year follow-up.

It is important to note that while married couples tend
to come from similar SES backgrounds, wives tend to have
less education and be of lower-SES backgrounds than their
husbands. If high-aptitude women from *middle*-SES backgrounds were considered, the rate of noncompletion would be
considerably higher. The potential market size of almost
1,500 in Step 5 would be expanded by applying the chain-
ratio steps to the population figures for other suburbs just
west of these communities as well as areas of Chicago which
match the income/SES characteristics. A caveat: Able, interested candidates may also come from less affluent census tracts
than those analyzed here, which would further increase the
number of women in this market.

**Exhibit. Estimating the Market Potential for an
Undergraduate Education at Northwestern University
Among North Shore Women Between Ages 25 and 45**

| | *Total population
1980* (based on
NIPC [Northern
Illinois Planning
Commission]
forecasts in
August 1976) |
| --- | --- |
| *1. Base market (demographic)* | |
| North Shore communities (Evanston,
Glencoe, Kenilworth, Wilmette, and
Winnetka) | 138,000 |
| *2. Population of census tracts with
median 1970 income over $15,000
(demographic)* | 87,400 |
| *3. Females 25 to 44 (demographic)* | 10,300 |
| *4. Percent upper quartile on IQ*
Given the strong relationship between | |

IQ and SES, probably close to 50% 50% x 10,300	5,150

5. *Percent females 25 to 44 in top quartile on SES, in top quartile of age cohort on academic aptitude, and who did not complete college within five years after high school graduation*

   Probability of a female (top quartile on SES and academic aptitudes) graduating from a four-year college within five years after high school is .71.[a] Thus probability of noncompletion is .29.

   .29 x 5,150   1,493

6. *Percent interested in attending college (stage of readiness)*

   Some will decide to continue working, doing volunteer work, etc.   ?

7. *Percent interested in attending Northwestern (loyalty status)*   ?

8. *Further corrections must be made for*

   Percent able to arrange for household help, transportation, family agreement

   Percent willing to cope with application process

[a]This is a population estimate for the 1960 senior class in United States high schools, obtained by weighting the responses of 35,000 high school seniors (Claudy, 1971). This group is now in the midrange of the 25–44 age cohort.

Having determined the theoretical existence of a market of over one thousand women in five North Shore suburbs, what is the likelihood that they will be attracted to Northwestern? The answer depends on the success of Northwestern's marketing efforts to this market.

Professor Fox correctly presents the question. Consequently, the university is developing a special admission effort to identify and to recruit the re-entering woman student. The person appointed to manage this effort is expected to have a profile similar to the women she will be expected to recruit. The reason is that these women have special problems as returning students, and someone who has had similar experiences is likely to have a greater understanding of the demands to be placed on them by their families and their educational programs.

6

Pricing
Educational Programs

When students are asked why they selected a given college, they often cite such factors as the reputation of the institution and program options; they seldom mention price. These responses are based on their own self-concepts and the frame of reference of others they depend on for advice. If they had been exposed to and understood another set of options or had become acquainted with a set of criteria to evaluate their options, they might have made different decisions. This plausible assumption is the basis for the extensive promotional efforts of many colleges. At the same time, the interaction of price (tuition) and the perceived value of the experience and potential outcomes does affect college choice. Spies (1973, 1978) suggests that among high-ability students, price does not appear to be the main factor in applying to college. Yet, this conclusion reflects the interests and abilities of a small number of students and the market position of a small number of institutions. Moreover, applying to college is not the same as attending, for price does become a factor in the latter. For the vast majority of students attending college, the purpose is to get a better job. Consequently, if students perceive little difference in the value of the experiences offered by various colleges for achieving their career goals, then price, indeed, becomes a factor not only in the attendance pattern but in the application pattern as well.

This chapter addresses the significance of price and the factors that should be considered in determining price. The administration should be cognizant of a few facts that tend to govern the behavior of the market. As suggested by the literature cited in previous chapters and in recognition of some regional differences, an evaluation of the applicant pools of different types of institutions leads to the following tentative conclusions:

1. Generally, the stronger the market position of an independent institution, the more likely that the greatest part of application overlap will be with similar institutions. In this instance, price does not appear to be a factor.

2. For this type of independent institution, when applicant overlap does occur with a public institution, it is likely to be with the major state university in the state where the prospective student lives and/or with a few highly prestigious public universities, such as the University of Michigan, the University of North Carolina, and the University of California at Berkeley.

3. This group of independent institutions does not exceed seventy-five. Almost all other independent institutions compete on a regional or local basis with other independent institutions and with public institutions in their own states.

4. Students who apply to independent colleges located only within their states are also likely to apply to at least one public institution within their states.

5. Students who apply to at least two independent institutions are likely to apply to at least one public institution, but students who apply to two public institutions are not as likely to apply to an independent institution.

6. There appear to be two dominant markets, one independent and the other public, with limited overlap between the two. This separation is likely to increase, the independent market further reducing in size because of the apparent differences in tuitions and what are considered marginal differences in value.

7. Because students have become increasingly dependent on financial assistance, there appear to be fewer students transferring from one four-year institution to another. The reason is the lack of portability of most state grant programs and of all institutionally based aid programs.

The message that should be extracted from these observations is that most independent institutions are competing directly with public institutions and at a significant price disadvantage when only gross tuition differences are considered; however, the net price difference may not be nearly as great. Today, we compete in a massive price-discounting environment, but in both public and independent institutions, tuition increases are seldom determined by taking into consideration the vast amount of government grant assistance available. Notwithstanding the expressed fears of many public officials that increases in government student aid will stimulate tuition increases, over the past five years median tuition and fee charges in the private sector have grown faster than the Consumer Price Index by only 4 percent (Life Insurance Marketing and Research Association, 1979), while government grant aid increased by more than 500 percent. Although tuition and fees have increased at a greater percentage rate in the public sector, in neither sector have tuition and fees over the past ten years increased at the compounded rate of inflation. One reason that we have not observed greater increases is that the financial officer seldom talks with the financial aid officer, and too many financial aid officers view themselves as processors rather than planners. The result is a lower price or a price structure that does not maximize tuition revenues. Financial aid in the form of grant assistance from external sources is a price support and a significant source of revenue—a fact that few administrators realize.

Price and Market Position

Although the congressional debate in 1978 over tax credits for higher education raised considerable doubt about whether tuitions had increased faster than family incomes (Esenwein and Karr, 1978), public opinion persists in questioning the value of the perceived experiences in relation to the announced prices. Moreover, if one assumes that we are going to continue to live in an inflationary economy, then the gross price to the education consumer would appear prohibitive as we look toward 1990. Table 3 indicates that, assuming tuition increases of 4 percent in the public sector and 7 percent in the independent sector and increases of 6 percent in expenditures for room, board, and miscellaneous items in both sectors, the annual cost will increase at least $2,000 in the public sector and will double in the independent sector by 1990. The cost of attending an independent four-year college or university will range between $10,000 and $17,000 annually by 1990.

Table 3. Projected Annual Prices of Higher Education, in Dollars

	Public[a]			Private[b]			
Year	Univ.	4-year	2-year	Select[c]	Univ.	4-year	2-year
1979	2,905	2,784	2,473	8,020	5,930	5,278	4,243
1986	4,235	4,075	3,679	12,626	9,270	8,222	6,560
1990	5,259	5,072	4,590	16,371	11,973	10,599	8,421

[a] Assumes annual increases of 4 percent in tuition and 6 percent in other costs.
[b] Assumes annual increases of 7 percent in tuition and 6 percent in other costs.
[c] High-priced colleges and universities with strong market positions.
Source: Larry Hough, Student Loan Marketing Association.

Although the increases in price that have been observed in the 1970s seem excessive, the gross price of attending a four-year independent institution in 1990 is staggering. Few people could afford it, and a portion of those who could might not value it. However, the fact is that very few parents must absorb the entire price of their children's education. Through federal, state, and institutional financial aid programs, the price is significantly discounted for the vast majority of those enrolled in institutions of higher education. Every indication is that these trends will continue. The question is how the institution should interpret this information in relation to its market potential.

Every college should assess the interaction effects between its price and the potential of its primary and secondary markets, understanding the difference between its net price (tuition minus grant assistance) and its gross price. Theoretically, a college could announce almost any price if it were willing to discount the price for all students. Doing so, of course, would serve no useful purpose, but at times the institution must adjust its net price upward or downward to improve its market position. In other words, it must increase or decrease the amount of price discounting by offering more or less grant assistance. Whether the net or the gross price is adjusted depends not only on economics but on psychological factors as well.

For example, Northwestern University has been a price leader. The university's tuition historically has been within the top ten in the country. At the same time, because of a substantial institutional grant program, the university's net-price position with regard to most other private institutions and in its various markets has been quite competitive. However, as operating costs demand that the university's revenue from tuition continue to increase, it may be more desirable to increase the net price substantially and to increase the gross price modestly or to hold the tuition (price) constant for one year. Such a decision would communicate several messages to the consumer: (1) the university would be offering less grant assistance and expecting students to work and borrow more, a Proposition 13 message; (2) the university would be indirectly stating that it is concerned that prospective students, regardless of financial need, are selecting themselves out of the university's market; and (3) Northwestern would be realigning its gross-price position among its competition.

A study of the pricing policies of higher education leads one to two conclusions: First, in the independent sector, pricing appears to be more of a residual policy matter than one related to market forces— that is, historically, increases in tuition have been determined after revenues from other sources have been forecasted in relation to expected operating costs. The price has been set at whatever residual amount is necessary to balance the institutional budget. Second, in the public sector, the price charged is more related to political influences and the apparent willingness or unwillingness of the taxpayer to continue underwriting most of the cost of public higher education. Often, operating costs have been depressed, sometimes at the expense of educational quality, to limit tuition increases.

The constant fear among management in the independent sector is that increases in price will continue to widen the tuition gap between public and private institutions, thus decreasing the potential market for the independent sector. This fear is not unfounded, because the gap has continued to increase. At the same time, legislative politics have placed considerable constraint on increases in tuition in the public sector, and, increasingly, there have been shortfalls in appropriations, with the concomitant demand that productivity increase. An increase in productivity has been defined as either fewer faculty members teaching more courses or fewer faculty members teaching more students in either fewer or the same number of course sections; in either instance the faculty-student ratio increases.

A thesis that will be developed in this chapter is that not only has price been unrelated to demand because management has not understood the variation in pricing models, but most institutions are underpriced, and others should consider implementing different tuition policies with regard to the pricing of courses or terms. The pricing objective should be to maximize tuition revenues at the least net cost to the individual student. In developing a proper price structure, management should ask these questions:

1. Is the price charged adequate to generate enough revenue to improve or at least maintain the quality of the educational services offered? A marketing or admission officer should be less concerned with increases in price and more concerned with improvement in quality.
2. Is the price charged maximizing income from price supports available through government student aid without reducing the size of the potential market?
3. Is the price charged adequate to either maintain the size of the present market or increase it? This objective may be best achieved by charging a higher tuition in order to generate more dollars for the financial aid program. The effect is to reduce the net tuition for a significant number of students and thereby broaden the potential market. This proposal assumes that the institution is able to attract a sizable number of full-pay students.
4. Do the pricing and credit policies of the institution interact in such a way so as not to create pricing systems in which one group of students substantially subsidizes the cost of education for another group? Such subsidization occurs when students are offered the option of accelerating their education without being required to pay the price related to that acceleration.

Questions 3 and 4 may appear contradictory because question 3 implies that to broaden the market subsidization may be a desirable management objective, whereas question 4 discourages pricing/ credit policies that reduce expected revenue by having one group of students subsidize another. This latter form of subsidization may or may not be a desirable management objective. The decision depends on the market position of the institution and the system by which it awards advanced standing in relation to the price charged. However, many schools have been offering credit by examination and/or for life's experiences without considering the financial implications. Such policies have been implemented to expand an institution's market. The question is "Could the market have been expanded through other promotional efforts without a loss of revenue?" The apparent contradictions involved in this matter should be resolved as the reader acquires a more comprehensive understanding of the differences between gross and net price.

Net Price as Differentiated from Cost and Tuition. Although it is generally recognized that a large percentage of college students do not pay the full price, it is often not understood that no undergraduate student pays the full cost of his or her education. In addition to the relative discount received by many students in the form of grant assistance, there is an absolute discount received by all students. The latter represents the difference between the average cost of educating a single student and the price paid in the form of tuition. Thus, in both the public and independent sectors, the pricing policies include both absolute discounts (instructional costs minus tuition) and relative discounts (tuition minus student grant aid).

Instructional costs in the public sector are heavily subsidized from the purse of the taxpayer, for usually tuition represents no more than 20 percent of the cost of education. In the private sector, tuition, or the price charged to the consumer, generally represents at most two thirds of the cost but often much less. In addition, as indicated above, the discounting of tuition is prevalent in both sectors, but in the independent sector the cost of price discounting, excluding government assistance, is underwritten by deficit financing out of operating revenues. To put this in the language of financial aid, grant assistance subtracted from the gross price, or tuition, results in a net price. It is common practice for all institutions, both public and independent, to discount their prices for as many as 70 percent of their students, and at some community colleges 100 percent of the students receive discounts. Price discounting based on a systematic assessment of family financial need is analogous to progressive taxation. In contrast, discounts unrelated to financial need, such as tax credits or non-need-based grants, are regressive, for the more affluent benefit to the same degree as, or even more than, the less affluent.

One prevalent assumption is that price discounting or financial assistance is absolutely necessary in order to maintain a given enrollment of a given quality. Although this assumption is true for some schools, for others it is not even a matter of maintaining a highly qualified or diversified student body, it is simply a matter of maintaining minimum levels of enrollment. In the latter schools, a more satisfactory pricing policy may be one that balances the budget by reducing the gross tuition for all students while limiting or eliminating institutional financial aid that discounts the tuition for some students. For some independent schools a lower tuition might broaden the potential market; for others a higher tuition may be required to achieve the same objective. The objective is to maximize revenues in relation to the potential market. To achieve this end, an institution must study the probable effects of a change in price in relation to both the changes in availability of government financial assistance and the changes in per capita disposable income among the institution's primary market. The focus of such a study should be the net tuition students are paying on a per capita basis and the extent to which tuition increases have paralleled increases in per capita disposable income or after-tax income over a given period of time.

Because of the massive infusion of government grant assistance over the past ten years and because of the sophistication of staffs in some financial aid offices, the per capita student price has decreased at many institutions even though tuition has increased. Since this decrease seems contrary to the more-publicized fact of dramatic increases in tuition, it is necessary to examine some specifics. Between 1970 and 1978, federal grant assistance through Social Security benefits, Supplemental Educational Opportunity Grants, and Basic Educational Opportunity Grants has increased from $700 million to $4 billion (Hansen and Gladieux, 1978; Roark, 1977). Likewise, grant assistance through state programs during the same period has increased from $236 million to $829 million (Boyd and Pennell, 1978–79). These figures represent a 415 percent increase in the last eight years in federal and state assistance combined. During this same time span, per capita disposable income increased only 78 percent. The result of this significant increase in government student aid was to broaden the potential student market and to act as a price neutralizer for tuition increases. The impact is even more dramatic when veterans' benefits are taken into consideration. From a management perspective, these rather significant increases in student assistance should be assessed in relation to an individual college and its primary market. If over a period of a few years per capita disposable income within an institution's primary markets has increased faster than tuition, then tuition increases should have little or no effect on demand. Moreover, an examination of net price increases on a per capita basis may indicate that an institution is underpriced or that its potential student market should have expanded. Figure 4 illustrates this conclusion.

If government financial aid increases faster than tuition, an institution has at least two options. First, it can decrease the amount of institutional grant aid from general revenue sources; this move will have the effect either of suppressing future tuition increases or of diverting needed dollars into other areas. Second, it can continue to stabilize or increase institutional aid, thereby expanding its potential student market by further reducing the per capita net price.

Table 4 shows examples of the changing ratio of government assistance to tuition at several institutions. These data represent the amount of financial aid allocated from the Illinois State Grant Program, the Basic Educational Opportunity Grant Program, and the Supplemental Educational Opportunity Grant Program to students at these institutions in relation to the amount received in tuition. For example, in 1972–1973, for every dollar of tuition Augustana College received, students received an average of thirty cents in grant assistance. Thus, from these three programs alone tuition was discounted 30 percent. Data collected in support of Table 4 (see Appendix A) show that even though tuition and fees in a representative sample of public two- and four-year institutions in Illinois increased 38 percent from 1972–73 to 1977–78, student-grant aid increased 214 percent, while full-time enrollment increased only 4 percent. More dramati-

Figure 4. Interaction of Tuition, Per Capita Disposable Income, and Government Grant Assistance

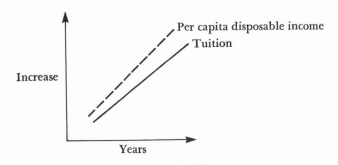

In this instance the market should be broader because disposable income has increased faster than tuition. This example illustrates what generally has happened in the public sector and at those independent institutions that are underpriced.

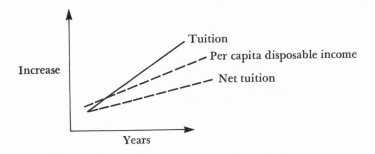

In this illustration of the effect of federal and state grant assistance, tuition has been significantly discounted on a per capita basis as a matter of public policy.

cally, in the Chicago Community Colleges, for every tuition dollar collected in 1972–73, students received $1.15 in grant assistance. In 1977–78 students received $1.63 in student aid for every tuition dollar paid, even though tuition had increased from $40 to $360, or 800 percent. This analysis does not include Social Security and veterans'

Table 4. Ratio of Government Grant Assistance to Tuition Revenue
at Selected Colleges in Illinois

	1972–73	1974–75	1977–78
Private			
Augustana	.302	.286	.281
Lake Forest	.065	.118	.174
Loyola	.285	.276	.313
Milliken	.263	.247	.266
Northwestern	.083	.077	.091
Public Four-Year			
Southern Illinois (Carbondale)	.253	.435	.518
University of Illinois (Urbana)	.246	.213	.265
University of Illinois (Circle)	.286	.413	.751
Western Illinois	.203	.249	.312
Public Two-Year			
Belleville	.101	.208	.503
Blackhawk	.207	.229	.278
Chicago Community Colleges	1.152	1.261	1.634
Joliet	.087	.168	.237
Triton	.071	.119	.252

Sources: Illinois State Scholarship Commission Reports of April 1973–1978. Basic
Grant Program Institutional Agreement and Authorization Report,
1974–1975 and 1977–1978. Notification to Congress Report, Department of
Health, Education, and Welfare, April 23, 1973; May 1975; May 1977.

benefits; with them, the increase in grant assistance in relation to
tuition would have been even greater.

In independent institutions, as shown in Table 4, the ratio of
government aid to tuition revenue remained relatively constant
except at Lake Forest College. The increase in government student
aid at Lake Forest is a result of a greater emphasis on recruiting
students from Illinois, which has the third-largest state grant program in the nation. Except for Northwestern, which as a matter of
policy seeks a nationally diverse student population, the other independent colleges listed have for years had a high concentration of
Illinois residents among their student bodies.

In conclusion, this table and the supporting tables in Appendix A indicate not only that the gross tuition gap is increasing between public and independent institutions in Illinois but a fact of even greater significance—that the net tuition differences are increasing at a faster rate. Clearly, at least in Illinois, the data suggest that a substantial tuition increase in the public sector would have little impact, if any, on a student's ability to meet an increase in tuition. If students are to make choices based on educational rather than economic factors, the net price differences between public and independent institutions must be reduced. This position is consistent with earlier recommendations of the Carnegie Council on Policy Studies in Higher Education, the Committee on Educational Development, and the College Entrance Examination Board. This objective can be achieved by increasing tuition in the public sector and at the same time increasing government aid for students in the independent sector. As a matter of public policy to encourage educational choice based on individual needs, maximum state grants available to students in the independent sector should be related to the differences in tuition between the public and independent sectors.

In this study Illinois was cited because the information is readily available to the writer. However, similar analyses in most other states would lead to the same conclusion.

Willingness to Pay for Higher Education. Few students have the *ability* to pay for higher education, based on family income and asset structure, even among those of relatively high ability (Doermann, 1976, p. 35). An analysis at Northwestern indicated that there were no more than 30,000 high school graduates in 1979 who could have scored 550 on the verbal scale of the SAT, who had achieved a B average in a college preparatory program, and whose parents could contribute $6,000 a year to their education. However, what price a family is *willing* to pay to achieve a given educational goal is related to a number of personal values that are difficult to quantify and are not necessarily related to the family's current ability to pay. Not too long ago economists and financial aid officers were asking whether families were willing to borrow to meet the increasing price of higher education. Today that question appears to have been answered, since families borrowed well over $2 billion in 1978-79 to finance the cost of higher education. What is not clear is what price should be charged for the opportunity to achieve a particular educational objective. Individuals and agencies involved in financial aid have developed a uniform method of analyzing a family's financial circumstance to determine the price a family with a given level of income and assets should be able to pay for higher education. Whether this derived price is realistic is debated annually. The most significant related issue is whether a need-analysis formula based on a uniform method should be used to assess the family's ability to pay for higher education or whether the formula should simply be used as a tool for allocating scarce financial aid resources. A recent study indicated that the need-analysis process for determining the parents' contribution may be more fantasy than fact. Boyd and others (1978) found that the parents of high-ability students contributed only 42.9 percent of their expected contribution in 1976–77 and that this percentage had been decreasing since 1967. For students of average ability, the gap was even greater.

The market position of a given institution generally is unrelated to the method of determining financial need. Clearly, many families are willing to pay more for an educational experience at one institution than at another; the prestige and perceived utility of education differ among institutions. In other words, how much a family is actually willing to pay for a given higher educational experience has yet to be determined, because the present system is based on a series of assumptions that educators and politicians have made about the amount that a family with a given income should invest in either public or independent higher education. Logic would suggest that the net price should be a function of the strength of each school's market position, and to some extent it is. For example, a college with a strong market position may require more self-help—a larger amount of educational loans and work in relation to a student's total financial need—than might be required by another college with a weaker market position. Thus, the variation in price discounting through increases and decreases in self-help in relation to various amounts of grant assistance is one way of assessing an institution's market position.

To expand this analysis: Institutions with comparable tuitions may have quite different market positions. One school may find that its market position is strong enough that it can offer less grant assistance as a percentage of total financial need without affecting its acceptance/enrollment yield than another school with a similar tuition must offer. The latter school may find that it must reduce the percentage of self-help required in order to maintain or improve its market position. Theoretically, it should be possible to neutralize marginal differences in the perceived quality of the educational experiences at different institutions through relative price discounting. If it can be assumed that each school has a primary market, the question becomes "What is that market willing to pay for the quality of the experience offered?" Once the net price (tuition minus grant aid) has been determined, then how the student finances the residual costs becomes the primary concern. The options appear to be to draw directly on present family resources and to defer much of the present cost through loans.

Some economists argue that how the cost of education is financed should not be a concern of the management of higher education and that government-subsidized educational loans are unnecessary. Those families who are willing to invest in a given educational product, the argument goes, are also willing to find the resources to pay for that investment. It does appear that many institutions are offering price discounts unrelated to demand and to the present financial value of the expected degree. The fact that tuition at Harvard Law School is one of the lowest among independent institutions in the country is but one example. The difficult task for management is to assess the interacting effects of relative price discounts in relation to the institution's market position. Institutions that have opted for scholarships not based on need are indirectly stating that they have a rather weak market position. Grants not based on need, excessive grant assistance in relation to need, and give-away credit policies are forms of price discounting that increase the direct cost to the institution.

The revenues that might be allocated to discount price or lost through give-away credit may be better utilized in improving the quality of the institution. Price discounting cannot neutralize all the differences between institutions. If there is a dollar to be spent and the question arises whether that dollar should be spent for financial aid or for improving the educational program, an institution really has no choice. Regrettably, too many schools have made a choice with the hope that by discounting the price they would attract more students to the institution and the quality of the student body would improve. Rather than attempting to improve the institution's market position through price discounting, the first objective of management should be to improve the educational experience for its undergraduates. A quality educational experience generates satisfied customers, who become salespersons for the institution. That is the first step in improving an institution's market position.

Marketing Position and Price Discounting. Now that I have argued for greater investment in the quality of the educational experience rather than price discounts as a long-term market strategy, to what extent will discount practices affect college choice?

This question can be answered by analyzing the behavior of students who fall within certain cells of the student mobility paradigm. Students who fall within cells M3 and M4, for purposes here, are defined as those who might be able to attend public institutions without any financial assistance but who would need considerable aid to attend an independent institution. The question is then whether the independent institution can neutralize the price differences by offering an attractive financial aid package and whether a student is sufficiently interested in the private institution to want to substantially invest in his or her education through self-help. Thus, the stronger the market position of an independent college, the more it can expect in the way of self-help from its financial aid candidates. Conversely, a private college with limited visibility might improve its market position by limiting the degree of expected self-help and increasing the amount of grant assistance as a percentage of financial need. However, if the student's first-choice college is a public institution, probably no degree of price discounting will change the candidate's mind.

As indicated previously, the degree that self-help must be limited is related to the market position of the college. The more prestigious an institution's market position, the more self-help can be expected. Those few colleges that have extremely strong national market positions can expect a specified amount of self-help from every candidate who applies and qualifies for financial assistance. These colleges will not find it necessary to vary the self-help component in relation to total financial need. The poorer the market position in relation to a college's main competition, the more likely that a college will have to reduce the amount of self-help required. Therefore, the market position of a college will affect the financial aid packaging policies for all students who fall within cells M3, M4, L3, and L4. However, for all types of high-priced institutions, students falling in cells L3 and L4 appear to be the most difficult to attract (Bracken, 1975, 1976, 1977). Students who fall within these cells come from families who would be expected to contribute $4,000 to $6,000 to their education. They are able to attend a public university in their state for about $3,100; therefore, even though these students would receive some financial assistance at many private and out-of-state public institutions, their families would still be required to make sacrifices in sending them there rather than to a public university within the state. Such families also may be looking toward the future when they will have other children entering college. For these families the decision is based on what is referred to in economics as "marginal utility." Is the perceived superiority of the benefits to be received from the more expensive college as great as or greater than the price differences between the two colleges being considered? The marketing technique applied by some independent colleges in an effort to attract students who fall in cells L3 and L4 is to offer grant assistance in excess of a student's financial need. However, there appears to be no evidence that suggests that this method of recruitment is successful either in attracting students who normally would not have enrolled or in expanding an institution's market.

The acceptance of a student into a special program may improve an institution's market position as much as offering a more attractive financial aid package would. In fact, special programs may have a market position that is separate from the institution's. One example is an honors program in medical or law education in which a student is admitted to the program as an entering freshman. Another example is combining B.A. and M.A. degrees within the same period normally required for a bachelor's degree. This is not only a form of portfolio packaging, but it is also a form of price discounting. If a student is able to accelerate his or her education and thus save a year of tuition and forgone income, then this is indeed a very attractive financial aid package even if the student does not have

a financial need. Such programs should be marketed for their financial advantages as well as for their academic significance.

A Market-Sensitive Financial Aid Program. Under a market-
sensitive model the amount of self-help required in relation to grant
assistance would vary, within reason, across groups of candidates
and/or from individual candidate to individual candidate within
groups. The variation in self-help would be based on the following
factors.

1. *The market position of the college, compared with other
colleges in which the candidate is interested.* Each financial aid form
identifies the other colleges to which a prospective student is likely to
apply. This permits the institution to assess its relative market
position.

2. *The market position of a program or a school within the
institution.* A program or school may have a stronger market position
than other programs or schools at the same institution, than its
counterparts at other institutions, or than the institution itself. For
example, within a region, a program in fine arts may have a very
strong market position compared with those offered by other institutions. The demand for a program is determined by the number of
applicants over time, compared with other programs offered by the
institution. Students accepted into a program in great demand may be
offered more loan and work assistance and less grant assistance.
Another example would be accelerated programs whereby a student
completes both a bachelor's and a master's degree within four years.
Since such a program already provides for a reduction in the required
investment in education, it should be possible to offer less grant
assistance and more self-help as a proportion of financial need. Conversely, a candidate with strong credentials who applies to a program
with a weak market position would be offered more grant assistance
and less self-help.

3. *The market position of the college in relation to student
ability and financial need as defined by the student mobility paradigm.* Since students in cells H3 and H4 are not very mobile with
regard to college choice, the greater the amount of self-help, the less
likely that students in these cells will attend a given college if another,
located nearer a student's home, offers less self-help and more grant
assistance. The idea of incurring considerable debt to acquire an

education is a foreign concept to students from such families. Accordingly, the greater the distance between such a student's residence and the college, the less responsive the student will be to a large self-help component. Colleges that apply a policy of a set amount of self-help for all financial aid candidates may want to reconsider their positions with regard to students from such backgrounds. The same analysis can be applied to students within cells M3 and M4 but to a lesser extent. Prospects who fall in these two cells will be influenced by the amount of self-help required by a private school, particularly if the parents of these students have graduated from a public university and if these students are also considering a public institution with a good market position.

4. *The credentials of the candidate, compared with the market position of the college or university.* Is the candidate's market position stronger than the institution's, compared with the typical student who enrolls? It may be desirable to offer students with strong market positions substantial grant assistance in proportion to self-help.

The awarding of financial assistance based on this model can be effective in attracting students who are undecided with regard to college choice. At the margin, adopting the concept of competitive financial aid packaging is an effective method of improving a college's market position. Such a process is really no different from the type of price discounting that takes place in other industries, and it has proved to be a successful marketing technique. However, the evidence does suggest that in the aggregate students with financial need will elect to attend their first-choice college regardless of how financial aid is packaged as long as their families believe their financial need has been met (Gwinn, 1976; Spies, 1973).

Some admission and financial aid officers believe in total equity in the packaging of financial aid and find it unethical to vary the amount of grant assistance among students with similar financial need in order to improve an institution's market position. However, many of these same admission and financial aid officers are willing to offer scholarships not based on need in an effort to attract a certain type of student. This is a rather paradoxical market philosophy and one that generally does not work. If such discounts (scholarships) are offered to students with high ability and no financial need, these students will select a college on the basis of reputation, program offerings, and prestige. They seldom can be bought. Consequently, given a choice and limited dollars, the wise investment is to improve the quality of the product and not to discount the price on strictly a merit basis unrelated to financial need (Spies, 1978).

Hints on the Management of Financial Aid. If an institution has been meeting the financial needs of most of its students who demonstrate need, the expansion of federal and state grant programs permits a dollar-for-dollar substitution of external grant assistance for institutional grant assistance. This process should increase the institution's revenue base and should limit future tuition increases. At the same time, colleges and universities that offer non-need-based scholarship programs will not qualify for as much federal assistance, because the federal formula requires an institution to estimate the total need of its student body and to subtract from that figure the amount of institutional grant assistance available. Therefore, those dollars unrelated to financial need work to the financial detriment of the institution.

The federal work-study program has tremendously expanded the opportunities for students to help pay for their education. Institutions also have benefited in that they can utilize student help at nominal costs. Under the federal formula, institutions must provide 20 percent of the total dollars paid to students. An institution can pay more and should do so to expand its employee force where needed. The institution that is not using part-time student employment in its libraries, student centers, and laboratories is wasting money. Presidents and vice-presidents for finance in most colleges and universities have little or no idea of the vast savings that could accrue to their institutions through greater use of work-study funds. These savings, even for rather small institutions, can easily reach $100,000. The question then is "Are you as a college president aware of this resource, and are you fully maximizing its potential?" A good guess is that you may be aware but that you may be suffering from myopia.

The Guaranteed Student Loan Program has become the primary source for education loans, and in the academic year 1979–80 students are likely to borrow at least $3 billion through this program. From an institutional perspective this is not only an excellent financial aid resource, it has become a financial investment. For example, the Middle Income Student Assistance Act has made all students eligible for interest benefits. Therefore, any student should have access to an education loan without being charged interest while he or she is in school. For the student who has no need to borrow but who elects to do so anyway and places the loan funds in the bank, the interest earned on the loan, in effect, is a tuition discount. Moreover, if the institution is a lender under the Guaranteed Student Loan Program and uses general operating funds to support the loan program, the institution will gain greater earnings—about 2 percent more—through federal interest benefits than by investing in short-term securities. When an institution needs to liquidate its loan paper to meet its financial obligations, the Student Loan Marketing Association, as the chief secondary loan market, will purchase the loan paper. Most purchases are at par. Summarily, a college or university will earn more money as a lender of guaranteed student loans than by investing in short-term paper.

Pricing Models

As stated previously in this chapter, most pricing policies have evolved through accretion rather than through specific objectives. To determine the appropriate pricing policy, the factors that should be considered are (1) the effects of a given pricing policy on the nature and mission of the institution, (2) the effects of a given pricing policy on enrollment, and (3) the degree to which a particular pricing policy may unnecessarily encourage acceleration and therefore decrease revenue. Present pricing policies at many institutions appear to reflect the following: the expected, but generally untested, effect that a given price will have on enrollment demand; the desired amount of revenue necessary to balance the budget; some stability in revenue forecasting; and, for some institutions, a lack of interest in encouraging part-time study and/or acceleration. Thus, many pricing policies have been derived from the negative consequence that alternative policies might offer—simply a reduction in revenue.

Historically, equity pricing has been the common tuition model: all students, irrespective of year in school or field of interest, are charged the same gross price. However, today it is not unusual to find variable pricing patterns within a single institution. Variable pricing has two basic forms—differential and graduated. Under a differential pattern students in medical school would be charged a price far greater than those enrolled as undergraduates or in a Ph.D. program. Under a graduated pattern, students are charged a set rate based on year in school. Freshmen pay less than seniors, and seniors pay less than graduate students. This form of pricing is more closely related than other pricing models to the cost of providing the education and to the potential income of the graduates within a certain professional field.

Prices on a per course basis should be monitored and compared with the cost of offering a single course and the incremental costs of offering additional sections of the same course. Increasing the number of courses offered may or may not achieve economies of scale. If it does, the price should decrease for the second, third, or fourth course a student registers for. However, the incremental cost of offering an additional course may be greater than the cost of offering the first course. In addition, courses obviously vary in their costs across departments. Such an analysis would suggest that courses in medical technology should be priced higher than those in the humanities and that within each department prices could be graduated to correspond with instructional and servicing costs.

In a pricing system that is the same for all students or one that varies depending on academic discipline or year in school, the following objectives should be sought (Marquand, 1974):

1. Course programming should be maximally flexible.
2. There should be no price disincentives to discourage students from taking additional courses to enhance their education.
3. Financial pressure on students to graduate earlier than they wish should be minimal.
4. There should be an effort to minimize the financial distribution between scholarship and nonscholarship students. Students in neither category should be required to make educational decisions on the basis of financial considerations.
5. Subsidization by nonaccelerating students of those students who have chosen to accelerate should be minimal. Since such subsidization reduces revenue, compensating increases in tuition must be charged to either the current or the next generation of students.

6. Management should seek simplicity, ease, and low cost of administration to save overhead costs for educational purposes.
7. All students who are registered should have equal access to all
   facilities at all times.
8. There should be a sense of stability and predictability in tuition
   income to facilitate budgetary planning.
9. A policy should exist that avoids placing either the institution or
   the student in a position of having to decide educational or peda-
   gogical issues solely, or even primarily, on the basis of pricing
   questions.

In applying these principles to different types of institutions,
it should be helpful to focus on four basic pricing models: scaled
pricing, two-part pricing, term pricing, and unit pricing. These four
do not exhaust the possibilities, but they serve as examples to permit
the administration of an institution to assess its present method of
pricing. For purposes of understanding, these pricing models should
be considered macroconcepts: within any one of these concepts the
equity or variable pattern can be applied.

Scaled Pricing. Under a system of scaled pricing the student
pays more for the first and second courses, less for additional courses
up to the accepted norm, and more for additional courses. If the
normal course load is considered to be four, a student's fifth course
costs considerably more than the fourth course. In other words, a
surtax is charged to discourage acceleration. The effect of this type of
pricing policy, as well as any other, is to preclude various educational
options. In this instance, the student is discouraged from taking too
few courses and from taking too many courses for either acceleration
or enrichment. Such a policy monitors income, but it also establishes
educational policy, for it controls, through price disincentives, acceleration, enrichment, and consequently the time of graduation.

Educationally, according to the aforementioned objectives, a
desirable pricing policy is one that encourages taking courses for
enrichment but not necessarily for acceleration. Acceleration entails
subsidization of one group of students by another, and either the
present generation of students or the next generation must pay an
increased price. The recommendations of the Carnegie Commission
(1971) may be sound educationally for some students, but it should be

recognized that such a policy has a cost that must be absorbed either by raising the price for the current or next generation of students or by increasing the number of students enrolled.

Two-Part Pricing. Two-part pricing partitions tuition into two parts: a fixed price associated with enrolling a student, independent of the number of courses taken, and a price per course. The fixed price requires analyzing and segregating instructional and noninstructional costs. For example, by analyzing an institutional financial report, one can extract such noninstructional fixed costs as instructional support (for example, executive management, fiscal operations, administrative data processing, student services, public safety), libraries, maintenance of physical plant, other expenditures (including interest on indebtedness), and depreciation. This amount can then be distributed among students in a number of ways: over all students or over all students minus part-time and summer school students, if these programs are self-supporting, or in such a way as to discount a certain percentage for the differential cost of housing and offering different programs. For example, the fixed overhead in the sciences is greater than the fixed overhead in the humanities.

In support of a two-part pricing model, it could be argued that, whether a student takes one or five courses, there is a fixed overhead cost to the institution that must be included as a part of tuition. This fixed amount can be reduced or expanded depending on which variables one wishes to include in overhead and how many students are affected. The point is that, regardless of the number of courses a student takes, there is a fixed overhead component to whatever price is ultimately charged.

Effectively, there would be no additional cost to the student for acceleration other than the price of the course. In fact, savings would accrue through acceleration because the student would pay fewer overhead charges and because the same course taken a year hence might be offered at a higher price.

Two-part pricing might be desirable for schools with large numbers of part-time students in recognition that, whether a student is enrolled full-time or part-time, there is a fixed overhead component to the cost equation.

Term Pricing. Under the term-pricing model a flat tuition is charged each term. A student takes as few or as many courses as desired. This schedule discourages part-time study but does not penalize a student who wishes to take additional courses for credit. Students who elected to take more than the normal course load would not be charged an additional amount unless they wished to accelerate their graduation. At the time a student decided to graduate earlier than normally expected, he or she would be charged a prorated amount of the tuition currently in effect. Every student would be expected to pay for four full years of education unless credit was allowed for advanced placement, for foreign or summer study, or for work done by transfer students. Such a pricing system is most desirable for institutions with few part-time students. The advantages of this system are as follows:

1. It limits the degree of subsidization of one group of students by another.
2. It provides greater flexibility in course selection, because a student may take five or six courses one term and only three the next.
3. Because fewer seniors will be graduating early, it allows reduction of the number of entering students, thus providing for a better distribution of students across classes and among course offerings, and also makes possible improvement in the quality of the entering class.
4. It reduces the amount of financial aid necessary because the cost of assisting seniors averages lower than that of assisting freshmen. (More self-help is required of seniors who are receiving financial assistance, and the average parental contribution is more because the parents of seniors are closer to their peak earning power.)
5. It presents a method for improving a school's market position through pricing, since management can offer the option of charging no additional tuition to a student for studying an additional term, once he or she has paid for four full years of tuition.
6. It provides the option of suppressing tuition increases while still generating the desired amount of total revenue from tuition, because fewer students will be graduating early through acceleration. This option is plausible because it will cost less to underwrite a financial aid program for seniors than for additional freshmen.

The disadvantage of such a system is that it would be market-insensitive for a school that normally attracts a large part-time population. For such a school the two-part or unit-pricing model is more appropriate.

Unit Pricing. Under a unit-pricing system, students are charged so much per course. Whether a student takes one or five courses, the price per course is not varied (some institutions charge on a credit hour rather than per course). This system is generally in effect at institutions with large numbers of part-time commuter students. The disadvantage of this system is that it makes it difficult to forecast tuition revenue, which is likely to vary with economic conditions such as the availability of jobs, the amount of financial aid available, and to some extent even weather conditions. The advantage of a unit-pricing system is that it invites students from a much broader market. Students who are interested not necessarily in seeking a degree but rather in improving their skills in a particular area may be more attracted to a school that charges on a per course basis than to a school that discourages part-time enrollment through either term or scaled pricing policies.

Although a unit-pricing system may be inappropriate for schools that attract primarily full-time students from the traditional eighteen- to twenty-four age cohort, some such schools do use unit pricing. Generally, such a policy results in more students enrolled part-time, and it becomes necessary to attempt to increase the total enrollment in order to generate the desired amount of revenue. The unit-pricing model is desirable only for an institution that attracts large numbers of commuters and working students, who generally wish to study part-time.

Although unit pricing has been the typical pattern at colleges serving large numbers of part-time students, a two-part system is more defensible financially. Clearly, there are fixed costs whether a student is enrolled in one or three courses, and to an extent these costs should be covered either by a separate fee for registration or by a surtax on the first course, as under scaled pricing. A natural concern of management is that a change in pricing policies will decrease the potential market. However, because of the massive infusion of federal dollars for financial assistance, changes in price structure will have little effect on enrollment if the financial aid options are properly marketed.

Comparison of Pricing Systems. What is needed if the vast majority of colleges and universities are to survive with limited erosion in quality is a price structure that will more appropriately reflect costs without substantially increasing the net price to the individual students. The objectives of any pricing system should be to maximize revenue and minimize cost to the student, but these aims cannot be achieved unless the nature of the student body is considered in relation to institutional costs, growth in disposable income, and available financial assistance. There is no one desirable pricing policy for all institutions, but there is a single best pricing policy for each institution if the marginal costs and price supports are considered. The revenue accruing under each pricing model is presented in Table 5.

Table 5. Revenue Under Various Pricing Systems, in Dollars per Term

Pricing System	Number of Courses Taken[a]				
	1	*2*	*3*	*4*	*5*
Scaled	175	175	500	500	675
Two-Part[b]	230	320	410	500	590
Term	500	500	500	500	500[c]
Unit	125	250	375	500	625

[a] A normal course load would be four. If forty-five courses were required for graduation, this could be achieved in eleven quarters by taking one additional course in one quarter.
[b] In this example a fixed charge of $140 is applied plus $90 a course.
[c] Unless fifth course is applied to graduation; then an additional fee would be charged.

To illustrate the revenue generated from different pricing systems, Table 6 summarizes a student's total tuition over twelve quarters and over eleven quarters at a hypothetical university. In this illustration forty-five courses are required for graduation. Under scaled pricing and under unit pricing, the cost is the same for graduation in eleven quarters as in twelve. The greatest incentive to graduate early is provided by term pricing, in which a student would save $375. Such a pricing policy is economically indefensible for an institution with a pattern of full-time enrollments, since fixed costs remain when students accelerate their education; hence, a surtax beyond the per

Table 6. Tuition Revenue by Pricing System for Graduation in Twelve Quarters and in Eleven Quarters if Forty-Five Courses Are Required for Graduation, in Dollars

	A. Graduation in 12 Quarters (student takes 1 course in 12th quarter) Pricing System				B. Graduation in 11 Quarters (student takes 5 courses in 11th quarter) Pricing System			
	Scaled	Two-Part[a]	Term	Unit	Scaled	Two-Part[a]	Term	Unit
Tuition in 11th quarter	500	500	500	500	675	590	625[b]	625
Tuition in 12th quarter	175	230	500	125	0	0	0	0
Total for both quarters	675	730	1,000	625	675	590	625	625
Gain (loss) compared with scaled pricing	0	55	325	(50)	0	(85)	(50)	(50)

Pricing System			
	Scaled	Two-Part	Term	Unit
---	---	---	---	---
Savings to student by early graduation (incentive)	0	140	375	0
Net gain (loss) if 25 percent of students graduate 1 quarter early, averaged across all students (compared with scaled pricing)[c]	0	20	231	(50)

[a] Based on a fixed charge of $140 plus $90 a course.
[b] $500 plus $125 for applying addition: 1 course toward graduation; the $125 could be any amount.
[c] Calculated as .75 of the gain in Part A plus .25 of the gain in Part B.

unit price should be charged at the time an accelerating student decides to receive his or her degree. As shown in Table 6, the term-pricing system would provide the greatest increase in revenue. If one assumes that 25 percent of each class of 1,000 students were to graduate early, a term-pricing policy would increase revenue by $57,750 ($231 x 250) annually.

Cost of a Three-Year B.A. Northwestern University implemented a three-year bachelor's program in 1973 in response to the Carnegie Commission's (1971) recommendations. About 100 students a year enroll in the program. The availability of this option is based on the student's admission credentials. The typical student in the program has a composite SAT score of 1400 and has graduated in the top 5 percent of his or her high school class. When the program was implemented, it was assumed that the applicant pool contained a given number of students whose credentials were of such quality that it was not necessary to require them to take the Advanced Placement Tests of the College Entrance Examination Board. It also was assumed that, if those students were advised that they were accepted into a three-year B.A. program at the same time that they were accepted into the university, this option would increase the likelihood of their attending Northwestern, thus improving the university's market position. We have been able to conclude that this additional option does increase the likelihood that a student of high quality will enroll at Northwestern; however, as many as 60 percent have elected to extend their studies for an additional two or three quarters. Therefore, this option has proved to be an effective marketing device but not necessarily an incentive to graduate early.

Students in the three-year B.A. program must take thirty-six courses. This means that during their three-year residence program they must take four courses a quarter, and the current pricing structure does not allow them to take three courses one quarter and five courses the next without an additional charge.

An analysis of the cost of this program indicates that replacing a group of 100 four-year students with the same number of three-year students would result in a revenue loss, since there would be 100 fewer students in attendance the fourth year. If, however, 33 additional three-year students were enrolled each year, the number of students on campus would be the same.

In fact, replacing 100 four-year students with 133 three-year students would increase the number of course registrations, thereby increasing revenue. A three-year student must take twelve courses each year to reach the thirty-six courses required for graduation in three years. In comparison, a four-year student, who is required to take forty-five courses to graduate, needs only nine courses his or her senior year. Under the present pricing system, 400 three-year students generate $1,704,000 in gross tuition income per year. A group of 400 four-year students, however, would generate, on the average, $1,613,000 in tuition income. Replacing 100 four-year students with 133 three-year students in each freshman class can therefore generate as much as $91,000 in additional tuition income once three classes are enrolled. This argument assumes no attrition or early graduation. Table 7 compares the revenue accruing under the two programs.

The purpose of this chapter has been to discuss various pricing options, the related costs, and the interaction effects of pricing policies and market position. Clearly, the content of this chapter does not exhaust the discussion, but I hope that it will serve as a stimulus for similar discussion within various educational environments.

The one program option discussed, the three-year degree, was not presented as a marketing recommendation, for few students are so highly qualified that they should consider such an option. Rather, the comparative costs of a three-year degree were presented as an example of a systematic assessment of the underlying cost related to the impact of one program—a type of comparative cost analysis that has not often taken place before changes in program offerings.

Table 7. Tuition Revenue from Three-Year and Four-Year B.A. Programs, in Dollars

Group	Revenue		
A. Three-year B.A. students			
400 FT ($4,260 per student)		1,704,000	
B. Four-year B.A. students			
Model 1			
300 FT (Fr–Jr)	1,278,000		
100 seniors			
FT 2 quarters	284,000		
1 course 1 quarter	51,000		
		1,613,000	
Difference			91,000
Model 2			
300 FT (Fr–Jr)	1,278,000		
100 seniors FT fall	142,000		
90 seniors FT winter			
(10 percent graduating)	127,800		
75 seniors spring			
37 1 course	18,870		
19 2 courses	19,380		
19 FT	26,980		
		1,613,030	
Difference			90,970

7

Improving Communications and Promotion

Sandage and Fryburger (1975), in their book on advertising, identify five fields of research required for effective advertising: consumer research, product analysis, market analysis, media research (size and character of the audience that each medium reaches), and testing the effectiveness of alternative communication strategies. The first two sections of this book have addressed the potential consumer market, the variation in product and the related demand, how to segment that market to forecast demand, and the interaction effects of market and price. This section will discuss alternative communication strategies, but no effort will be made to assess the size and the character of the audience that each medium reaches. It is assumed that institutions that are serious about addressing the communication process will refer to an advertising agency. What follows is related more to developing specific communication strategies than to determining the most appropriate medium.

Forming the Communications Network

In creating a communication strategy, the main question is "How can we maximize prospective-student contacts in the most efficient and personal manner?" In response, the roles to be played by alumni, faculty members, and students in designing and modifying the marketing plan should be clearly defined as they relate to the different markets. A comprehensive communications strategy should include people external to the admission staff who can assist in the communications effort. The interaction of these sources with the admission staff and the roles of these external sources as defined by the marketing plan are called the "communications network." The network is basic to developing a marketing team.

The marketing team can be almost any size desired. The chief criterion should be the admission staff's capability to serve the network. If a director of admission who is asked "What is the size of your staff?" responds by naming only the size of the professional staff or the size of the professional staff plus the paid supportive staff, then this person is not marketing-oriented. The communications network should include faculty members, members of other offices, students, alumni, and media personnel. In a major university this network should provide human resources numbering as many as 1,000. Thus, the answer that a director of admission should give to questions about the size of his or her staff should vary depending on the size of the school but should not be restricted to the professional staff.

To have an effective organization that maximizes personnel size and diversity, it is necessary to be well organized and to serve that organization with relevant information. As indicated in Chapter Four, involvement is a key concept, and any member of the community who wishes to be involved should eventually be given the opportunity, but there are limitations of time, staff, and money to support the efforts of all those who may wish to be involved. Consequently, at times the answer must be "Yes, we want you to be a part of our overall effort, but we will need some time in order to provide you with the necessary direction and to support your efforts."

If the admission office is to have such a philosophy of inclusiveness, then individual members of the staff must be given the responsibility for organizing the faculty, the alumni, the students, and other offices. About 150 Northwestern faculty members are involved with on-campus programs. In addition, they visit with individual candidates and their parents on a regular basis. Faculty members appear to be the most effective in discussing their disciplines, not as interviewers or as general representatives of the institution. To use faculty members in any capacity other than to represent their disciplines is a poor use of their time. They can best assist the institution's marketing efforts by meeting the intellectual needs of students.

Students who believe in their institution can be a strong adjunct to the marketing program. They can help organize information programs for candidates either on campus or in their home communities. They can also provide special technical skills that are not readily available among the professional staff. Some admission offices pay undergraduates to work for them and coach them on what to say to prospective students. If such coaching creates a lack of candor, this will be recognized by prospective students. Although volunteer student representatives may be critical at times, such openness generally has a positive influence in enhancing the kind of environment a college should wish to portray. On occasion an undergraduate may advise candidates that this is one school they should not attend. However, such a statement, unsupported by evidence, has little or no credibility with candidates or their parents. If the undergraduate is able to provide a substantive reason, though, it may very well be the best advice that the candidate has received. Seldom, however, does such a statement stand alone. The most critical undergraduates will always find something good to say if they have elected to participate in the admission program, for they, too, have their own vested interests at stake. It is self-demeaning to be overly critical of one's educational experience and at the same time maintain an active role in representing the institution. Besides, the student would probably be asked why he has not transferred. Thus, whether the institutional representatives are alumni, faculty members, undergraduates, or staff members in other offices, it is constructive criticism that will better serve the needs of students and add credibility to the marketing effort.

The marketing molecule shown in Figure 5 is an effective device to clarify the process and to further illustrate the relationship

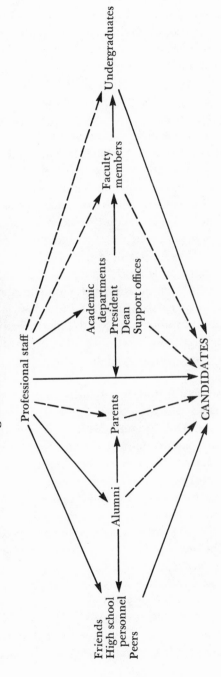

Figure 5. Marketing Molecule

Professional staff

Friends
High school personnel
Peers

Alumni

Parents

Academic departments
President
Dean
Support offices

Faculty members

Undergraduates

CANDIDATES

Note: Solid lines imply direct influence in the college-choice process; dashed lines indirect influence.

between the professional staff and other audiences. As indicated in the figure, based on philosophy and research, candidates are affected differently by the various audiences who either are an integrated part of an institution's overall recruitment effort or have some continuing contact with the institutions (Ihlanfeldt, 1975, p. 142).

As Figure 5 shows, some influences on the candidate are direct, some indirect. For example, whether faculty members, in general, are having a positive or a negative influence on undergraduates will affect the degree to which undergraduates are willing to represent the institution. The professional staff directly influences alumni to the extent that alumni are organized to participate in the overall marketing effort. Professional staff members influence high school personnel and friends of the university by the quality of the information that is distributed, by their personalities, and by the types of workshops that the institution offers for secondary school teachers and counselors. The professional staff is more likely to affect candidates unfavorably than favorably. A candidate's expectations are generally positive, so that a good experience with a staff member only reinforces what was expected. If a candidate has a bad experience in an interview or a member of the staff poorly represents the institution at a high school, "minuses" are remembered to a far greater extent than "pluses."

Alumni and representatives of units within the university, such as presidents and deans of schools, can have a direct impact on parents of candidates. Alumni and deans are often more effective in communicating with parents than with candidates. Contact between an alumnus and a parent often means a talk between members of the same age group who live in the same community. A sense of local identity is created for the institution, and the parents feel more secure in guiding their children toward that college. Academic deans have a different image: They are perceived as authority figures who have instant credibility because of title and responsibility. Their message is frequently taken at face value by the parents of candidates. Because they are not perceived to be salespersons for the institution in the same sense as are members of the admission staff, their opinions and philosophies tend to have more credibility.

The marketing molecule is nothing more than an attempt to conceptualize the nature of the communication network and the flow of communication from one constituency to another. Such communication can be in the form of a telephone contact, a letter, an interview, or a personal conversation. The quality of that contact and how it addresses the concerns of the candidate and his or her parents cannot be overemphasized. Contact must be individualized because people tend to hear what they want to hear; hence, the quality of communication and the nature of the audience should be the focus of the communication effort. The marketing molecule illustrates the importance of the coordinating role of the professional staff and emphasizes the interrelationships among other members of the communication network as they relate to candidates and their families.

Developing Faculty Support. Through proper cultivation the faculty can become an effective part of the marketing team. However, the admission staff that has failed to include faculty members in policy discussions will often find them unresponsive to the problems of recruiting students. To begin to create an awareness among the faculty of institutional enrollment needs, market interests, and the potential number and abilities of eligible students, there should be a standing committee of the faculty senate responsible for determining admission policies and for reviewing recruiting practices. At some colleges where committees do exist, the responsibility of the committee is to make and to review admission decisions. Although this may be a prudent assignment to provide faculty members with some first-hand knowledge of the quality of the student body, the reading of applications should not be a central function of the committee. The faculty's time can be better spent addressing policy questions as they relate to admission and by addressing, through good teaching, the problem of attrition.

The admission committee should also include students, alumni, and several administrators. Tenured faculty members who are opinion leaders should serve on the admission committee, and the president and senior faculty administrator (that is, the dean of faculties) should not. Often, the presence of the latter two will inhibit discussion among faculty members and middle management. The director of admission should be an ex officio member of the committee and should be assigned the responsibility of providing information and sources of information.

Since financial aid should be an integrated part of the marketing plan if enrollment objectives are to be realized, the responsibilities of the admission committee should include policies and practices governing the awarding of institutional assistance. If a single committee is assigned the responsibility for both admission and financial aid, the name of the committee should reflect both functions, and the director of financial aid should also be an ex officio member of the committee. Having one committee assume the policy responsibilities for both offices will facilitate communication between them and will help the faculty develop a more comprehensive understanding of the costs of recruiting a student body of a given size, quality, and diversity. Moreover, recommendations are not likely to emanate from the committee unless it has realistically assessed the financial aid cost implications. The responsibility of the ex officio members is to keep before the committee the main issues and the probable consequences of alternative policy recommendations.

By establishing a committee that includes faculty members, students, alumni, and staff members, the admission and financial aid staffs have the opportunity to create a forum for discussion and to develop informed citizens of the community. Members of the committee can become ambassadors of goodwill and can assist the admission staff in soliciting the support of their peers to become a part of the total marketing effort. However, the director of admission should not believe that with the establishment of a committee the involvement and credibility problems are solved. In fact, the work has just begun, for the opportunity now exists to keep before the community such concepts as the relation of student satisfaction to enrollment (attrition), the demands of the marketplace, the market position of the institution, the quality and size of the potential pool of students, and the related operating and financial aid costs. If these kinds of topics are not brought before the committee, members' interest will soon subside, and the opportunity to increase community participation in the marketing effort will be lost.

Although the establishment of such a committee is absolutely necessary if a legitimate forum is to exist, the director of admission should initiate other outreach efforts to sensitize faculty members to the critical role they play in maintaining or in improving enrollment. Written or oral reports addressing enrollment issues should be presented to the faculty and to other potential members of the marketing team. In addition, research should be initiated to identify students' attitudes toward their educational experiences, and faculty members should be informed of the results. Further, the admission staff should meet annually with faculty members in each department to learn of program changes and developments as well as faculty concerns about enrollment distribution and student quality. Such meetings provide the admission staff with an excellent opportunity to share the demand problems it faces that result from prospective students' changing interests.

Establishing a working admission committee, issuing reports, initiating research, and hosting small group meetings to exchange information ought to arouse sufficient faculty interest to secure involvement in the overall marketing effort. The better informed the faculty is about student satisfaction and market needs, the more likely that it will be responsive to the concerns and interests of the admission staff. Faculty involvement is not necessary to meet the adjunct staffing needs of the admission office, but it is necessary if faculty members are to understand that the quality of their performance as teachers and scholars transcends the boundaries of their departments and affects the market position of the institution.

As faculty members develop a better understanding of their role as a part of the marketing effort, their interest in the college's student recruiting program will increase. They will take the time to assist the admission office with its communications between prospective students and the institution. They will be willing to make themselves available to talk with prospective students, to help with the writing of publications about their departments, and to provide technical skills in research, data processing, and communication. Through the adoption of this suggested organizational model, which perceives the faculty as an integrated part of the marketing team, the faculty becomes a significant and necessary resource. To the extent that such a model becomes operational, the admission staff not only has substantially improved the communication network but has created a greater concern among the faculty about the quality of the educational experience. The result, over time, is likely to be a much improved product and a reduction in attrition.

Developing Student Support. At one time or another, almost all college administrations have been suspicious of students who ask questions about their separate domains. Often, our attitude is that we must protect our territory rather than share it. We fear that any information we provide, unless prefaced with pages of qualifications, will be misunderstood. The attitude is almost paranoia.

Before one objects too strongly, let us recall the late 1960s. Almost everyone associated with the admission profession was suspicious that formalized student involvement in recruiting other students would create more administrative problems. How could minority students who knew little about admission criteria recruit other minority students? For many, such a question today strikes a chord of disbelief, but for other administrators the question is still pertinent. Well, the answer is that students are probably the college's best representatives, and the more information made available to them, the better representatives they are. Numerous studies indicate that the involved student is likely to be an involved and loyal alumnus.

As members of a university community and as administrators, we have a responsibility to be teachers. To share information with students who want to assist the admission staff is the beginning of a learning experience. The learning experience teaches responsibility and accountability, and students who volunteer are eager to learn. In such an environment, undergraduate students become an important component of the marketing team. The objective of the organizational plan should be to match undergraduate students who represent various backgrounds with prospective students. As a part of the marketing team, as represented in the marketing molecule, currently enrolled students not only tend to influence prospective students more than any other group of representatives on the marketing team, but they tend to affect the attitudes of other members of the communication network. Alumni and secondary school personnel who have contact with satisfied and informed undergraduates are most gratified, particularly if they encouraged the student to attend the institution. A sense of collegiality develops among the three parties—a bond that every college should want to encourage.

How structured should the program of students recruiting other students be? Should students be paid for their efforts? Can they be held accountable for meeting their responsibilities? What tasks should they be asked to perform? What are the advantages to be gained by their involvement? The last question has been answered— except to add that having undergraduate students around the admission office creates an alive atmosphere, and, as a result, one's work becomes that much more satisfying.

Now to the other questions. I do not believe in paying students to recruit other students. If the long-range goal is to create an attitude of volunteerism by alumni, then the admission office should be a training ground. The exception is that needed technical skills that would have to be purchased elsewhere if a student were not available should receive some remuneration. One should keep in mind that how we respond to the interests of undergraduates will have lasting effects once they are alumni. However, they must be held accountable for accepting any responsibility, whether it be conducting a tour, hosting a party, contacting prospects, or visiting secondary schools. They must realize that failure to meet their accepted responsibilities affects many other parties. If they fail, then their actions must be called to their attention, and, for a period of time, they should be excluded. Generally, this is not a problem, for failure to follow through is rare; undergraduates remember when they were prospective students and how anxious they were at times. Many undergraduates also view their work with the admission office as creating the possibility either for future employment or for a good recommendation. One year, I wrote, for one student, forty-six recommendations to different law schools. He was finally accepted, and he has not forgotten. Today, he plays an active role in Northwestern's Alumni Admission Council.

Finally, what should students' responsibilities include? In every student body a variety of skills can be identified and developed, from identifying good conversationalists to developing computer-programming skills. Each year a list of items should be identified that will require a variety of skills to enhance the marketing effort. As suggestions, one can begin by identifying various skills, such as research, computer, public relations, writing, and political. For example, research skills represent a continuum from creating a questionnaire to typing envelopes, to collating responses, to reporting the data. Computer skills might include developing systems, understanding how to use canned programs, writing programs, interpreting the data, and so on. Public relations would include skills varying in scope, from developing a total communications plan down to typing letters. Once the general concepts have been identified, then achieving the goals defined by the concepts requires various skills from the sophisticated to the mundane. Students should be included at every level, within the limits of the time and skills of professional personnel.

Because of the tremendous source of manpower within the student body and because of the federal work-study program, no director of admission should say that he or she does not have the staff or the money to get the job done. A college may not be attracting enough students, but the reason should not be a lack of effort by the admission office. No other unit in a college or university has the potential to be as well staffed as the admission office. Not only are the complementary abilities of students cost-effective, but student involvement adds credibility to the communication effort and provides the opportunity to increase the number of future well-informed alumni.

Developing Alumni Support. Historically, alumni have been involved in many areas relevant to the activities of their alma mater, particularly athletics, fraternity and sorority affairs, fund raising, and various special events. However, not until recently, except for a few colleges on the East Coast, have alumni been involved in recruiting students other than athletes. Most professional admission officers have opposed the idea of involving alumni in recruiting the typical student. Admission staffs have been concerned about the overzealous alumnus who might make false promises of admission independent of university authorization. They also have been concerned about alumni who simply would not represent the institution very well because of the generation gap, a lack of propriety, a lack of professionalism, and so forth. However, in the past, an underlying reason appeared to be that most directors of admission were threatened by the idea of the involvement of any constituency in the admission process over which they did not have direct control. Regrettably, this does not speak well for those still in the profession who have similar feelings.

The experiences of a number of eastern schools have shown that alumni can be a successful adjunct to the marketing effort. By their presence and, ideally, their pride in their alma mater, they can project an image of their college or university into hundreds of communities throughout the nation. Further, they provide a sense of local identity between their alma mater and people in the community. Well-informed alumni serve as institutional representatives throughout the country who can explain institutional policies to fellow alumni, prospective students and their families, and secondary school personnel. However, this last group, at times, also has expressed reticence about the participation of alumni in admission activities. The reason is that too often colleges and universities have asked willing but uninformed alumni to represent their alma mater at a college day or to visit a number of high schools. Some colleges match the ZIP codes of prospective students with those of alumni and mail a blind letter to an alumnus requesting that he or she contact the prospective student through the local high school. This kind of mismanagement has over time undermined the credibility of alumni in the eyes of secondary school counselors. Yet, most alumni, if properly instructed, can be as effective in representing their alma mater as can an admission counselor.

A caveat that must be mentioned is that it is a mistake to have alumni involved unless the admission office is prepared to support their activities and to hold them accountable for their efforts. It takes more than the willingness of alumni and the eagerness of an admission office to solve an institution's enrollment problems. The alumni represent a significant part of the marketing team as long as they are well organized, are well informed, understand their responsibilities, and are held accountable for the completion of those responsibilities. This implies that the admission staff must impose the same requirements on itself.

Organizing the Alumni Team. What should be the organizational structure of the alumni admission council? If one were to survey a variety of colleges, it is quite likely that one would find that over the past ten years alumni involved in admission activities have been organized through the alumni office. It also is likely that this type of organizational structure would be found ineffective because the alumni office is not abreast of admission policies, financial aid information, and secondary school contacts. Another problem that often occurs when the organizational function is placed in the alumni-relations office is that a conflict of interest develops. The alumni office may be courting a potential donor whose child has an interest in attending the institution. If the child is not admitted, the alumni office has lost its credibility in the eyes of the potential donor.

If the alumni are to be an effective part of the marketing team, they must be made to feel that they are a part of the overall organizational structure of the admission office. Such an attitude is easily developed if the admission office practices a posture of openness and involvement; the alumni will feel welcome and want to become actively involved. If they are to be involved, they must be served adequately, and this will require that at least one member of the professional staff in the admission office be assigned the responsibility of organizing the alumni. As a rough estimate, for a school with an undergraduate population of 6,500, the management of the alumni admission program will require that one admission officer devote 70 percent of his or her time to developing and subsequently serving the alumni council. The objective should be for alumni to become an integrated part of the staff. As the program evolves, secretarial and computer time will be required. The amount of each will depend on the sophistication of the total marketing program. Thus, the support for the alumni component of the marketing program should be an integrated part of the total support system.

In addition to having the alumni admission council administratively located in the undergraduate admission office, the degree to which alumni can successfully assist the admission office in its overall marketing effort will depend on the organization of the alumni in the field and what kind of contact they have with the office of admission. As one model, in each area where alumni are involved in the admission effort, one alumnus should be assigned the responsibility of coordinating the activities of the alumni admission council. When both a husband and a wife are graduates of the institution, they should be assigned as codirectors. All assignments should be channeled through the alumni directors in the field to other alumni who are members of the alumni marketing team. On completion of assigned tasks, field reports are cleared through the alumni directors to the admission office. Figure 6 summarizes this model.

If the alumni are to be well informed and to maintain an interest in campus events, a communication program must be implemented to keep them abreast of campus activities. An integrated

Figure 6. Alumni Admission Council

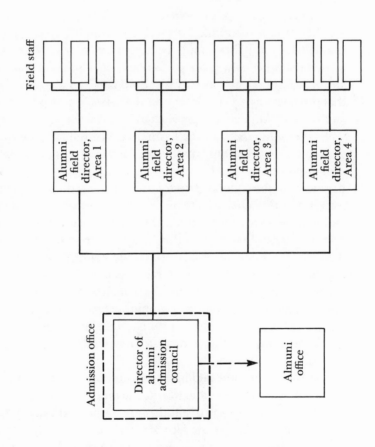

Field staff

| Alumni field director, Area 1 |
| Alumni field director, Area 2 |
| Alumni field director, Area 3 |
| Alumni field director, Area 4 |

Admission office

Director of alumni admission council

Almuni office

Field-staff
assignments

1. Visit secondary schools
2. Contact prospects
3. Host various events
4. Facilitate parent communication

part of the communication plan is required attendance at workshops, both on and off the campus, monitored by professional staff members. The workshops should include information on admission, financial aid, and institutional programs and visits with faculty members, students, and deans. As the program develops, it is particularly instructive to have alumni visit with students they helped recruit. Although on-campus workshops should be busy and at times intense, it is synergistic to permit the alumni to participate as freely as possible in other institutional activities that are not necessarily part of the workshop. The opportunity to reflect during such occasions facilitates dialogue during instructional sessions. Other forms of communication should include newsletters from the office, a subscription to the campus newspaper, and other items of general interest about the institution. To assist the alumni in feeling a part of higher education, they should be encouraged to read books on issues related to higher education, particularly on admission and financial aid. In addition, each alumnus should be given a resource manual that provides answers to most questions asked by prospective students and parents. Appendix B provides an example of such a manual.

Selecting the Alumni Team. In developing an alumni admission council the regional director or coordinator is the most significant appointment. Such a person must be a good manager. It is not necessary for the regional director to be involved in specific recruiting responsibilities other than to coordinate the activities of other alumni and to make sure that the alumni follow through. Interest is of key importance, and most often this interest is generated because of the desire to have some informal contact with young people. In selecting regional directors, time, secretarial assistance, and money are also necessary ingredients. Since the regional director is a conduit between the admission office and other alumni, a lack of follow-through on his or her part impairs the credibility of the admission office. Selection of an alumnus who is interested and well organized is therefore essential.

For the alumni regional staff, alumni who have been out of school for ten years or so and who are no longer job-hopping or being transferred from one job to another are the best candidates. Obvious sources are alumni who are secondary school teachers and those who work in communications. A recommended procedure is to focus on alumni who graduated within a given period and to check their activities and interests as undergraduates by canvassing old yearbooks. Alumni who agree to participate generally were quite involved in extracurricular activities when they were undergraduate students and wish they had had the opportunity to talk with alumni in various professions when they were prospective students.

Alumni who are invited to assist in the marketing effort should thoroughly understand that they have no other responsibilities than to give their time. They should not be required to join an alumni club or to give money to the university, although these are likely outcomes.

Once a list of alumni has been developed for a given area, a letter should be sent inviting their participation. If they are interested, they should be required to attend a workshop to be held in their area. If they do not attend the workshop, they should not be permitted to participate in admission activities. At each workshop it should be made clear what the time constraints are and what the responsibilities of the alumni will be.

Responsibilities of the Alumni Admission Council. The primary responsibility of the alumni is to create a sense of local identity for the institution. Faculty and staff members from the institution who visit a community once or twice a year simply cannot provide the sense of identity and continuity that involved alumni can who live and work in a community. Alumni who are opinion leaders in their communities can have a significant influence in projecting an image of their institution. A successful doctor, lawyer, educator, businessperson, or politician who frequently mentions his or her alma mater is an ambassador for the institution.

Alumni who become a part of the field staff should be required to obtain as much information about the institution as a typical member of the admission staff. Some of the responsibilities that can be assigned to alumni are as follows: to identify high school sophomores and juniors who the alumni believe have the potential to meet the criteria for admission; to visit specifically assigned high schools; to represent the institution at college nights; to become well acquainted with secondary school personnel; to meet with prospective students and their families; to attend local university-sponsored events for prospective students; to interview candidates for admission;

to become acquainted with the parents of admitted students; and to host or attend summer parties for entering freshmen.

Alumni not only should be expected to be a source of information for prospective students and their families but also should be requested to maintain contact with parents of present students. This encourages parents to believe that the college continues to be interested in them and their child long after the college decision has been made. During the period of campus upheaval in the late 1960s and early 1970s, parents often sought relief by talking with alumni; alumni who were kept informed of the exact facts about a demonstration or some other form of campus disruption were quite helpful in counseling or allaying the concerns of parents.

A primary responsibility of the professional member of the staff who is responsible for the alumni marketing team is to maintain biweekly or monthly contact with alumni, informing them about the admission process and campus events. An alumni admission program should not be developed unless there is adequate staff support to meet the demands that interested alumni will make. The more information they are provided and the better they are served, the more interest they will show as a part of the marketing team. If frequent contact is not made, interest in program activities will quickly subside. To solicit the interest of alumni and then not follow through will discourage alumni from getting involved in future institutional efforts.

To have an effective alumni admission program, the professional staff should be uncompromising with regard to the responsibilities alumni agree to accept. Alumni who do not fulfill their assignments should be counseled into other alumni activities of a less critical nature by either the professional staff or the alumni regional director. If alumni understand that the admission office is making every effort to accommodate their needs by keeping them informed, they will also understand that they have responsibilities that they must meet if they are to be retained as members of the alumni admission council.

Relations with the Alumni Office. In some colleges and universities the alumni office is unwilling to let the admission office manage any part of alumni affairs. However, the admission office has something to offer alumni that can also benefit the alumni office. For example, many alumni are willing to give time but are unwilling to give money. Interestingly, it appears axiomatic that the more alumni get involved in any activity of their alma mater, the more money they are likely to give—if not presently, at some future time. A well-run alumni admission program is a form of seduction that in the long run may benefit the alumni office.

Over time, alumni who are involved in admission activities are likely to get involved in other alumni functions. These often include raising money. If alumni are involved in the affairs of their alma mater, they will naturally want it to provide the kinds of services and programs that students desire. Ultimately, they will therefore want to assist the institution in improving itself. This requires more funds, and thus the commitment is made. Of course, this sequence of events will not take place in every instance, but it should certainly make sense to utilize alumni to whatever extent they wish to commit their time.

The only responsibility the admission office should have in its relation to the alumni office is to keep the appropriate personnel informed of the activities of the alumni admission program. Names of the alumni field staff members, the workshop itinerary for alumni, problems that may affect other alumni activities should be passed on to the alumni office. Coordination of activities between the alumni and admission offices can be fruitful. For example, to have the alumni admission campus workshop at the same time as the alumni office is hosting some other alumni event promotes a spirit of cooperative solidarity. As indicated in Chapter Four, openness and involvement add considerably to the marketing effort. Alumni want to be informed and they want to be involved. It is simply a matter of tapping the appropriate interest.

Developing Parental Support. Although relatives have limited influence on college choice (Astin, King, and Richardson, 1978), parents of most dependent students do provide some, if not all, of the financial support. If price is a factor in attending a given college, parents do play a more significant role, and if they are not supportive of a particular college or type of institution, their child is not likely to apply. Therefore, for the more expensive colleges and universities, communication with parents should be an integrated part of the promotional plan. Parents are often most concerned about why they should invest in a particular college when less expensive alternatives exist. They are naive about admission and financial aid practices and are interested in such areas as housing options, security, counseling, health services, religious alternatives, extracurricular programs, and job-placement opportunities.

It is wrong to assume that parents become informed and reassured through information sent to their children. In fact, the communication between parents and their teenage children is probably at its lowest ebb. Consequently, from a marketing perspective, a prudent course is to assume parents know very little about the process of college admission and financial aid and about your institution. Therefore, the marketing plan should include a systematic effort to educate them. One avenue is through counselors in secondary schools, and although many secondary schools offer college information programs for parents, far more do not.

A promotional campaign directed at parents would include some of the same tactics that are applied to cultivate the interests of prospective students: direct mail, on- and off-campus programs, interviews, and personal contact with alumni and with parents of currently enrolled students. Parents should not be overwhelmed with literature about the college, but their concerns should be addressed in special ways. An example of a direct-mail piece is reproduced below. Its intent is to justify the costs of high-priced private institutions by anticipating parents' concerns. This letter emphasizes positioning, opportunities resulting from the child's education, and methods of financing an education at a high-priced institution.

A Letter to Parents
from the Dean of Admission

Is Private Higher Education Worth It?

I am writing to you because your child is a student who will be graduating from high school in 1979. Therefore, you and your child are going through the difficult process of determining what he or she will be doing upon graduation from secondary school, and whether higher education, particularly private higher education, is a realistic educational opportunity. As you look at the prices of colleges across the country, it is quite clear that the differences in costs between public and private higher education are considerable. As a parent, you must ask yourself: "Is it worth it? Should I sacrifice to send my child to a private university when public higher education is less expensive? Are there really extra benefits? What is the difference in the quality of experiences, and what are the opportunities available upon graduation? Concisely, is there a difference in the value of the education received?" You will have to make that decision, but I would like to take a moment and share a few thoughts with you.

We are finding that many talented young people are not considering private higher education because their families are not looking beyond the price. It is our position that price should not be a determining factor as to who enters Northwestern. We are committed to an admission policy based upon intellectual and not monetary criteria. We do believe that there is a considerable difference between the educational experience offered at Northwestern University and that available in the public sector, as well as that in most other private institutions. Although the quality of the intellectual experience based upon the excellence of our faculty, student body, and library is one way of assessing this difference, we believe that you also are interested in what happens to the Northwestern student after graduation.

First of all, compared with 45 percent nationally, 80 percent or more of those who enter Northwestern graduate from Northwestern. At the time of graduation, 75 percent of the men and 45 percent of the women who graduate from the College of Arts and Sciences enter either graduate or professional schools. Of these, 38 percent continue their graduate education at Northwestern. We continue to be advised by our director of placement that the Northwestern graduate is a desirable employee in the corporate world, and that most of our graduates are able to find preferred employment upon graduation. This fact is true not only of students graduating in such fields as engineering, speech, music, journalism, and education, but of the typical liberal arts graduate, who has mastered a broad range of intellectual skills and learned to communicate effectively. However, liberal arts students majoring in the humanities or social sciences will improve their employment options if they take at least one or two courses in the following areas: economics, statistics or mathematics, and computer sciences. I call these facts to your attention because of the increasing need to spell out the more quantifiable benefits received from a college education.

The Economics of Higher Education

During the past several years with the rampant growth in inflation, the economic constraints placed upon public higher education by the state legislatures, and the deficit spending that has occurred in much of the private sector, there has been little opportunity for improving the quality of educational programs offered to the nation's young people. In fact, since higher education budgets have not been able to keep pace with inflation, there has been little alternative but to reduce the quality of the overall educational experience offered to college students. This has been reflected in increasing student-faculty ratios, greater utilization of graduate students as instructors, elimination of programs, and a reduction of student services offered. The significance of what I wish to say is that this has not been the case at Northwestern University because of sound fiscal management and continued financial support from the university's many friends. During the past ten years, the physical size of the campus has doubled while enrollment has been held constant. Concurrently, the size of the faculty has been increased, and the programs offered to undergraduates have been increased in number and enriched in quality. Of course, you may say that this is all well and good, but at the same time Northwestern is a very expensive institution. This is quite true, but many schools equally expensive have been operating on deficit budgets and have been required to reduce program offerings. Nevertheless, the question remains for each of you: "How can I finance the high cost of private higher education?"

Financing the Northwestern Education

Northwestern's administration has taken the position that it will not hold down tuition at the expense of reducing the quality of the undergraduate educational experience. Consequently, we anticipate that tuition will increase on the average at about the same rate that incomes increase across the country. Families that can afford the price of a Northwestern education will be expected to pay for it. Those families would be defined broadly as having gross incomes in excess of $40,000 with considerable home equity and assets and no more than two children. Students of other families who are admitted to Northwestern will qualify for tuition discounts commensurate with their financial need. Currently, in excess of 50 percent of Northwestern undergraduates are receiving financial assistance. This past year the university administered more than $12 million in undergraduate financial aid. Of those receiving financial assistance, 65 percent of the families have an income between $15,000 and $35,000; 5 percent have in excess of $35,000; and 30 percent have incomes less than $15,000. These figures and the university's overall position with regard to those who qualify for financial assistance clearly indicate that the middle class has not been excluded at Northwestern.

Consider the example of a four-person family with two children, one in college, with gross earnings of between $18,000 and $20,000 a year and limited assets. Such a family would be expected to contribute $1,600 a year toward their child's education. A student from such a family could expect to receive approximately $5,800 in financial assistance. This is in addition to $500 we expect a student to contribute from summer earnings. The $5,800 would be subdivided into work, loan, and gift assistance. In this example, a student would be offered a $1,000 loan that is interest-free during the in-school period; a $1,000 job for working 10 to 12 hours a week; and a grant of $3,800. Part of the grant assistance might come from other sources such as the state and federal governments. This example, of course, represents what might be considered an average case. Some students will receive grant assistance of as much as $5,000; others may not receive grant assistance but simply be offered a loan or a job as determined by the family's financial condition.

Those of you who do not qualify for financial aid should view the university's financial aid program as an *insurance plan*. Should your family suffer an economic setback, the university would come to your assistance in order to ensure that your child would not be forced to transfer or to discontinue his or her education. For families who do not qualify for financial aid but who have a cash-flow problem, the university offers an installment credit option and, through an external agency, a deferred payment plan. A prepayment plan is offered at the time a student is accepted for admission. Under this plan the family pays so much a month and earns 5 percent interest on the balance outstanding up to the point when tuition is due each quarter. Thus, instead of paying in one lump sum, a family may pay monthly and receive an interest benefit of 5 percent at the same time. In addition, all families, independent of income, are now eligible for interest-free guaranteed student loans while a student is in school. Seven percent interest begins to accrue nine months after one terminates his or her education. These loans are made through financial institutions.

In closing, I would like to share with you the results of a study which included 200,000 students and which reports the personal and intellectual benefits derived from their college experiences. The study is reported in a book entitled *Four Critical Years,* which was written by a well-known scholar on the faculty of a major public university and published by Jossey-Bass, located in San Francisco. I was heartened by the results of this study because it confirms my conviction that there clearly is a difference between the education offered by public and private institutions, and I quote: "Practically all the effects associated with college attendance are more pronounced among students at private institutions . . . if favorable impact on students is the desired goal for the higher education system, private institutions seem to foster greater student change than public institutions in almost all areas. In addition, students become much more involved both academically and nonacademically in private colleges and are more likely to implement career plans."

I encourage you to read this book, because it clearly indicates that private higher education is indeed worth the investment. I would like to encourage your responses and inquiries to the statements that I have made. You may be assured that you will receive a personal response. I urge you to look beyond the price and to make your own judgment with regard to educational quality and opportunity.

Cordially,

The response to this letter has been very positive and extensive. Even if a family is not interested in Northwestern, the letter provokes questions to measure the programs of other colleges and thereby acts as a public service.

Appendix C is an example of a handout that can be used at off- and on-campus information sessions. The objective is to provide families with a method of measuring impressions of a set of colleges as well as a device to assist families in determining their eligibility for financial assistance. In this instance the emphasis is clearly on public service, but the message is "This university cares." Again, the idea is to qualitatively improve Northwestern's market position by providing information that differentiates Northwestern's communication from that of other institutions.

Finally, the role of the interview must be explained as it relates to parents. Parents should have the opportunity to visit with a member of the professional staff any time they accompany their child to an interview. I do not recommend that they be present during the interview, but they should have at least ten to fifteen minutes to ask the interviewer questions, and in some cases the interviewer may want to offer the parents advice. Moreover, one should keep in mind that the parents of prospects become the parents of enrolled students. If they are properly educated during the prospect phase, they can become informed members of the communications network once their children have enrolled.

Maintaining the Interest of Volunteers

The faculty members, students, parents, and alumni who join the marketing team as volunteers need to belong to an effort they believe in, and they need to be recognized for that effort before their peers. Consequently, as part of the planning effort to create a volunteer organization, one should know why people will give time and for what reasons and under what conditions they should be recognized. Volunteers need a sense of belonging as identified by J. Donald Philips, retired president of Hillsdale College, Hillsdale, Michigan:

If you want my loyalty, interests, and best efforts, remember that . . .

1. I need a sense of belonging, a feeling that I am honestly needed for my total self, not just for my hands, not because I take orders well.

2. I need to have a sense of sharing in planning our objectives. My need will be satisfied only when I feel that my ideas have had a fair hearing.

3. I need to feel that the goals and objectives arrived at are within reach and that they make sense to me.

4. I need to feel that what I'm doing has real purpose or contributes to human welfare—that its value extends even beyond my personal gain or hours.

5. I need to share in making the rules by which, together, we shall live and work toward our goals.

6. I need to know in some clear detail just what is expected of me—not only my detailed task but also where I am given an opportunity to make personal and final decisions.

7. I need to have some responsibilities that challenge, that are within range of my abilities and interest, that contribute toward reaching my assigned goal, and that cover all goals.

8. I need to see that progress is being made toward the goals we have set.

9. I need to be kept informed. What I'm not *up* on, I may be *down* on. (Keeping me informed is one way to give me status as an individual.)

10. I need to have confidence in my superiors—confidence based upon assurance of consistent fair treatment, or recognition when it is due, and trust that loyalty will bring increased security.

In brief it really doesn't matter how much sense *my part* in this organization makes to *you*—I must feel that the whole deal makes sense to me! (Rivchun, 1979, p. 29.)

Remember that for most alumni it is easier to write a check than to give time. Yet, for many of the reasons cited above, they would prefer to give time. If they feel gratified by their affiliation, they may eventually give money as well as time.

Effective Use of Time, Personnel, and Capital

Within any plan there will be different strategies for different markets. The strategies define the various options available to management to improve or to expand the demand for the product, as well as the options available to the director of admission to develop effective systems of communication between the institution and prospective students. The type of plan—its philosophy and organization—will determine the admission office's capability to develop different strategies for various target markets. As the effort is made to create different strategies for a number of target markets, the timing of the promotional efforts becomes critical.

The earlier a communication plan is developed and implemented, the more easily it can be altered. The later a plan is introduced in the recruitment cycle, the less likely it is to be effective. Timing, therefore, is a management strategy. A concept implemented at the wrong time is likely to fail, whereas it may be quite effective if introduced at another point in the recruitment cycle. The importance of timing is emphasized because I frequently get calls from presidents asking what can be done to reverse an admission trend in the middle of a recruitment cycle. An appropriate response is "For the coming fall, very little; but for the following fall your timing is right." Unfortunately, these callers often are interested in short-term solutions to long-term problems. Timing, if properly managed, is a critical resource in developing marketing strategies. The more sophisticated the marketing effort and the larger the marketing team, the more critical the dimension of time becomes in each phase of the marketing process.

If the office of admission has created a marketing team that includes alumni, undergraduates, parents and faculty members, the responsibilities of each subgroup should be defined in relation to the three markets—primary, secondary, and tertiary. For example, the auxiliary undergraduate student admission council as a whole may be totally involved in the primary market because of related on-campus recruitment activities as well as off-campus recruitment efforts in the immediate area of the college. In addition, undergraduates who are a part of that auxiliary force and who come from secondary markets can be given specific assignments of contacting candidates from their local areas. This plan would include visiting the high school each attended as a representative of the college with a letter of introduction sent by the admission office before the visit, contacting candidates directly by phone or by letter, and working with the local alumni in organizing information programs and parties for candidates and their parents during term breaks. As a general guideline, freshmen and sophomores serve as more effective liaisons with their high schools than upperclassmen do. Since freshmen and sophomores are the most recent graduates of secondary schools, they are remembered best not only by teachers and staff members but by high school students who are now in their junior and senior years of high school and who want to learn more about colleges and universities from people they consider credible sources. This concept is particularly significant if the undergraduate representative achieved considerable visibility in high school as a result of activities or academic performance.

Although faculty members are most effective on their own turf, from time to time having them participate in off-campus programs or contact candidates directly can be helpful under the proper circumstances. This activity can be effective if the faculty members previously lived in the area they are visiting and/or are responsible only for talking with candidates interested in their disciplines. We have had one interesting experience that I would like to share. A member of the faculty from a rather unsophisticated background approached us about the possibility of contacting candidates from the area where he had spent his childhood. In this instance, he simply wrote a letter to candidates explaining that he, too, was from their area and could understand their concern about attending college in a major metropolitan area. At the same time, he stated, he had made the transition, and the value received was well worth the effort. Although the numbers were small, his letter and his availability when students from his area visited campus increased the flow of applications and matriculations. *This is just one additional example of how important it is to match profiles of people in developing exchange relationships as part of the marketing plan.* Matching faculty members, alumni, and undergraduates with candidates who have similar interests is far more productive than matching on a random basis. Strangers need a binding interest; it is the responsibility of the admission office to create that match.

In the admission marketing effort, alumni and undergraduates are more effective in secondary markets than in primary markets. A member of the admission staff can have little impact in a secondary market as a result of a once-a-year visit to a high school or hosting a single-evening information session. Alumni provide a sense of local identity that is ongoing after a representative has come and gone.

However, using alumni directly in recruiting students who live near the campus may not be as productive as having a series of ongoing programs that encourage candidates to visit the campus. As the geographic distance between the alumni and the institution increases, their involvement in admission activities becomes more important. In the primary market, particularly within fifty miles of the college, the institution is easily accessible. However, to maintain the visibility of the college in any market there should be a systematic effort to publicize contributions of alumni to stimulate candidates' interest in the institution. There appears to be an inverse relation between distance from the institution and direct involvement of alumni as part of the marketing team. To increase the effectiveness of the activities in the secondary market, alumni should be actively involved in making the institution not only more visible among high school juniors and seniors but more visible in general. The more public recognition individual alumni receive, the greater the level of public awareness of the college. The institution can facilitate this awareness by writing stories about the achievements of alumni for the local press.

The more involved in secondary market activities alumni become, the less time the professional staff must commit to these areas and the fewer dollars expended. Again, this principle does not imply that there should be no contact between candidates who live in secondary markets and representatives of the institution. However, the contact may take other forms than a personal visit. Although total institutional operating costs related to secondary market activities may decrease, mailing costs in these areas are likely to increase because of more frequent mailings to alumni and to candidates and their parents. It is necessary to visit most of the areas identified as secondary markets, but through the involvement of alumni, instead of spending a week each in major metropolitan areas visiting secondary schools, it is possible to spend only one or two evenings. These should be devoted to alumni workshops and evening information sessions for candidates and their parents. Such sessions can be conducted at a club, a hotel, or an alum's home that is centrally located. After such programs, the names of candidates and their parents should be turned over to alumni for the purpose of follow-up activities. Instead of spending five weeks in five different areas, under such a plan the professional staff member need spend only five days—a Sunday through a Thursday in five different areas. This type of recruitment plan is credible, efficient, cost-effective, and yet quite personal because its focus is on orchestrating communication between the prospective student and those who either directly benefited from the institutional experience or helped create the experience.

Admission operating budgets vary considerably. In a study of recruitment practices of small liberal arts colleges by the Academy of Educational Development (1978), an average of $380 per matriculant was spent in the fiscal year 1976–77. The range was considerable. One institution spent $1,939 per matriculant to a low of $197. These costs are similar to those I have found as a consultant to a number of small colleges. The costs per matriculant are related to the strength of the institution's market position. The weaker the position and the lower the enrollment the more likely the cost per matriculant will be high— an assessment truer of regional institutions than of national institutions. Although national institutions with strong market positions often have high costs for personnel and computer support to monitor the substantial flow of inquiries and applications, these same institutions will achieve some economies of scale if they enroll a rather large number of entering students. In comparing costs one has to be careful to include the costs of all publications and computer support, which often appear in the budgets of other offices. Finally, costs that never appear are those related to the time given by faculty members, alumni, and undergraduates to the overall recruitment effort. However, after all realized costs are considered the management question remains: "Is there a more cost-effective process to achieve the same or better results?"

Developing a Promotional Strategy

There are few colleges and universities whose administrators are satisfied with the public recognition of the institution. Most colleges are not household words beyond their immediate areas. Colleges with similar names are often confused by both the public and the media. For example, in the northeastern region of the country, Northwestern is often confused with Northeastern. Even if the college is known, its image may be outdated. We have all said at one time or another, "If only a national magazine would write a feature article about the institution or at least some part of it!" We continue to strive to get some mention somewhere about our college or university, and we know it is even better if the story is unsolicited. However, to put such fantasies in the proper perspective, the only section of the daily newspaper that continuously has news about colleges and universities is the sports section.

For those institutions that consistently make the front page of the sports section, there are some disadvantages. Few colleges want to become known as football factories; yet, as one college president stated, "I would rather be known as the president of a basketball school than not be known at all." Consequently, because of public interest and particularly the interest of newspaper editors, the quickest way to acquire public recognition is through the sports pages. Even the University of Chicago was recognized first for its feats on the gridiron led by the distinguished coach Amos Alonzo Stagg. In recognition that an athletic program does keep the institution's name before the public, the extent to which a college should invest in the intercollegiate athletic program is part of the marketing plan.

Since most colleges desire more public exposure, what are the alternatives in a promotional campaign, and what should be its objectives? The alternatives are paid advertising, public relations, institutional publications, and personal-contact programs. Variations in the format within any one category are restricted only by one's imagination. Paid advertising might include the use of radio, newspapers, magazines, or television. Public relations could include newsletters, public-service announcements, feature stories, special events, and special letters. Publications can range from a simple handout on one topic to a comprehensive catalogue of courses, student services, and fees. Personal-contact activities vary in degree of structure and range from activities for large and small groups to one-on-one contacts. Examples include on-campus information programs, interviews, telephone contacts, high school visits, and correspondence.

In developing a promotional campaign, focus should be first on the institution and second on subunits within the institution. There should be a single institutional strategy, which should be modified by time and events, with individual subunits developing separate promotional efforts to achieve rather specific goals. Examples might be recruiting more students, increasing gifts, and attracting better faculty members. The institution should have a message it wishes to communicate that is consistent across subunits as it is projected to various audiences. A common problem is that most institutions are unable to develop the message they wish to communicate, and as a result each subunit will tend to create an image, which may or may not be consistent with the primary purpose of the institution. Unless an institution's mission and the related message are defined, it is likely that individual subunits will generate messages that will be at cross-purposes. The alumni office will generate one message, the admission office another, and the public-relations office another.

There are a limited number of institutional messages. They can be defined along several continuums: the institution is either research- or teaching-oriented or perhaps both if a college is both relatively small and well supported financially; the college's admission practices may vary from selective to nonselective; it may be a two-year or a four-year college or a university; historically the character of the college may be denominational and private, nondenominational and private, or public; the college may be coed or single-sex, may be military or nonmilitary, and may offer an environment that is predominantly intellectual, academic, collegiate, or vocational (to use the typology of Clark and Trow, 1966). The problem is that every institution is a combination of several of the above descriptive traits, and the question is therefore what message should dominate to strike a position in the market. Individual subunits may communicate a multitude of messages through letters and institutional publications, and some may even take out paid advertising without seeking the approval of the central administration. The basic requirement is that whatever the message, it must stand the test of believability. In 1978, John Wayne was named "Advertising Personality of the Year" by the Advertising Club of Los Angeles for straight talk on behalf of a bank. His presentation was perceived to achieve three primary goals of all advertising: honesty, directness, and believability. Because there are few John Waynes to speak on behalf of individual colleges, the messages generally are easier to convey through the written, rather than the spoken, word. When one speaks to any person or group, selective hearing takes place. People tend to hear what they want to hear. The spoken word must therefore be clearly enunciated. Analogies and examples are often useful to clarify the spoken word and to maintain the interest of the listener.

To achieve a sense of institutional consistency in promotional efforts, one suggestion is to assign such a responsibility to a committee on institutional advancement. The committee's responsibilities would include testing internal and external perceptions of the institution, identifying program strengths and weaknesses, proposing changes, seeking outside consultation if necessary, and auditing current promotional efforts. The goal of the committee would be to increase awareness of the institution among different audiences. A successful promotional effort will stimulate interest in the institution among desired audiences and in the long run will encourage identification with the institution among preferred markets. As one tactic, all institutional publications and letterheads should have a logo or a style that easily identifies the institution. Over time, the design itself will remind people of the name of the college or university. Whether this result is national or regional will depend on the nature and size of the institution.

In the admission office, the promotional effort should begin with dissemination of general information about the institution. As prospects express an interest, specific information should be available in different formats. A personal contact should be made on a timely basis, but only after specific written information requests have been accommodated. Initially, information in the form of either a letter or a flyer should focus on opportunity as defined by available programs and activities and by careers of alumni. Comments by students and alumni will permit prospects to identify with the institution and will enhance their interest. As soon as a prospective student expresses an interest through inquiry or by replying to a general mailer, information should be made available that focuses on the student's interest. Replies by the institution should be in the form of a personal letter prepared by the academic department in which students are interested, and shortly thereafter a personal contact should be made by either alumni, current students, or faculty members. However, this is not a good use of faculty time unless the prospective student is visiting the campus.

It is not the intent of this section to suggest the best promotional methods, for there are better professional sources. However, experience and trial and error do permit me to provide some suggestions, if for no other reason than to be thought-provoking. Generally, a school with a strong market position does not need an "awareness" campaign. It does need to maintain its visibility, and this can best be achieved by a well-planned public-relations effort. Such an institution seldom has to align itself with other schools. In fact, it is probably to its advantage to differentiate its product by not associating itself with other institutions. The college with a modest or weak market position, however, may want to align itself with other institutions with stronger market positions by mentioning them in its literature. For example, a college that is a member of a consortium or an athletic conference may improve its market position by aligning itself with better-known institutions that are also members. For instance, the fact that Monmouth College in Illinois is a member of the same conference as Carleton and St. Olaf colleges in Minnesota strengthens Monmouth's market position, but that relationship has little or no effect on Carleton's or St. Olaf's market position.

In the Ivy League, the situation is somewhat different. Each institution in the Ivy League does have national name recognition. However, those that are currently at the bottom of the pecking order in the Ivy League are likely to achieve a stronger market position by not identifying as closely with Harvard, Yale, or Princeton. The objective of the other colleges in the Ivy League should be to achieve a separate identity without losing the prestige garnered by being a member of the Ivy League.

An institution with a weak or an unknown market position, if not affiliated with another college or group of institutions with a strong market position must seek to establish its credibility through other means. Perhaps such a school will have a few well-known alumni who will provide a source of identification for the college. If the alumni are better known than the institution, the college should be promoted through its alumni. Or, if the location is desirable, such as Colorado, Boston, or San Francisco, then to associate the college with the location is an effective marketing strategy. All these strategies are attempts to capitalize on name association, whether it is another institution, famous alumni, or a desired geographic location.

Assorted Thoughts on Promotion

A psychologist will often ask a client to lean back in the chair and to talk about anything that comes to his or her mind. At times a more restrictive technique is used: the client is given a word or a topic and asked to discuss it. What follows is a collection of free-associated thoughts focusing on promoting a college.

The Blitz. A brief, intense promotional effort is called a "blitz." It should be used only to focus on a limited objective. In concentrating on a restricted geographic area, a college might implement all of the following in sequence to meet a specific recruiting goal, such as adding ten more students to the entering class: radio announcements; newspaper ads; a letter of introduction to prospective students advising them that they will be contacted in the near future by an alumnus, an undergraduate student, or both; and a subsequent phone-o-thon using alumni and undergraduates. All these activities should occur in a span of about two weeks with a special event at the end. Prospects would be invited to attend the event when the phone contacts were made.

The blitz focuses on increasing awareness by maximizing available resources during a short period. To a great extent, it eliminates prospect initiative, but it does tend to increase recognition of the college. Prospects who attend the special event are likely to gain a greater sense of identification with the college. The blitz is not very cost-effective unless a continuous, but less concentrated, promotional plan is implemented in the defined market area. The objective of this latter plan is to keep the name of the college before the desired audience.

Distributed Practice and Intermittent Reinforcement. Psychologists tell us that material learned in several sessions spread out over time, rather than all at once, is likely to be remembered longer. To those of us interested in audience development, this principle suggests that messages need to be repeated with some frequency. Learning theorists also point out the greater efficacy of positive reinforcement on an unscheduled, rather than a scheduled, basis. This principle suggests that interest in a college is likely to be sustained at a higher level if contact with candidates is frequent but unscheduled, rather than frequent and scheduled. As an example, a series of contacts of different kinds when the candidate is not expecting them is likely to be more effective than sending the candidate a copy of the student newspaper every week. However, for an uninterested prospect, no strategy is likely to be effective.

Educational Aids. How to make young people aware of a particular college in the seventh or eighth grade or even earlier is a question that I have often asked myself. One suggestion is to develop educational aids for use in the classroom. These might include films on various subjects, experiments, or books that could be rented at a nominal fee by elementary schools. Faculty members who write textbooks or develop films for young children should be encouraged to use the name of the college in illustrations or examples. Although such aids are often developed by members of the faculty, their institutional affiliations are seldom mentioned other than as a postscript. Administrators should encourage such activities as long-range investments in marketing the institution and should, if necessary, pay faculty members a subsidy for using the name of the college in the text of the product.

Public-Service Announcements. Every radio and television station is required by the Federal Communications Commission to commit a certain amount of time each day to free announcements of general interest to the community. These announcements can come at any time of day and are sixty seconds long at most, but quality announcements will receive frequent play. Several years ago, Northwestern developed a record disk with four public-service announcements on opportunities in engineering; Northwestern's name was mentioned twice in each announcement. The result of this effort was that individual announcements were played over 3,000 times on more than 400 radio stations. About the same time, Carnegie Mellon University created a film for television on opportunities for women in engineering. I do not know how many times it was shown, but I remember seeing it just before the national evening news at least three times. Another example of ingenuity, but not a public-service announcement, is that several radio stations in Indiana that play the national anthem as they leave the air each evening acknowledge that *The Star-Spangled Banner* will be played by the marching band of St. Joseph's College.

Less dramatic than these examples but perhaps of greater consequence is to place on radio as public-service announcements the great variety of campus events open to the general public.

Public-service announcements are among the best of the promotional activities. They are inexpensive but keep the name of the institution in the public eye.

Listening and Seeing. The written word certainly is an effective way to communicate, particularly if the message is clearly stated, but the written word accompanied by a picture is even more persuasive. Posters and billboards tastefully designed and strategically located serve a number of purposes: they create awareness, the message is consistent, and they reinforce an idea through frequent exposure. The main objective of the poster or billboard message should be to stimulate inquiry.

A more sophisticated form of advertising, but one that requires customer initiative, is the use of records or cassettes. Some colleges have found these to be effective, but they should be complemented with a viewbook. Although colleges and universities have not yet mass-mailed audiovisual cassettes, the day is rapidly approaching. An increasing number of secondary schools are encouraging colleges to create such communication devices, and with the rapid improvement in audiovisual technology, playback equipment may in the near future be in as many homes as television sets are. An audiovisual cassette would be more than an adequate substitute for a college viewbook, and it would be less costly to produce. Presently, a college should consider developing a small number of cassettes to assist alumni, particularly if the institution recruits nationally. Such devices complement the regular mailings of the institution and tend to bring the college to life.

Packaging Information. Whether we are writing a letter, an announcement for a poster, or an advertisement for radio, the core message should create in the reader's mind an image of opportunity. This may be achieved by talking about people interacting with people or people performing a skill, but the message should be that through this progam offered by that college, I will improve my life. Higher education has not always delivered, but its track record is as good as, if not better than, that of any other industry. The message of all higher education is programs, people, and opportunity, and the significance of that message is not restricted to any one segment of a person's lifetime.

Effective Distribution. An attractive, well-written pamphlet is not effective if it is not delivered on a timely basis. The objective should be to get the right information to the right prospects at the right time. Timing is as critical as any other variable in the promotional effort, and different markets tend to have different time demands. Almost all admission staffs believe that getting information out early, at least by the beginning of the senior year in high school, is desirable, but for some colleges and their markets, the beginning of the senior year may be too late, and for others it may be too early. The fundamental question to be asked by the admission staff is "When do students who attend our institution begin to think about attending college?" Generally, the more sophisticated the market, the earlier students begin to plan for higher education. The timing question is related to the degree of readiness, and the markets of many small private and state colleges are not thinking about college until the middle of the senior year or late in that year. This is not to imply that no contact should be made until that time, for a market must be cultivated. The question is when a college should maximize its communication effort. This can be determined by evaluating the flow of applications in relation to time. One might assume that several days before students complete an application, they go through a mental sorting process. The right piece of information at that time is likely to encourage them to apply to a given college. If the information does not mesh with the students' sorting process, they may no longer be interested. Few institutions have studied the market response to sending information in relation to the admission calendar. An admission office should trace the flow of applications and seek to determine whether the timing of an institutional mailing is related to an increase in the flow of applications and whether application flow is related to the vacation periods of secondary schools. The answer should either suggest a change in the direct-mail plan or provide reassurance that the plan is working.

Developing Advertising Strategies

Developing an advertising strategy in student recruitment differs little from developing an advertising strategy for a tangible product or a political campaign. In politics the goal is to convince enough voters to win an election; in admission the goal is to convert a significant number of potential students into matriculants. The process of achieving the goal will include identifying a large number of potential candidates, creating a desirable image in their minds, and cultivating their interest through various forms of communication, which, one hopes, will result in their submitting applications. The strategy should have a threefold objective: it should be informational, educational, and persuasive. During this process the potential students will be making a series of judgments related to various alternatives. In the student's mind the college will be positioned in relation to not only other institutions and specific program offerings but other alternatives besides higher education.

The choice of tactics used should take into consideration those aspects of the market plan that appear to be the most appropriate in terms of timing, geographic distance from the institution, and the image of the college that a particular market is expected to have. For example, it is inappropriate, bad timing, and a poor use of resources to send a catalogue to a prospect before he or she has received an introductory informational piece. The various tactics that can be considered are direct mail, on-campus information programs, high school visits, college nights, off-campus information sessions, and collective activities, such as college fairs sponsored by the National Association of College Admission Counselors. Other tactics of a more personal nature are on- and off-campus interviews and various kinds of contacts by alumni, faculty members, undergraduates, and staff members with prospective students. Thus, different communication strategies for different markets are a part of the general marketing plan. The tactics used as a part of a general strategy should vary depending on what is known about a particular market and the market position of the institution.

A more substantive analysis of the principal marketing tactics should help define their functions. Each tactic is a part of the overall promotional process, and no single one should be considered primary in and of itself. The various tactics represent a series of efforts by the admission office that are parts of the overall marketing plan.

Direct Mail. Every college, to some degree, uses direct mail to contact prospects. The form and the number of contacts vary by institution, but direct mail has become the principal process for contacting substantial numbers of prospective students. Direct mail, as an avenue of communication, became attractive as soon as names of secondary school students were made available by the National Merit Scholarship Corporation in the 1960s. Individual recognition by the National Merit Scholarship Corporation implied academic distinction, and many colleges sought to attract these students. With the development of the Student Search Service of the College Entrance Examination Board in 1972, colleges and universities were offered the opportunity to contact prospective students as early as the spring of their sophomore year in high school. Now, it is not uncommon for a college to request annually from the Student Search Service as many as 60,000 names. The popularity of this process has been facilitated because of the acknowledged credibility of the College Entrance Examination Board, the fact that students select themselves into a national pool, and the ability of colleges to specify the academic and demographic parameters of the pool of students in which they are interested.

However, direct mail can be effective only if a first-contact piece is attractive and expresses a message that either explicitly or implicitly permits a substantial number of students to identify with the institution. If the markets contacted are properly segmented, a quality first mailing should generate a return of as high as 25 percent from the primary market. The return from secondary and tertiary markets is likely to vary from less than 1 percent to as high as 5 percent; returns will depend on the national market position of the institution. Hence, a rifle approach in the use of direct mail through market segmentation will increase the rate of return, in contrast to a shotgun approach. However, a shotgun approach is necessary for many colleges that have small primary markets. Such an approach may be necessary not only to elicit prospective students' interest but to increase the visibility of the college. To increase applications from nonprimary markets, the college must institute a series of mailings to cultivate individual interest. The mailings should vary in form, content, and frequency and should attempt to position the college and its programs in relation to better-known institutions.

The main disadvantage of the extensive use of direct mail is cost. As the price of mailings continues to increase because of the cost of postage and paper, one is inclined to look toward less expensive forms of communication. For example, certain kinds of media advertising may be cheaper. Such a decision should recognize that this form of communication depersonalizes the process and requires the prospect to initiate inquiry. Before a decision is made to reduce the number and frequency of direct-mail contacts, the various mailing rates should be considered in relation to the cost increases in other forms of contact. Third-class or bulk-rate mailing may be cost-effective and achieve the same purpose as first class. The move to a cheaper and a slower mailing process will require a college to establish more lead time in preparing its direct-mail pieces. Periodically purging the files of those prospects who have not responded to one or more mailings will also help reduce costs.

On-Campus Programs. Many colleges offer special on-campus programs for prospective students, few colleges include the parents, and even fewer try to evaluate the experiences of these prospective students by canvassing them for their opinions. Nonetheless, special campus programs, if properly organized, are the most effective way to recruit new students. When prospective students visit a college campus, they have certain expectations, including a hope that they will find students who are like themselves and faculty members who are interesting and interested in them. Consequently, the objective of such programs should be to place prospective students and their parents in contact with faculty members and undergraduates. The responsibility of the admission staff is to organize the program, but once such programs begin, its role becomes custodial except for answering questions about admission and financial aid. Members of the faculty, talking about their programs on their turf, are the college's best recruiters. Undergraduate students can reinforce the value of faculty contact by sharing their experiences, both good and bad. This adds credibility to the marketing effort.

Although on-campus programs may be the most desirable form of recruiting, they are restrictive, in the sense that prospects who have some interest in the institution are the most likely to visit the campus. Thus, on-campus programs provide not only a captive audience but one that already has some interest in the institution. Since most prospects attending campus events are somewhat interested, there is the risk that the biggest problem is a negative sell by a cynical member of the faculty or a disenchanted student. This should be expected and can be moderated by permitting prospects and their parents to have a variety of contacts and experiences when visiting the campus. A tour of the campus guided by an undergraduate, an interview with a member of the admission staff, and the opportunity to visit classes and to meet with faculty members will tend to mitigate any single poor experience. Remember, most students will visit more than one campus, and it is a total set of experiences that permits prospective students to discriminate among institutions. If members of the admission staff perceive their roles as building bridges and making friends rather than recruiting individual students, the college is more likely to achieve its enrollment objectives. Every visitor has the potential of becoming an ambassador of goodwill for the college. Consequently, the more people visit a campus, the more likely that a college will maintain high visibility.

High School Visits. Except for the experiences offered at a few secondary schools, there are only two reasons for a college representative to visit a high school: to exchange information between two professionals and to make new friends. High school visits, as differentiated from college nights, are probably the least effective method of direct communication between colleges and interested students. The exception would be preparatory schools whose students are predominantly residents and are restricted to the campus or to the immediate area. In recognition of these constraints, administrators at these schools make a considerable effort to permit students to spend substantial time with college representatives, including arranging for individual interviews at the school.

If a college elects to continue to visit high schools, it should recognize the cost of such visits, compared with other forms of communication. If the high school visit still appears to be the most desirable form of student recruitment, then the representative should not overwhelm the secondary school counselor with information. One should seek to find out what is of interest to the counselor that may be offered by the college. The objective should be to strike a common chord, for it is more likely that an impression will be remembered than any amount of information. Also remember that one of the benefits of the school visit is to exchange information. After the visit, one should ask what has been learned that may better direct the marketing activities of the college. Should the school be visited again, and how frequently?

Off-Campus Information Programs. The potential of off-campus programs increased measurably with the expansion of the opportunity to collect and maintain the names of potential students.

These new options permit institutions to contact students often to share information and to invite them to activities sponsored by the institution.

Off-campus programs should be held in the evening or on Sunday afternoons at either a public or a private facility. Whether they are held in large facilities or in the homes of alumni depends on the size of the college and its market position. The value of such programs is similar to that of on-campus programs: they provide a college with the opportunity to communicate with a captive audience in a convenient location.

An institution with a strong market position might follow a procedure whereby prospects and their parents are invited by mail to an information session. In this instance, a meeting room in a hotel or a private club is the most suitable. For a college with less visibility, alumni can be requested to contact students who have expressed some interest in the college and to personally invite them and their parents to attend a special program in a smaller setting.

Such programs permit the involvement of alumni and are cost-effective and efficient. Instead of spending one or two weeks in one large metropolitan area visiting twenty to forty secondary schools, the college representative can visit a different city each evening. Alumni admission workshops can be held before or after such meetings, and the alumni can be assigned the responsibility of contacting at a later date students who attended the information session.

Substitution of these programs for high school visits still permits counselor contact. Since these programs are in the evening, counselors can be invited to the program, and selected secondary schools can be visited during the day.

Collective Activities. A collective activity is defined here as any forum in which representatives of a number of colleges talk with prospective students and their parents. Typical examples are college nights sponsored by one or more secondary schools and, more recently, the college fair. The college fair is usually conducted at one central location in a large metropolitan area. College representatives rent space at the fair to talk with interested students as well as those who are shopping. The fair is promoted widely through secondary schools and often the media. This is a promotional activity that tends to provide higher education with a considerable amount of visibility for a short period. It adds to the visibility of those colleges present that have a rather limited market position, but it inhibits the ability of a college to differentiate itself from hundreds of others. Further, the arena-type atmosphere does not lend itself to good communication between colleges and prospective students. It is the least desirable recruitment tactic if the purpose is market positioning and differentiation.

However, a college night can be a productive experience because it is likely to attract a high percentage of parents as well as students. Its effectiveness depends on its organization. If the institution already has a relatively strong market position, then a separate room is most desirable. The interest of colleges with rather weak market positions is served if they are placed in an open area that is likely to have considerable traffic. A rather unknown college can thus acquire some visibility and some contact with a small number of students and parents. For such a school to be located in a separate room works to its disadvantage.

The advantages of the college night over college fairs or secondary school visits are that parents are more likely to be present and that there is a source of community identification among the parents, the students, and the high school. This is good public relations for the high school, and for some colleges the college night improves visibility.

8

*Developing Program and
Institutional Strategies*

The continuous dilemma for management is whether the college or university offers the appropriate market mix: does the current academic program structure make it feasible to package new programs that are more market-sensitive without investing substantial resources? As a result, individual institutions as well as boards of higher education continue to try to anticipate the needs of potential students and assess whether the present educational delivery systems are capable of meeting those needs. On campus, as well as off, educational delivery systems have been improved through changes in scheduling, variations in the academic calendar, and outreach programs, with courses offered in a variety of places, including the home via television. Moreover, institutional inquiry continues along the following lines: if we should offer a new program, how should the program be priced, and is our current physical location appropriate to maximize the demand potential of the courses we wish to offer? Some examples of questions being asked by particular types of institutions, along with possible answers, are as follows:

- Should a small college that has limited business course offerings create a business major to accommodate the career mentality, or is there another way to respond to such pressures by packaging current program offerings differently? One suggestion is to consider packaging programs along a corporate typology. For example, IBM is likely to prefer a different set of technical skills than Amtrak—if not in content, then in degree. However, in each instance, a major in a traditional liberal arts discipline may be more desirable than an undergraduate major in business. The question is how the major is to be packaged along with other academic or work-study experiences. Possibly, the only investment required would be to upgrade the promotional process and the job-placement office.

- How does an institution respond whose location is a hindrance but whose programs are in demand? What outreach efforts should be made? Many comprehensive state colleges find themselves in this situation. Their alternatives appear to be to offer extension courses, home-study courses, campus weekend programs, or a combination of these. Another alternative is to use the electronic media in various ways—closed-circuit television, two-way cablevision, an electronic blackboard with video capability, and so forth. If the demand exists for various programs, the physical location of a college can be overcome. If the consumer cannot easily get to the program, the program should be taken to the consumer. The options exist; all that is required is a little ingenuity.

- What about a small college that offers programs for which demand is low, suffers from a remote location, and has little name recognition? The chances for survival are bleak, and major surgery is required. Resources would have to be concentrated in as few as one or two areas along with an upgrading of the promotional process and the job-placement office. Other possible ingredients include a major change in the curriculum, such as block study or contract learning, along with field experiences and work-study options. In other words, the institution needs to be repackaged with a totally new look. If necessary, the programs should be taken to the consumer by offering courses in a more desirable location and by busing students to the campus on some weekends. Name recognition can be improved in the least expensive way through posters placed in strategic locations, but probably a formal advertising campaign would be required.

Managing Change

Large universities, four-year state colleges, and community colleges have historically offered enough program breadth to accommodate changes in demand. In contrast, many small liberal arts colleges that were founded for an explicit purpose are finding it difficult to respond to the increasing demand for career education.

In response to changes in market interests and the expected decrease in the number of students, there are basically three courses of action for the traditional liberal arts college. The first is not to change, in the hope that the market position of the institution will remain strong or that it will improve because of the college's uniqueness as other institutions change. This course implies a transitional period of market interest. Therefore, during this period demand is likely to decrease unless the college has a strong market position. The second alternative is to adopt a philosophy which maintains a core curriculum of the liberal arts but which repackages program options. This can be achieved by offering a variety of field opportunities to mix theory with practice. For example, science majors would have the opportunity to acquire actual laboratory experience in corporations or to spend time working in hospitals. For students in the social sciences, a variety of field-study examples already exist. Many college students spend their summers or a single term working for city governments or doing field research for a professor on the problems of a particular community. A third option is to develop new core programs that are specifically career-related. This may be the most difficult to achieve, because of the cost. For example, to establish a new program in accounting or commerce would require a substantial addition to the faculty. The question becomes what is feasible given institutional philosophy and ultimate costs, but no matter what the costs, for some colleges curriculum changes will be required and substantial risks will be necessary.

Regardless of the changes required, the basic philosophy should be one that adheres to developing a quality experience by insisting on rigor and evaluation and by keeping ever forward the difference between certification and education. Too many institutions have opted for certification in an effort to increase the number of students. This is a short-term philosophy and will not bear fruit in the future. Although most people have want-satisfying needs and are improvement-oriented, one can improve only in an interactive environment that encourages personal growth by insisting that all students achieve a given level of performance before they are granted a degree. Educators who are willing to give away credit for life's experiences will find that the market will soon diminish. Academic rigor and individual evaluation (not just providing grades) will provide an institution with credibility in tomorrow's marketplace.

Previous chapters have discussed meeting the needs of students through educational programming and improvement in student services, thus reducing attrition. Information was also presented on designing the pricing structure of a college so as to maximize revenue at the least cost to individual students. However, if an institution is offering a quality experience and has maximized its revenue potential with its traditional students, it still may find the need, during periods of rampant inflation, to generate additional revenues. Questions must be asked: how the institution can accommodate different markets, how it might better utilize its physical plant, what options exist to create extension programs, whether faculty productivity can be improved, and whether there are programs that the college could offer at the right place and at the right time to attract additional students.

For some institutions, it may be a prudent decision to offer evening and weekend courses. For others, the current academic calendar may not be demand-sensitive. Those on the quarter system may find it more appropriate to offer a full program during the summer months and a modified program during the winter quarter. Such a change may be particularly beneficial for institutions in the northern part of the country. For a college located in northern Minnesota, a calendar that begins in April and ends in December may expand demand in contrast to the present calendar. Under such a calendar, the winter term could be changed to offer students an off-campus work-study experience funded through the federal program. The fact is that very little thought has been given to the demand nature of the academic calendar. Too many institutions continue to operate on a traditional basis at a time when financial problems require nontraditional responses. One example of success is Mundelein College, located on the northeastern border of Chicago. Mundelein College, a women's college, almost closed its doors until an enterprising nun became president. The institution now thrives as a weekend college. Working women and women busy with small children during the week become full-time students on the weekend. They live on the campus on weekends and return to their homes and work during the week. Demand is high and the college is alive and flourishing. Mundelein's response was demand-sensitive. Other college administrators have similar opportunities. This repackaging of academic programs and the altering of class schedules in order to stimulate demand or to meet an existing market need is called "portfolio planning" by market theorists (Kotler, 1976, p. 59).

Case Studies and Strategies for Change

The following are actual case studies with slight modifications to dramatize problems and possible solutions. The profiles represent two Catholic colleges, one community college, and one Protestant college. These briefs are presented to demonstrate the commonality of the problems that many colleges are facing and the commonality of the methods required to solve marketing problems. Implicit in these studies are the significance of the necessity for change, the interrelationships between leadership and the willingness to take risks, the significance of basic personnel skills and the use of those skills, the internal organizational structure of the college and the degree to which it facilitates communication across boundaries of subunits, and the functional purposes of the institution and how those purposes are communicated to various markets. Alterations in any one of these areas will introduce change.

College of St. Hope. This is a four-year Catholic college of 435 students located in a residential area of an industrial city of 100,000 people. St. Hope had been a women's college and within the last ten years had become coeducational. Moreover, because of dispirited management, the institution had been placed on probation by the regional accrediting association. The college's mission was unclear, there was no curriculum plan, and the debt of the college was excessive in relation to its net worth. Morale among faculty and students was at a low ebb. The question was whether to remain open; if the college did so, a change in management would be required. Because of the present state of affairs, it was not a matter of the trustees' selecting someone from a large pool of candidates; rather, the question was whether someone with foresight and management skills would step forward who was prepared to take risks. Someone with such traits did come forward. He had been following the fate of the college through his wife, an alumna. Within four years the college had paid off its debt, had stabilized its enrollment, and had begun to develop an endowment. The regional accrediting association removed the college from probation with plaudits.

Today, the college's financial position is relatively sound because of this president's foresight, his ability to establish reasonable goals, his willingness to hold staff and faculty accountable, and his personal recognition that he did not have all the answers. More specifically, he did the following: he sought out local opinion leaders to take an interest in the college, he brought about curriculum reform by forcing the faculty to share the economic burden, and he sought creative ways to develop name recognition for the college. As a result, the composition of the board of trustees was changed to provide access to new financial sources and to the media. Departments were eliminated and divisions created. For small colleges it is hard to justify, financially or educationally, the maintenance of departments. An interdisciplinary approach was taken, and academic programs were developed that were demand-sensitive.

Because the college had recently become coeducational, it suffered from the past image of being a Catholic women's college. To transcend this history and to develop name recognition, men's baseball and basketball teams were created, and adequate funding was provided for athletic grants. The president attended admission and financial aid workshops to develop an understanding of the market and of pricing, for he well understood that these two areas are the lifeline of a college. He wanted to know whether the college was attracting its fair share of students and government financial aid dollars. As a result, new admission and financial aid plans were developed. Members of the staff were required to become involved in their professional associations, if for no other reason than to assist the college in its quest for name recognition.

The following was found after a consultant was brought in: Publications were outdated, unattractive, and untimely. Although the recruitment cycle was half over, the first-contact brochure was not yet printed. The contact pool was small, and there was no systematic strategy to maintain or to follow up contacts. The contact pool had not been matched to the profile of students currently attending the college, nor had it been segmented into target markets. The contact pool had been created mostly through high school visits, the Educational Opportunity Service of ACT, and score reports from ACT and CEEB. The admission staff had elected not to contract with the Student Search Service because few of the prospective students in its current markets took either the Preliminary Scholastic Aptitude Test or the SAT. Consequently, the admission staff had no way of contacting a large number of potential students who might or might not have heard about the college. The initiative had been left in the hands of the prospective student. Moreover, the admission staff had been required to visit an inordinate number of secondary schools, thus limiting the amount of time that could be devoted to servicing inquiries on a personal basis. However, the personnel in the admission office had developed the basic skills required to be an effective admission staff. The problem was a limited contact market and an inappropriate use of time.

The primary student market was within twenty miles of the college. The greatest percentage of the students would be identified as "locals," even though many of them did live on campus. Beyond the immediate local market area, the college was not at all known except in traditional Catholic communities. Even among this constituency, it was still perceived to be a women's college. Subsequently, the decision was made to try to expand the market in those areas which were immediately adjacent to the current primary market and which were also predominantly Catholic. The college had considerable interest in expanding the religious backgrounds of its students, but the immediate problem was to cultivate the market with the greatest potential. It was too late in the year to create a new plan or to use the most appropriate Student Search. The alternative was to identify the most accurate list of names of high school seniors that could be provided by another agency. After evaluating the capability of a number of such agencies, the American Student List Company was selected. However, the chief problem in renting the names of students from such companies is that the lists are void of academic interests or parameters. Lists are provided by ZIP-code area and often by religious background.

The infusion of about 12,000 names into the prospect pool in the middle of the recruitment cycle required the reassignment of staff members. Moreover, it was a catalyst to change the recruitment approach. As the process of initiating contact with 12,000 prospective students evolved, it became clear to the staff that the basic market plan and the contingency plan had to be developed 18 months in advance of the desired date of enrollment. The prospect pool had to be identified early and segmented by interest area and potential yield. It became apparent that a quality first-contact piece had to be developed as well as various follow-up pieces. The types of inquiries were to be anticipated and appropriate responses developed. The objective was to move from a general piece that described the college to specific responses related to expressed interests, and then to personal contact by undergraduates, faculty members, and alumni. Alumni had been identified in two target market areas to assist in student recruitment.

To accommodate the demands of an expanded prospect pool and of an earlier schedule for market contact, the admission staff was required to reassess its schedule of high school visits. Subsequently, it was decided that only feeder high schools and high schools in the immediate area serving a constituency with an economic and religious profile similar to that of the students attending the college would be visited. This decision decreased the number of visits from nearly 600 to 200. Many schools eliminated from the visitation schedule had never produced a student for the college but were visited once or even twice a year. Staff morale immediately improved, for the staff's efforts could now be devoted to creative work with secondary schools where the college was known and with prospective students interested in attending the college. In addition, the initiative was now in the hands of the college to contact students whose names were readily available from several national sources.

The administration in the College of St. Hope was able to engineer all these changes because the faculty knew there was no alternative. This was the only hope that the College of St. Hope had. The president has acquired the confidence of the faculty, for he has provided a new breath of opportunity. He successfully marketed and managed the concept of change. In retrospect, it is unfortunate that the college almost had to close its doors before it was prepared to change.

Identity College. Identity College is located in a residential section of a major metropolitan area. It is a four-year college for women, of whom the vast majority are commuters. The president is a nun, as are a significant number of the faculty members. Historically, the college has educated the daughters of blue-collar Catholic families, but for several years it had observed a substantial decline in its enrollment. The facilities of the college are attractive, but space for resident students is limited.

Several features of Identity College, individually and collectively, created market problems. The president is very competent intellectually and is somewhat impatient with those less competent. With the president acting as the catalyst, the college changed its evaluation system from one of grades to one of written evaluations. The written evaluations were to be based on a defined level of competency. In addition, the college had made an effort to attract the older woman student by publicly supporting the feminist movement. Administratively, there were two admission offices—one identified as such and the other identified as the office of enrollment planning. Little or no attention had been given to how students were to finance their education.

The faculty members, although supportive of changing the evaluation system, did not feel they had contributed meaningfully to the decision. As a result, they were not very responsive with regard to submitting written evaluations rather than grades. Many students argued that one of the reasons they had elected to attend Identity College was that they intended to transfer to a different college, farther from home, after two years. They argued persuasively that a written evaluation would not be the same as a grade on the transcript. They contended that many other prospective students looked at Identity College also as an institution from which to transfer.

The faculty, although sympathetic with the president's public support of the feminist movement, was not prepared to offer courses in the evening or on weekends, and there were no daycare facilities. The rhetoric of the college communicated one message and the actions of the college another. The combination of changing the evaluation system and publicly supporting the feminist movement was not received well by the parents of the traditional student market. What appeared to be happening was that the traditional market had become alienated by the public actions of the college. Moreover, the faculty was confused about the purpose of the office of enrollment planning in relation to that of the office of admission. The staffs in both offices appeared to be frustrated over what they perceived to be similar responsibilities. As a result, neither office had done much planning, and neither office knew much about the potential of the college's desired markets.

Because the college did have a traditional market and because its financial position was reasonably strong, one had to question why the college created its own problems. There was no need for a total competency-based evaluation system. If students had the option of either a grade or a written evaluation, the marketplace would be unaffected. The college could have responded to the needs of older students simply by changing its scheduling of courses and promoting opportunities for the older woman student. This could have been achieved by offering courses in the evenings and on weekends and by offering daycare facilities. It did not appear necessary for the president to make public pronouncements in support of the feminist movement. In this instance, the president failed to separate her own philosophical position from what was in the best interest of the institution. A compromise clearly was available without public pronouncements.

Now that the faculty and the market were confused about the basic mission of Identity College, what options did the institution have?

First, because of the location of the college and because of its excellent reputation, the older-student market could be attracted to the college if course programs and services were available at convenient times. This was a matter to be resolved between the administration and the faculty, and as financial exigencies became paramount, an accommodating resolution was to be reached.

Second, the office of admission and the office of enrollment planning needed to be combined to maximize the use of resources, including individual skills. Since neither of these offices had developed a marketing plan, doing so was in order. As a beginning, the size of the potential commuter population had to be determined. This was to be achieved by studying the demographics of the current student body and by using the consulting services of the College Entrance Examination Board. Through the Student Search Service, CEEB would be able to advise the college of its market potential based on specific parameters.

Third, to expand the traditional market, the limited amount of housing space would be reserved for students who lived beyond a reasonable commuting distance. These markets had not been tapped in the past and, therefore, represented a considerable amount of potential. Alumnae in these markets would begin to contact secondary schools and their parishes to promote the interests of the college.

Fourth, to assess the potential of the older-woman-student market, the following processes were recommended: A questionnaire was to be sent to alumnae of the college to determine their interest in enrolling in minicourses or advanced degree programs. Chapters of the League of Women Voters were to be contacted to express the interest of the college in offering courses of a prescribed nature for older women. The cooperation of parish priests was to be solicited. At some future date, when more goodwill had been created, the college would run ads in local newspapers, in parish bulletins, and over the radio to explain its new programs for the older student.

Fifth, because the administration had failed to stay abreast of financial aid activities, it was not fully benefiting from federal support. For all practical purposes, there was no financial aid staff, and the college had not taken into consideration the interaction effects of price and market potential. Therefore, when the federal financial aid application was completed, the college expressed limited interest in work-study funds and National Direct Student Loan monies. An analysis of the college's price position in relation to its traditional market indicated that, if the college would maximize its opportunities for federal support, it could increase tuition without increasing the net price to 90 percent of its students. In all likelihood, students would end up paying less regardless of any reasonable increase in price.

There is no end to this scenario, for Identity College is still struggling to initiate and to accommodate change constructively and efficiently. Its enrollment and financial aid problems have improved, but its faculty remains uncertain about the purpose of the college. Consequently, the potential quality of the experience has not been fulfilled.

Electorate College. Electorate College is a two-year community college serving a densely populated area of about 150 square miles. The college was built in the mid 1960s and had observed, until recently, substantial increases in enrollment each year. In 1976, the college observed an increase in "head count" enrollment and a decrease in full-time enrollments. In 1977 and 1978, there were net decreases in both head count and full-time enrollments. From its beginning to the present, Electorate College had observed a change in interest among students from transfer programs to terminal programs. More recently, student interests had changed to career development and non-degree programs. The population that the college was created to serve was a cross-section of income, racial, and ethnic groups. In 1978, the median income for the district was about $25,000.

An analysis of the college's problems produced a number of findings. First, during the past five years the college had moved from providing courses in a number of locations to a single campus location. Courses that had been taught in a number of secondary schools at different points in the district, as well as in other modified facilities, were now being offered at a single location. Although the new campus was most attractive, it was not located conveniently for a high percentage of the district's population. The outreach programs that had existed previously had been eliminated without considerable thought. This, more than any other factor, appeared to be the reason for the decrease in enrollment.

Second, the average age of the student population—as in most community colleges—was in the late twenties. In order to expand its market, the college was going to have to attract either an increasing number of students over age forty or an increasing percentage of the decreasing eighteen- to twenty-four-year-old market. The former was the more attractive choice, but there was no marketing effort to communicate the types of services that were available to people who may have been out of classrooms for more than twenty-five years.

Although the evidence suggests that people indeed want to continue to learn throughout their lives, they also want to feel secure about the learning process. Not only do they want to know there are specific counseling and compensatory services available to them, but they also want to know there are other people like themselves attending the college. Although much has been written about the fact that the community college population is an older population, a fifty-year-old widow does not believe that the writers are talking about people like herself.

Third, faculty members perceived their teaching responsibilities as a job that they performed at specific hours, a certain number of days per week. Even within their own departments, they did not identify with their colleagues, nor were there opportunities to do so. Although offices were available to them, they prepared for their courses at home and were seldom available to either colleagues or students. In addition, most of the faculty members, although paid quite well, had other jobs. The fragmentation that existed among the faculty reinforced the fragmentation that existed among a part-time student body. The development of a single campus location unattended by faculty members, with high attrition among the student body, created an environment that inhibited communication among students and among members of the faculty. The result was limited or no interaction between faculty and students except within the classroom. The student services staff was expected to provide the academic counseling normally provided by the faculties at most four-year institutions.

Fourth, the promotional activities of the college were of a general nature, and the use of academic jargon in all materials was rather blatant. No communication focused on specific target markets or provided detailed information about selected programs. Rather, before the beginning of each term, the district was blanketed with a mailing that presented course listings for the next term and enrollment procedures. The pamphlet was hard to read and was unattractive. It reminded the reader of the typical advertisements tossed on doorsteps by supermarkets.

Each of these problems is resolvable, and the college is taking steps to redevelop its outreach programs by again offering courses in various locations throughout the district. The administration has undertaken some studies to determine needs of the over-forty market. Through negotiations the faculty has been asked to spend an increasing amount of time on campus and to assume responsibility for academic counseling. A professional consultant has been employed to assist the college with its promotional process. The resolution of these problems should reverse the enrollment trends observed by this community college.

Since these problems are not unique to Electorate College, other community colleges should learn from this institution's experiences. If a community college is to realize its potential by meeting the needs of its constituency, it must have an outreach program, and the faculty must provide a sense of identity for the college. Without an outreach program and with a highly fragmented faculty, a community college cannot fulfill its purpose.

Opportunity College. Opportunity College, a coeducational Protestant college with about 900 students, is located in a small community fifty miles from the suburbs of a large urban area. Its facilities are more than adequate, and its environs are attractive. The college participates in an athletic conference for both men and women. The primary problem was an erosion in enrollment; the optimal size was 1,200 students.

In addition to the buildings on the main campus, the college owns a rather large building in the center of the urban area proper sixty miles away as well as a facility located at a weekend resort area fifty miles from the college but in the other direction. The facility in the urban area is unoccupied, and the facility in the resort area is used sparingly for educational purposes during summer.

A series of interviews revealed that the students, faculty, and administration were extremely loyal to the institution. Students who were interviewed came from lower-middle-class, religious backgrounds, and most of the students enrolled at Opportunity College were the first in their families to attend an institution of higher education. The vast majority were receiving financial aid. The college offered need- and non-need-based grant assistance. Students in the top quarter of their high school classes who had a composite score of 1100 on the SAT or 26 on the ACT were automatically offered $1,000 scholarships. Those who wanted financial assistance beyond the $1,000 were expected to have their families complete a financial aid form.

The president and the director of admission viewed the office of admission as responsible for recruiting students, and faculty members and currently enrolled students had little or no involvement in admission activities. Alumni were involved to the extent that they were sent a letter annually requesting that they refer prospective students to the admission office. The admission office did have a written recruitment plan, which was very traditional and lacked imagination. The college had made no effort to become more marketing-oriented, nor did the admission office understand that its role was to orchestrate the communication process between prospective students and alumni, faculty members, and undergraduate students.

The main components of the recruitment plan were visits to high schools (the same ones that had been visited for years), contacting National Merit commended and semifinalist scholars, a community college transfer program, and a proposal to attract more foreign students. The college's markets were not segmented. There was no viewbook, and the catalogue was sectioned in such a way that prospective students would receive only that portion of the catalogue in which they expressed an interest. No first-contact piece was available other than a letter, and prospects who were contacted had to write a letter in order to request additional information.

Opportunity College had a marketing "process" problem. The recruitment plan was too restrictive to permit the institution to achieve its enrollment objective. Currently enrolled students were reasonably satisfied with their experiences, and the college was well regarded in its primary market area. The consultant believed that this was not a college with a limited future. To the contrary, it was thought that, if the college expanded and segmented its prospect pool and involved faculty members, alumni, and undergraduates in admission-program activities, its future would be secure. With some modest changes in institutional programming and the adoption of a marketing approach to attracting students, the college should easily increase its enrollment from 900 to 1,200 students, the desired objective. In addition to suggesting the development of a marketing rather than a recruitment plan, a number of specific recommendations were made, including the following:

1. With the development of the Student Search Service, it should no longer be necessary to request names from the National Merit Scholarship Corporation. These same names are readily available six months earlier through the Spring Search of the Student Search Service. This search allows the institution to contact prospective students before the summer of their senior year to stimulate college visits during vacation.

2. A quality first-contact piece with a postage-paid self-mailer should be developed. A viewbook is needed independent of the catalogue. Interested candidates should receive the entire catalogue, not just sections. Parents and students are interested in cross-departmental offerings and want to develop a rather comprehensive picture of an entire college. Information pieces should be developed that encourage a student to compare an institution with other colleges, with specific criteria in mind.

3. The expanded transfer recruiting plan proposed by the admission staff to attract and enroll more community college students was viewed as rather optimistic, because not enough community college students are interested in a baccalaureate degree. In the long run, the only effective way to recruit these students is through faculty-to-faculty contact.

4. It was suggested that a foreign student recruitment program be abandoned, mainly because it is a high-cost budget item, since most of these students required scholarships. If full-paying foreign students can be attracted with a marginal effort, that is all to the good, but the college must recognize that additional support services will be required.

5. It is impossible to properly monitor a large contact pool without being able to generate mailing labels when needed and to update the file with regard to the kind of information each candidate has received. A system should be developed that will permit using a card deck or a tape to support the prospect data file. If such a system is not implemented, costs can be excessive, and a single-mailing-label system does not permit an effective direct-mail campaign. The software options available through the Student Search Service should be carefully evaluated to determine which of them best meet the needs of Opportunity College.

6. The college should eliminate the awarding of scholarships unrelated to financial need. The more a college discounts its price without regard to financial need, the more it is penalized by the federal government with regard to the funding of campus-based programs. Because of the nature of the student that Opportunity College attracts, it is highly likely that most of the students who are currently receiving $1,000 scholarships would qualify for at least that much grant assistance based on financial need.

Two recommendations were also made on academic strategies:

1. Because the college is relatively small, there is no need for many of the departments that currently have only one or two faculty members. The college should be reorganized along divisional lines. This would provide for more flexibility, and it is more cost-effective.

2. Continuing education programs should be offered at the facility in the urban area. They would increase the college's income as well as its visibility. In addition, special program activity is recommended to increase the utilization of the resort facility.

Opportunity College quickly responded to the recommendations. Enrollment has surpassed the 1,200-student objective. This college really did not have many problems. It suffered from a lack of imagination, but it did have skilled administrators in the traditional sense. All that was needed was the willingness to listen and to try new ideas with limited risks.

Next Steps for Admission Directors

As all of higher education leaves the period of nirvana and enters what appears to be a long enrollment recession, individual institutions will be affected differently. Colleges and universities that currently have strong market positions may be able to continue to exist as they are, but that, in and of itself, may be too bad. Others will wither and still others will die because of forces beyond their control and a history of poor management. Yet, many institutions will prosper, though possibly not initially; after internal realignment and some retrenchment, they will be better prepared to provide new educational services to new markets as new needs are identified.

What can institutions do that are experiencing or expecting shortfalls in enrollment? First, program demand must be determined, as must be whether there is additional elasticity in the institution's primary markets. Second, if it appears that elasticity does exist, it must be asked what additional promotional efforts should be initiated. Third, it should be asked what additional markets could be tapped, based on current program offerings or a modification of those offerings. Fourth, if it is necessary to adopt a posture of institutional realignment, of the available alternatives, what recommendations are in the best interest of the institution rather than of individual schools or departments within the institution?

The application of marketing principles to higher education has been brought about by a combination of forces. Existing or expected decreases in enrollment, decreases in real faculty income because of inflation, erosion in investment income, tax-conscious legislatures, and the increasing cost of fuel have placed the nation's system of higher education under severe stress. With stress comes the search for new responses, changing whatever variables appear to be the easiest for the institution to control. In this instance, one of the first responses is an attempt to stabilize enrollments without any redefinition of academic programming. The result has been that time-honored but outdated methods of student recruitment are being discarded for more aggressive and sophisticated promotional efforts.

Presidents who heretofore expressed little interest in student recruitment are now asking directors of admission what is needed to sustain enrollments, and many are attending seminars on marketing. This new environment creates an excellent opportunity for directors of admission to solicit the support of their presidents in developing a more marketing-oriented environment and to assume the role of director of marketing.

Marketing by definition requires a re-examination of the product offered as well as the market served. Until now, however, most administrators and faculty members have been far more willing to examine institutional promotional practices in an effort to increase demand than to assess how their markets are being served by the product offered. As it is learned that successful promotion efforts without substantive changes in the environment are usually haunted by high attrition rates, directors of admission are in the unique position of being able to educate their faculty and in many cases their president. Under such circumstances, they can act as a catalyst for institutional responsiveness and change. For admission officers, acting as such a catalyst is a rare opportunity to influence the quality of educational programs and services offered by involving the faculty, undergraduate students, and alumni in an institutional marketing effort.

To be effective directors of marketing, directors of admission will have to develop a comprehensive understanding of the demographics of the current student body and the institution's traditional markets, the nature and the strength of the competition, the factors that affect college choice, and how to organize a marketing team. They must perceive their staff to be inclusive of faculty members, students, alumni, and colleagues. They will understand that one of their responsibilities is to involve, inform, and to hold accountable willing volunteers in an extensive communication process between prospective students and members of the institution. They will perceive their role as managing people involved in an extensive information-exchange process.

To achieve this objective will require extensive research and planning, but from such efforts will evolve a methodology for identifying, segmenting, and penetrating primary, secondary, and tertiary markets. An effective plan will permit the development of forecasting models by market area so that it will be feasible to estimate the size of the entering class ten months before the date of enrollment.

In proceeding to achieve this management objective, admission directors should keep the following in mind:

- The market position of the college and its programs as related to its history, mission, affluence, and uniqueness compared with other institutions competing in the same market.
- The number of potential students by market area based on program offerings.
- The probable participation rates of these potential students, given prior trends and current alternatives to higher education.
- The application history of the institution and the degree of demand elasticity in its current markets.
- The number of admitted applicants and the operational efforts in relation to the admitted/applicant/enrollment yields.
- The number of students entering who are graduating and retention efforts.

An analysis of each of these concepts should permit institutional leaders to arrive at conclusions suggested in preceding chapters. Each of these concepts raises a series of questions for further investigation.

- Is the market position of the institution and of the various programs offered, as perceived by different audiences, accurate or outdated? Does the institution suffer from a lack of name recognition?
- Will location or program changes or both increase the interest of new markets?
- Will additional promotional efforts by a consortium of institutions within a given market area increase the participation rates in higher education?
- Has the application history of the institution been consistent with that of similar and competing colleges and universities? In relation to participation rates in the primary markets, has the college been attracting its fair share? Will new programs result in more applications?
- Does the college have a sufficient understanding of why students attend the institution? Has there been an effort to increase the admitted/applicant yield? Should the recruitment effort at this stage of the admission cycle—that is, after acceptance—be rethought? Are more of the same kinds of promotional efforts likely to be effective?
- Is the enrollment problem essentially a retention problem? Are the support services need-satisfying? Is the institutional community out of touch with student needs or changes in program demand once a student has enrolled?

As one thinks through these questions, participation rates (demand) are likely to receive increasing attention. Those colleges and universities that develop an understanding of how prospective students arrive at the decision to enroll in higher education and to select a given institution will not only be less susceptible to the vagaries of demand; they will be in the unique position of being able to apply sophisticated marketing principles, as presented in earlier chapters, because they will understand consumer behavior within their primary and secondary markets.

They will also be able to apply another component of marketing theory that has been overlooked by most colleges and universities: price and its relation to demand and optimizing revenues. The effect of tuition, or price, on demand for undergraduate education has been all but eliminated, with the exception of independent institutions with modest market positions, by the massive price-discounting policies of federal and state governments as well as those of institutions. Yet, most institutions remain underpriced because tuition has been determined through a residual budget process (tuition is set to equal the amount of revenue required to balance the budget) or because of political forces. The result is loss of revenue that could have been used to improve the educational experience. As colleges and universities become more experienced in applying marketing principles, prices will be monitored to maximize revenues as well as enrollments.

As we assess the present in our search for a future course of action, we already have observed the degree to which prospective students are responsive to market forces as they elect a course of study. Moreover, increasingly, students and their families are concerned with the rate of return in relation to the investment. Students are demanding more rigor in their courses and more evaluation of their course work. The true test of the market position of a given college may be the opportunities available to its graduates. Institutions that make a conscious effort to place their graduates successfully either in the best of the postbaccalaureate programs or in desired professional positions may find themselves fairly immune to the trends in what appears to be a zero-growth industry. To alter the present course and for higher education to expand in the next twenty years, the self-interest of the industry and its ability to meet the needs of the individual and of the society must be in greater harmony than when growth was an obvious outcome of the high birthrate of the 1940s and 1950s. The industry must move from responding to demand to creating demand.

For the managers of the industry, much of the problem may be in the way we think of ourselves. To continue to think of our responsibilities as working with people under age thirty before they begin their life's work may be a cause of the problem. Increasingly, people will have more time to pursue individual interests, and as there appear to be no limits to new knowledge, the demand for education is restricted only by our own imaginations.

Appendix A

Interpreted Information: Illinois State Scholarship Commission and Office of Education Reports

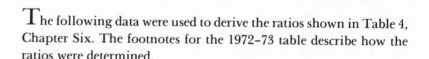

The following data were used to derive the ratios shown in Table 4, Chapter Six. The footnotes for the 1972–73 table describe how the ratios were determined.

1972–73

Institution	Tuition and Fees[a]	Enrollment[b]	Tuition Revenue[c]	ISSC[d]	BEOG[e]	SEOG[f]	Total Grant Assistance[g]	Ratio to Tuition Revenue[h]
Private								
Augustana	$2,043	2,065	$4,218,795	$1,187,634		$86,000	$1,273,634	.302
Lake Forest	2,810	1,043	2,930,830	118,771		70,320	189,091	.065
Loyola	1,850	6,732	12,454,200	3,260,424		295,074	3,555,498	.285
Milliken	2,200	1,349	2,967,800	712,957		67,600	780,557	.263
Northwestern	3,000	6,450	19,350,000	1,432,808		168,265	1,601,073	.083
Public Four-Year								
Southern Illinois (Carbondale)	589	17,298	10,188,522	2,286,294		294,442	2,580,736	.253
University of Illinois (Urbana)	686	24,147	16,564,842	3,217,601		864,076	4,081,677	.246
University of Illinois (Circle)	636	17,351	11,035,236	2,703,485		451,963	3,155,448	.286
Western Illinois	558	12,916	7,207,128	1,366,569		96,951	1,463,520	.203
Public Two-Year								
Belleville	184	3,053	561,752	56,741			56,741	.101
Blackhawk	400	3,080	1,232,000	207,941		46,644	254,585	.207
Chicago Community Colleges	40	25,275	1,011,000	21,363		1,143,394	1,164,757	1.152
Joliet	354	2,849	1,008,546	76,009		11,699	87,772	.087
Triton	308	4,988	1,536,304	91,073		17,984	109,057	.071

a,b,dIllinois State Scholarship Commission Report of 1978.
cObtained by multiplying (a) x (b).
eBasic Grant Program Institutional Agreement and Authorization Report, November 9, 1978.
fNotification to Congress Report from Department of Health, Education and Welfare, May, 1977.
gObtained by adding (d) + (e) + (f).
hObtained by dividing (g) by (c).

1974–75

Institution	Tuition and Fees	Enrollment	Tuition Revenue	ISSC	BEOG	SEOG	Total Grant Assistance	Ratio to Tuition Revenue
Private								
Augustana	$2,238	2,034	$4,552,092	$1,165,400	$64,520	$71,801	$1,301,721	.286
Lake Forest	3,230	994	3,210,620	201,700	48,174	129,387	379,261	.118
Loyola	2,110	6,198	13,077,780	3,326,200		287,818	3,614,018	.276
Milliken	2,598	1,452	3,772,296	854,500	43,135	33,906	931,541	.247
Northwestern	3,480	7,680	26,726,400	1,727,700	187,458	148,554	2,063,712	.077
Public Four-Year								
Southern Illinois (Carbondale)	440	14,855	6,536,200	2,089,300	587,114	164,578	2,840,992	.435
University of Illinois (Urbana)	690	25,316	17,468,040	3,013,700	434,514	272,412	3,720,626	.213
University of Illinois (Circle)	636	16,178	10,289,208	2,698,500	947,702	601,490	4,247,692	.413
Western Illinois	561	13,068	7,331,148	1,384,100	310,482	129,808	1,824,390	.249
Public Two-Year								
Belleville	286	3,584	1,025,024	111,500	101,553		213,053	.208
Blackhawk	432	3,223	1,392,336	173,600	97,380	47,475	318,455	.229
Chicago Community Colleges	140	22,579	3,161,060	576,200	2,068,985	1,339,370	3,984,555	1.261
Joliet	355	2,974	1,055,770	93,800	78,672	4,999	177,471	.168
Triton	372	7,369	2,741,268	168,200	116,012	42,781	326,993	.119

Note: See footnotes to 1972–73 table.

Institution	Tuition and Fees	Enrollment	Tuition Revenue	ISSC	BEOG	SEOG	Total Grant Assistance	Ratio to Tuition Revenue
Private								
Augustana	$2,691	2,119	$5,702,229	$1,318,500	$218,286	$66,232	$1,603,018	.281
Lake Forest	4,035	1,085	4,377,975	362,400	135,682	265,057	763,139	.174
Loyola	2,570	6,689	17,190,730	4,074,200	1,014,412	293,919	5,382,531	.313
Milliken	3,198	1,494	4,777,812	1,003,700	187,544	80,890	1,272,134	.266
Northwestern	4,620	7,545	34,857,900	1,773,800	652,182	747,676	3,173,658	.091
Public Four-Year								
Southern Illinois (Carbondale)	736	17,100	12,585,600	2,996,800	3,475,282	46,352	6,518,434	.518
University of Illinois (Urbana)	814	25,902	21,084,228	3,260,100	2,029,948	287,619	5,577,667	.265
University of Illinois (Circle)	789	16,239	10,445,571	3,541,900	3,751,108	554,103	7,847,111	.751
Western Illinois	677	12,012	8,132,124	1,329,800	1,144,921	60,747	2,535,468	.312
Public Two-Year								
Belleville	382	3,476	1,327,832	189,500	478,705		668,205	.503
Blackhawk	544	2,866	1,559,104	171,200	239,901	21,907	433,008	.278
Chicago Community Colleges	363	26,880	9,757,440	3,110,300	11,516,978	1,314,727	15,943,405	1.634
Joliet	448	3,542	1,586,816	137,600	233,143	5,088	357,831	.237
Triton	436	7,384	3,219,424	272,500	470,700	67,856	811,056	.252

Note: See footnotes to 1972–73 table.

Appendix B

Northwestern University Alumni Admission Council Handbook

The Alumni Admission Council Handbook is the reference used by the Northwestern Alumni Admission Council. This handbook defines the admission policies and the alumni's responsibilities and answers the questions most frequently asked by candidates and their parents. The handbook is updated annually and serves the needs of over 400 alumni. Supplementary materials are sent to the alumni every month. As an alternative, a community college might develop such a handbook to serve the needs of secondary school personnel, district leaders, and independent educational brokerage agencies.

Introduction

A Sense of the Future

Over the years you have received information from us that talks about what we are doing and the way the future looks. All of you know that the absolute number of students who will graduate from high school in the 1980s is substantially less than the numbers in the recent past. Many of you also recognize, either through the material you have received or as a participant in the workshops conducted in your area, that part of the Admission Office goal is not only to deal with the immediate concerns each year presents but to include, in our planning, activity that will solidify Northwestern's position for the future. If we succeed in this undertaking—and we have every intention of doing so—Northwestern will be less negatively affected by the declining student population than many other institutions will. This section of your handbook will attempt to focus on our view that the recruitment undertaking is a collaboration. In that way, I hope the role you play will become very clear.

Recruitment-Approach Premises

From time to time you have received samples of the research we do in the Admission Office. You know that we undertake evaluations of the admissions process each year not only with an eye to understanding how well we may have done what we attempted but to continually monitor student attitudes and their values. We are anxious to know how students make decisions. Further, we also recognize that students' decision-making habits and patterns may change from time to time. The nature of the times affects the way students think. This speaks not only to the point of the way prospective students select fields of interest but also to the sources they turn to for advice and counsel regarding college selection. The more we are sensitive to what students tell us, the better able we are to help them make good choices with regard to programs offered by Northwestern.

Over the years we have come to recognize that we play a facilitator's role in our relationship with prospective students. In my opinion this is as it should be. I would have grave suspicions of any student who indicated that he or she chose Northwestern on the basis of persuasiveness on our part. Students tell us that they do evaluate the quality of programs. They also want to know who teaches the courses and how well qualified those people are. Our freshmen also report that the diversity of our student population was extremely important to them. All of these characteristics of the university could be presented in a "spoken" form; however, we have chosen to address them not only in our public comments and in the university publications, but more important, we have made great strides in making the university community accessible to visitors. By that I mean we not only have the casual visitor or the person who comes to see us for an interview, but we have numerous on-campus programs which allow students and their families to interact with all segments of our population. The question is, who is better able to describe the quality of our programs than the faculty members who teach the courses? Also, who is better suited to describe the Northwestern experience than an undergraduate who is participating in that experience? Therefore, as we see the direction our activities will take in the future, we know that accessibility to the campus and the personal experiences prospective students will have with us, here in Evanston, will continue to be a dominant feature of our planning. It is also important for you to recognize that in addition to studying the habits and interests of prospective students, we continue to monitor the Northwestern environment. We regularly engage in studies that will help us know how our undergraduates feel about being here. This type of analysis, of course, submits the university to an ongoing critique. Some of what our students tell us is—to put it mildly—outspoken. Despite this the signs seem clear that more than 80 percent of the students who begin with us continue and graduate within four years. The point, then, is that keeping our ear to the ground forces us to be sensitive to the need for change when change may be important. This style of self-analysis suggests something about the strength of the university. Only institutions that are very strong can withstand the rigors of this type of soul searching. We are reassured that this inward analysis will only improve Northwestern's service to the members of its community. Therefore, the long-range benefits outweigh some of the short-range tensions.

　　Once again this year we are engaging in major research activity with respect to prospective students and their attitudes. One study we are doing will be similar to those you have seen before. We will closely examine the reasons why students selected Northwestern as one of their college choices and, if admitted, why they enrolled here or decided to go elsewhere. This type of study helps us understand our institutional "position" more clearly as well as to focus on many procedural facets of the admission and financial aid process. An equally interesting analysis that is being administered concurrently will focus on a group of prospective students who did not apply last year. In this study we are sampling the feelings of nearly 1,000 students who had expressed interest in Northwestern at some point during their senior year in high school. Despite the interest they expressed and the information they received, they did not apply. We are anxious to find out what prompted them to decide the way they did.

As you may surmise from the above, the focus of Northwestern's recruitment activity is directed toward a goal of matriculation and retention. The numbers of applications we receive are important, too. However, recruiting for applications implies that our efforts are largely sales-oriented and that we will engage in persuasion tactics rather than a counseling or facilitating approach. Over the years we have learned that persuasion simply does not work. In the short run it may appear to be successful, but students who have been "sold" on the notion that Northwestern can meet the needs of all people quickly discover that this is not the case. Northwestern is an institution that collaborates most successfully with students who have made solid commitments to their future. By this I mean those who have developed a strong set of academic and personal skills that will enable them to take advantage of the opportunities Northwestern presents. If a candidate for admission is not prepared both academically and personally for the pace and pressure of life at Northwestern, he or she will be seriously disappointed and become either an attrition figure or someone who may leave the university for academic reasons.

The Recruitment Model

As most of you recognize, we have participated in the College Board Search Service since its inception. This allows us to focus on a large number of prospective students who may then be approached via direct mail. The group of names we receive approximates 60,000. It may be interesting for you to know that the pool of candidates from which this group of 60,000 emerged originally numbered in excess of 1,000,000. This dramatic reduction from 1,000,000 to 60,000 was caused by our roughly defining Northwestern's minimum admission standards and asking only for students who met those standards. Further, we of course excluded from our potential group the names of students whose fields of interest did not match programs available at the university. This should convey an important message to you. You can see that of the more than 1.8 million students who go to college each year, a very, very small percentage meet Northwestern's minimum admission standards. It is also important for you to know that *if* we included in our College Board Search requests some qualification regarding the family's ability to meet the cost of a Northwestern education, this would reduce the number of potential prospects even more. (It is estimated that there are no more than 20,000 students who meet our minimum admission standards and who come from families that could easily contribute $5,000 a year for their education.)

Beyond decisions related to the direct mail approach we use in the early stages of our recruiting plan there are, of course, decisions to be made about how we will all use our time. By "we" I refer not only to members of the professional staff in the Admission Office but to you very important Alumni Admission Council members as well as Northwestern students and faculty members. Each year our admission plan is conceived with an eye to utilizing this force of some 700 people in the most effective manner possible. Over the years we have explored different ways to bring prospective students into contact with members of our recruitment force. Procedures and approaches have changed and probably will continue to do so as we strive to improve the method of dealing with an enormous potential prospective-student population. You have learned through your workshops that alumni in different regions of the country are asked to do different things. Not everyone has the same plan. We attempt to look at the nation, and, as you know, we have defined our market areas. Once the analysis and our definition are completed, we begin to make commitments on the time of our professional staff members. You have learned that the professional staff spends more time in certain areas of the country than it does in others. This is entirely due to our examination of application experiences and important demographic trends. At that point we also look at the Alumni Admission Council and try to plan ways for you to become involved not only in support of what the professional staff might do but to outline responsibilities you can initiate on your own. Further, our task requires that we find responsible work for Northwestern volunteer students and our faculty. I believe you understand how and why faculty members and students are utilized on the campus. We have found that they are extraordinarily valuable resource people for our visitors to meet. Further, we know that they deal from a position of strength when they are working from their campus base. In effect, then, our plan broadly covers many segments of the nation and some 700 people are engaged in activities that are all designed to meet certain kinds of short-run needs as well as to continue to reinforce the importance of Northwestern to serve our longer-range goals.

From time to time we are asked why we don't visit high schools or participate in college fairs. The key to all our thinking is tied very closely to the goal of differentiation. Northwestern must stand out as an institution with recognizable qualities if it is to be perceived as an important choice for prospective students. In many ways we differentiate ourselves most dramatically in the way we recruit students. We don't participate in college fairs because it would be difficult for students to see us differently from the hundreds of other institutions attending the same program, sitting behind similar tables in a huge auditorium. Also, our professional staff spends less time visiting high schools than do the staffs at other colleges. Aside from the fact that, again, this helps us to differentiate our approach, an even stronger reason for not visiting schools is related to the important role parents play in the college-selection process of their sons and daughters and the fact that we wouldn't see them if we did visit high schools. A question you might very well ask at this time is, "Why do you ask alumni to visit these schools for you?" That is a good question, and the answer has been carefully considered. In visiting schools you are serving an important public-relations function for us. The schools you visit are important to us, and the counselors you meet must have some good feelings about the university. The only contact they may have—aside from newsletters we mail or conferences we attend—will be the personal efforts you undertake on our behalf. Therefore, the role we ask you to play is entirely consistent with our long-range as well as short-range planning. The schools cannot function in a vacuum with respect to Northwestern, and the counselors, who may play only a minor role in the college-selection process for the type of student who chooses Northwestern, must nevertheless be informed about our programs and be able to recognize the existence of local resource people in their community who can be turned to when the situation calls for that.

As I have described this facilitating model, you will see that all of us are working in what appears to be separated activity, but at the heart of it all is an integrated plan which tries to take into account what you are doing in relation to what we as the professional staff of the Admission Office are doing. The College Board Search Service provides us with a source of names. The Search Service exists as an attractive feature in our recruitment approach because the quality of students may be controlled. The communication system we have developed functions because both of the above exist. Our immediate, as well as long-range, goals are designed to allow prospective students to participate in a college-evaluation process which considers not only the product as they see it but the reputation of the institution as they will personally learn about it. Further, these prospective students have the opportunity to interact with alumni, their own peers, students in college, and Northwestern faculty members as well as members of our professional staff. Our goal is realized if high school seniors actively interact with experiences and programs we conduct.

Our staff could not do this job by itself. Further, if we attempted to, we would not only fall short, we might be drawn dangerously close to a persuasion style of communication that could prove problematical for students who examine Northwestern. As alumni involved in this very important undertaking, you are helping us both in the sense of presenting an example of someone who has profited from participation in the Northwestern experience and by sharing updated information with students and counselors whenever the occasion permits.

We are extremely grateful to you for all of your hard work. We recognize and respect that as volunteers you are going far beyond the call of duty whenever you present Northwestern. I hope this message has helped you understand how strongly we feel about you. Also, we look forward to a continuing special relationship with you during the coming year.

Role of the Alumni on the Admission Council

As a member of the Alumni Admission Council, you are vitally interested in the future of Northwestern. You are concerned that it remain loyal to its rich heritage and traditions and yet be responsive to a complex, changing society. Northwestern is one of the major complex learning institutions in the country, and its responsibilities are to the nation. Because of these responsibilities, the students who are admitted to the university must be able to take full advantage of their education. It is your responsibility to help identify and interest the students with high scholastic and personal qualifications.

Identification of prospective students is a continuing process. You will be asked about the university by people who know you personally and those who have heard that you are from Northwestern. It is important that you notify the Admission Office when you contact a student who excites you. However, a note of caution is important. To oversell the university to a prospective student is a disservice to the student and to Northwestern. To overly encourage a student without fully knowing his qualifications is to court disaster, for the final decision on admission may not come from the Admission Office until February 15 (Early Notification) or April 15 (Regular Notification). It is important that while encouraging students to consider Northwestern, you know as much about the university and its various programs as possible.

As the role of the admission staff is in constant change and flux, so is the role of the alumni. We are well past the 1960s, when there was very limited space in colleges across the country. In the 1970s in some colleges there are empty dormitories, empty classrooms, and, in many cases, bankruptcies. The "prestige universities" are all competing for the same outstanding students.

In Northwestern's search for excellent students we have moved from a relatively modest admission program to one in which every idea is developed, and, if feasible, put into operation. Alumni are now active participants with the admission staff, visiting high schools, attending college nights, contacting students selected from the College Board Search Service, interviewing applicants, calling accepted students, visiting with parents, and hosting parties for incoming freshmen.

Today there are almost 500 active alumni in twenty-five cities across the country who are members of the Alumni Admission Council. Their role is to serve as a liaison between the Northwestern Admission Office and their own communities.

It has been our experience that wherever alumni are involved in admission work, there is better communication between that community and the university. And these alumni have discovered that it is very rewarding to be involved in the future of their university.

Recommendations for the High School Visit

Call the college counselor in the high school to make an appointment for a visit with him. In some cases, there are several counselors involved with college admissions, and only one will be available.

Introduce yourself and mention that you are Northwestern's Alumni Admission representative to the high school. Explain that we are very interested in students from the high school and you would like the opportunity to learn more about them and the school. The purpose of the visit is to develop communications between you, the high school, and Northwestern.

Do not ask to see students on this visit, unless the counselor requests that you do. Too frequently it is difficult for good students to leave classes, particularly during examination periods. Also, there may be other students who would skip classes to attend, although they are not interested in the university.

In some cases, you may be able to take the counselor out to lunch—or meet several counselors for lunch in the school cafeteria, where the atmosphere is more informal. Most counselors have received their degrees from colleges within their own state. Therefore, it is natural that they would recommend their alma maters to the high school seniors. They may not be familiar with the programs at Northwestern, so you should give them a catalog, "Northwestern University Now," and a few brochures on special programs (which we will send you). However, the counselors see admission representatives all year and will remember only a few programs you mention. *The main purpose of the visit is to learn more about the growth of the high school, the counselors' image of Northwestern, and the aspira-*

tions of their students (see High School Visit Report). If you can arrange an hour with the counselor(s), that should allow the time you need to establish the contact. Then ask him to call you whenever a question comes up or a student asks to see a representative from Northwestern.

Note: If you visited this school last year and have no changes to mention, please return this form to your director with only the date, high school, and your name.

Alumni High School Visit Report

Date of visit: _____

High school: _____

Address: _____

_____

Phone: _____ Principal: _____

Counselor contact: _____

Grades in school (check one): 10-11-12 _____ 9-10-11-12 _____

Enrollment: Total school: _____ Senior class: _____

Description of school (check one in each category):

1. public   _____   private   _____
2. coed   _____   all boys   _____   all girls   _____
3. city   _____   suburban   _____   rural   _____
4. blue collar _____   professional _____   other   _____
5. lower   _____   middle   _____   upper   _____
    income   income   income

Number of minorities: _____ Number of minority students: _____

Age of school: _____ Condition of school: _____

Percentage of graduates going to college: _____

Number of graduates attending four-year colleges: _____
                                           two-year colleges: _____
                                           Northwestern: _____

Where do the majority of graduates go to college? _____

Does this school have a "college night"? _____ Do you plan to attend? ____

AAC director: _____

AAC representative: _____

Address: _____

Phone: _____ N.U. class of ____ Major _____

In your discussion with the counselor, include questions like these:

> What can Northwestern do to improve communications with you
> and your students?
> What types of students do you advise to apply to Northwestern?
> To what extent are finances a problem for these students?
> Do they apply for financial aid?

On the basis of your discussion, what are your suggestions and evaluations?

Please return this to the Assistant Director of Admission.

We hope that within the next two years every high school counselor in the country with potential candidates for Northwestern will know an Alumni Admission representative on whom he can depend for current and expeditious information.

After your visit, please fill out the High School Visit Report and mail it to the Assistant Director of Admission at the Admission Office in Evanston.

College Night Report

Please complete and mail to: Assistant Director of Admission
                                Northwestern University
                                633 Clark Street
                                Evanston, Illinois 60201

College night held at: School: _____

                         City: _____

                         State: _____

Other high schools represented: _____

_____

_____

Date and time of college night: _____

Your accommodations: Classroom: _____ Table in gym: _____

                       Other (specify): _____

Schedule followed: Half-hour sessions: No. _____

                     One-hour sessions: No. _____

                     Other (specify):   No. _____

How many alumni represented Northwestern? _____

How many students did you see? Seniors: _____ Juniors: _____ Other: ____

How many parents did you see? _____

What were your impressions? _____

_____

_____

_____

_____

Is it worth visiting again? _____

Your name: _____

Address: _____

Phone: _____

Interviewing

The personal interview is an informal conversation between the candidate and the interviewer. It lasts about a half hour, although in some cases can extend for a longer period of time. It should not be a "hard-sell" exchange or a cross-examination. On the contrary, the interview should be an informative visit, leaving the student (and his parents) with a very good impression of the university—regardless of whether he (or she) eventually attends Northwestern.

The purpose of the interview is twofold: (1) to evaluate the student for admission on the basis of personal qualifications and (2) to give him information about Northwestern and his major interest. Although it is clearly not a "sales pitch," there certainly is a desire on the part of the interviewer to encourage the interest of the student *if* he seems qualified. It is also important to let him know that the final admission decision will be made by the Admission Committee.

After the interview, the interviewer will write a subjective evaluation of the candidate (Alumni Interview Report) but should attempt to be as objective as possible. The interview report will be read by the admission staff, who often do not know the interviewer personally; therefore, clarity is crucial in writing the report. This interview is an additional tool used to measure the ability of the student to succeed at Northwestern.

This year we are asking a number of alumni on the Council to conduct some personal interviews. These should be conducted in your home or office, not the candidate's home. If parents would like to come along, that is to be encouraged. However, during the actual interview time you should be alone with the student. Parents' questions, concerns, and interests should be handled upon completion of the student's interview. Parents are a very important part of the college-selection process and should be treated as such. The information and impression they receive from you may be extremely important in the later interaction between student and parent(s). We are searching for students with:

Intelligence, which is reflected in general conversation, grades, test scores, and ability to react to questions with some intellectual depth or creativity; *confidence,* which is reflected in discussions about peer-group associations, adult associations, and leadership roles in the school or community and during the interview situation; *energy,* which is reflected in motivation in high school (academically, socially, and emotionally) and in the community and in general interests of the student; *maturity,* which is reflected in ability to relate to the past and the future objectively—particularly evident in decisions about activities, jobs, colleges, and family and in discussions about relations with other people; *positive personal appearance,* which is reflected in dress, poise, and gestures; it is not necessary for a student to be dressed formally, nor do we expect conformity (in fact, individuality is encouraged); however, an individual's external appearance is clearly an expression of his self-concept; *commitment,* which is reflected in the student's sense of direction, not necessarily in a particular field, but in relation to the way he handles school, his community activities, and his time; *sense of humor; independent and critical thinking; sensitivity, awareness, curiosity*—which are reflected in the interview.

We are *not* looking for students who fall into particular molds. On the contrary, we are searching for a heterogeneous group, of which each member has something unique to offer and to gain from the university. In order to identify these students, it is necessary to remain very objective, which can be difficult at times. Some questions which are frequently asked during the interviews have been listed below:

They are only suggestions and should not be used in total. You will have your own style and manner in approaching the topics. You will find a sample copy of the Interview Report following the questions, which were compiled from staff suggestions.

Suggested Interview Questions/Topics

1. What do you think has been more important to you than anything else this past year? What have you been involved in (school/community) that you feel very pleased about?
2. Have you had any experience in the last two and a half years that has changed your mind about something? What kinds of things get you intellectually excited (fired up)?
3. Have you read anything or had an experience in the last year which in any way influenced you in your thinking or opened you up to things you were not aware of before?
4. What made you decide to come for a visit? Why N.U.? What kind of school are you looking for? What are you looking for in the next few years of college?
5. Who are you personally (not vocationally)?
6. Describe yourself and what you want to be doing in ten years. What's important to you in life outside of a career?
7. What things do you find yourself doing in a rather consistent way outside of school-related tasks? How have you arrived at the way you budget your time (meaning: Do you budget or plan your time)?
8. What are you interested in studying? (Establish how that relates to student's interests.)
9. Where do you live and what is it like there? The high school? Your town? How long have you lived there? Where were your formative years spent? What are your friends like?
10. How would you describe your present school? What have you done there? Would you say it is competitive? If yes, then are students competing for grades? How about learning? Do you think when you do not have to?
11. What changes could be made at your school that would benefit many people?
12. Where are you *now* in relation to your thinking about colleges? What are your expectations or standards? What personality traits

in teachers do you find most conducive to your best academic performance?

13. How would you create a college for yourself (not physical qualities, but the atmosphere)? What would it feel like? What kinds of people would you have at this ideal institution?

14. Defend your career choice to a person of opposite interests (for example, theater major explaining to an engineer).

15. What other colleges have you visited and why did you choose them?

Alumni Interview Report for: Student's name _____
(please print or type)   Last   First

Date _____ Home address _____
                                    Number   Street

Name of alumni interviewer   City   State   ZIP   Phone

                                                     Freshman _____
_____ High school _____
Phone   AAC area   Transfer _____

Describe the student on the basis of:

a. *Intellectual qualities* (for example, flexibility and scope, depth in some area, independence of thought, originality and creativity, ability to conceptualize, articulateness).

b. *Personal qualities* (for example, ability to relate interpersonally, resourcefulness, maturity, sense of humor, openness and sincerity).

(Please continue on other side)

Intellectual qualities: Personal qualities: Admission recommendation on basis of interview only:
_____ Well developed   _____ Well developed
_____ Potential for   _____ Potential for   view only:
     growth   growth   _____ Outstanding
_____ Limited evidence   _____ Limited evidence   candidate
_____ No basis for   _____ No basis for   _____ Strong candidate
     judgment   judgment   _____ Marginal candidate
                                                          _____ Weak candidate

Please return to your AAC director.

Admission Procedure

Operation of the Admission Office may be divided into various phases that develop throughout the year. There is obvious overlapping between stages, and the lines may not be drawn quite as clearly as they appear on paper. This permits definition and reevaluation of what we are attempting to do at various times during the year.

It is important also to note that the Admission Office may be divided between the external personal and professional relationships and the internal operational procedures. The goals of the Admission Office remain constant, but its role changes throughout the year.

The first phase, categorized as the *identification of candidates*, roughly extends from May 1 through December 31 of any year. During this period, prospective candidates are identified for admission. Externally, this is the period during which admission staff members conduct information sessions for prospective students and their parents throughout the country, interview individual students both on campus and in major cities, and visit high schools. At the same time, alumni contact these students and also represent Northwestern at area "college nights." Internally, this is the period for mailings to large groups of prospective students—to the outstanding students who take the PSAT/NMSQT (Preliminary Scholastic Aptitude Test/National Merit Scholarship Qualifying Test) in the fall of their junior year and to any students who have made inquiries about the university. It is important to remember that during this time no commitment is being made to these students by Northwestern, nor are the students committing themselves to the university.

The second phase may be described as the *descriptive phase*. During this period information is gathered regarding the students who have chosen to apply to the university. Externally, roughly from January 1 to February 15, candidates are interviewed by the Admission Office staff and alumni. Internally, the office receives the high school records, the College Board tests, recommendations from alumni, and any other information pertinent to the candidate's application.

The third phase, which we may term the *selection phase*, is roughly from January 1 to April 15, when admission decisions are made by the professional staff. We notify candidates of the committee's decision on their application as decisions are made. Letters of decisions are mailed from February 1 through April 15—Early Notifications are mailed by February 15; Regular Notifications from March 15 to April 15.

Phase four, *the follow-up on accepted students*, follows roughly the same time period as the selection phase. Externally, after the candidates have been offered admission to the university, alumni should contact them and encourage their acceptance of the offer of admission. These are the students we hope will attend Northwestern, and the personal contact is extremely important. Internally, this is a time of mailing campus brochures to candidates who have been admitted. Such information provides them with a better understanding of programs at the university.

The fifth stage, which is termed *re-evaluation and reassessment*, is from May 1 to approximately June 15. The primary concern is an analysis of the previous year. Results are scrutinized for faults in the system and for improvements to be made for the forthcoming year. Externally, this means a re-evaluation of the alumni program and the involvement of the alumni in the admission procedure. It also means a careful analysis of the relationship with our professional colleagues in the high schools—that is, discussing with them the decisions we have made on their candidates. Internally, it is a time of re-evaluating the procedures of the office and noting any deficiencies.

The sixth phase, the *planning phase*, roughly covers the summer months. During this period the Admission Office must plan and prepare for the coming year. The success of the year starting in the fall is determined to a great extent by what planning is done during the summer. It is important that incoming students now establish a direct relationship with the Office of the Dean of Students.

As indicated earlier, the various phases overlap to a great degree, and the role of each phase is not as clear-cut as it appears on paper. Admission is a continual process that occurs throughout the year, and it is imperative to keep in mind the identification of students throughout this time. The external and internal relationships coexist and really overlap, one dependent upon the other.

Notification Schedules

A student may choose to apply to Northwestern under one of two separate programs. One is Early Notification and the other is Regular Notification. The university discontinued its Early Decision Program in the fall of 1970. Students now may choose one of the two methods described below to register some control over when they will receive their admission decisions.

Students who request admission consideration under the *Early Notification* plan will receive admission decisions by February 15, on a rolling basis. To be considered for this earlier notice, a candidate must file his application no later than January 1. In addition, he must complete the SAT *or* the ACT (Scholastic Aptitude Test *or* American College Test) by the December test date at the latest. Students accepted who plan to matriculate, excluding those in the School of Music, must take three Achievement Tests by the May testing date. Earlier testing is encouraged.

Students who will apply to colleges whose admission notifications are normally sent later in the spring may apply to Northwestern under the *Regular Notification* plan. Decisions in this case will be mailed to students between March 15 and April 15. If a student is admitted, he will be expected to confirm his plans for enrollment by the Candidate's Reply Date of May 1, by submitting a nonrefundable tuition deposit of $200.

The majority of students choose to apply to Northwestern under the Regular Notification program. The prospective candidate should plan to apply by January 1 of his senior year. This is not a deadline, but the date is recommended so that all necessary information is on file by the time folders are read. He should note on his application whether he prefers a decision by February 15 or April 15. In either case he must respond to the decision two weeks later. All credentials must be received in our office by January 1 for Early Notification and February 15 for Regular Notification. By these dates a candidate is expected to have on file: (1) his high school record through the first semester of his senior year, (2) the results of the SAT *or* ACT, (3) the results of three Achievement Tests of the College Entrance Examination Board. The interview is recommended but not required. Most Early Notification candidates must arrange interview appointments before January 1. Regular Notification candidates should arrange appointments before March 1.

Members of the Admission Committee begin reading folders in the late fall and start notifying students February 15, completing notification by April 15. Northwestern's regular decision process is called "rolling admission," which means that notifications are sent out as decisions are made in the office. A student must respond to us with a $200 deposit by March 1 for Early Notification and May 1 for Regular Notification. May 1 is the College Entrance Examination Board's Candidate's Reply Date deadline.

Criteria for Admission

Complicating admission to the undergraduate school is the fact that each of the six schools within the university has different criteria for admission. Obviously, the Technological Institute is looking for a different type of student than is the School of Music. Each school also has a desired number of enrollments for the freshman class.

This is the approximate number of freshman students who will have entered the university September 1979:

College of Arts and Sciences	1,029
School of Education	11
School of Journalism	169
School of Music	100
School of Speech	221
Technological Institute	276
Total	1,806

Since each school has different criteria for admission, a student who has higher scores and grades may be turned down for one school, while a student having seemingly lower records will be accepted to another school of the university. This has to be considered when you are talking with prospective students and especially when you are talking with high school counselors. However, a student who desires to enter one school should not apply to another school within the university which is thought to have lower standards, with the idea of transferring to the desired school at a later date. This should be discouraged because internal transfer is difficult for the uncommitted student.

In reviewing a candidate for admission, the Admission Committee considers the following factors:

1. Candidate's high school program and his performance in specific courses.
2. Candidate's ability to compete at Northwestern, as indicated by standardized tests.
3. Activities he has participated in and leadership qualities demonstrated in these activities.
4. Recommendation of the high school counselor and, optionally, high school teacher(s).
5. Candidate's application, including the essay.
6. Personal interview with a Northwestern representative.
7. Audition Report for Music School candidates.

We must also consider the candidate's alumni ties with the university, geographical balance in the student body, and the number of openings in the particular school and department to which the student is applying.

However, the final decision is not based on any one of these factors alone but rather on the total picture of the candidate that they represent.

Evaluation of Candidates for Admission

Admission to Northwestern is competitive, and the Admission Committee is inclined toward a very subjective form of analysis. By this we mean we are searching for qualities that go well beyond the ordinary evidence provided by students' transcripts of credits or the results of their College Board examinations. In effect, there are three general classifications of information that can be discussed. The first represents the personal side of the student and would include the application for admission, the comments which come from secondary school people, and the personal interview. A second dimension of the student is demonstrated through the selection of courses and his high school performance. The third segment or dimension is presented in the form of the student's testing habits.

In the first instance, it is important for you to know that the application for admission is the most direct—and *personal*—contact the student will have with the Admission Committee. The application for admission truly presents a mechanism which allows the student to speak to the committee. It allows a candidate to share ideas and experiences with us. The student has complete control over what is said and how it is presented. In this fashion such matters as the student's style of thinking and use of time can be shared with the Admission Committee. Further, officials from the schools are normally very thoughtful in sharing information with us about the sort of impression a candidate for admission has made upon the school during his period of study there. Finally, a personal interview also allows the student to interact with a member of our admission staff or the Alumni Admission Council so that more subjective information can be shared with the committee of people who will read the admission file.

As you surmise, the decision period is a long one. The members of our committee work for nearly five months in this undertaking. Each candidate for admission has his file read by at least three different members of our committee, each of whom will vote. It is also frequently true that a file may be read four or five times before the decision is made. All of the above would not be necessary if deciding were based purely upon a student's grades, rank in class, and test scores. It is our assumption that students will understand the importance of these academic criteria and the commensurate responsibility they have in being serious students, particularly if they are considering competitive colleges or universities. By the same token it is vital to the admission decision for us to note something about their human nature. Our decision process, then, is one that tries to respect those personal qualities the students share with us. Such qualities as how the student chooses to use his time and, particularly, how he may care to share his time with others are valuable.

How Important Are Activities?

The members of our Admission Committee are interested in knowing how students use their time. I believe it would be correct for me to say that we do not try to establish biases in order to mentally credit some students who have done certain things while taking such credit from others who have not. We are anxious to know what the students feel is important and how they have supported their interest through their personal commitment of time. This might mean for one student becoming the president of the student body. For another it might mean involving himself in some community action program. For a third student it could possibly mean having a part-time job which would require working an unusual number of hours while still performing in a superior fashion in his academic program at school.

Are Activities in or Outside of School Best?

I would argue that the student should decide and then make every effort to become an active participant in whatever he or she feels is valuable. I don't want this to sound equivocal, but I hope that you will sense the admission process is one in which each candidate is respected as an individual human being. To do so presumes that we should respect the student's individual judgments and how he has supported those judgments with some form of activity.

Why Is This Involvement Important?

When a student is unusually involved in a principal interest, it most likely will be one that has some effect on others. The way others see this individual's participation and their evaluation of the student's commitment are frequently available in the form of recommendations or supportive commentary by officials at the school. We are attempting to look for something akin to a developing person. This implies academic development most assuredly, but it also includes a sense of others and a respect for becoming involved with others.

How Important Is It to Know "Your Major"?

We are attempting to try to find out something about how students think. This is true not only as it might be reflected in their academic performance in the classroom or on tests that they take but as they share ideas with us about their future plans. We recognize that many students will choose one area of interest only to find another one more appealing after they have been at Northwestern for a period of time. What we are looking into is the decision-making process and the evidence students present which clearly suggests that they do have a flair for original thinking and planning.

Educational Costs and Financial Aid

Northwestern rewards meritorious achievement and aptitude with an offer of admission to a community where high-ability students may grow more quickly in their abilities and interests than in the typical American college. Surveys of the highest-ability high school seniors—that is, students who can attend virtually any college they choose—indicate that an outstanding financial aid offer from College X will not lead the student to attend College X if the student is admitted to his first-choice college with adequate financial aid, which might in fact be less than the aid offered by College X. Simply stated, the evidence suggests that high-ability students cannot be "bought away" from the school of their first choice. (Therefore, as previously explained, our efforts are aimed at identifying high-ability students and assisting them in determining whether, in fact, Northwestern should be their first choice among colleges.) Therefore, Northwestern does not attempt to "buy" talent with financial aid. Rather, the financial aid program assists qualified students who would not be able to attend Northwestern without financial aid. In counseling a prospective candidate who wishes to apply for aid, this must be kept in mind.

Explanation of the Necessity for a Concept of "Financial Need"

The university must realize income in order to meet its expenses. Obviously, only families that can afford to pay some or all of their expenses can contribute to the university's income. Hence, these are the families who are expected to contribute a portion or all of the educational expenses incurred by their children. For those families who can meet only a portion, large or small, of the expense at Northwestern, the university maintains a financial aid program. This program is one of the most inclusive (involves about 60 percent of undergraduates) and largest (distributes about $7.9 million in 1978–79) in the nation. Total undergraduate scholarship money administered by the Financial Aid Office in 1978–79 was $13.7 million (including federal funds). At the same time, we do not have adequate assistance to award grant assistance (scholarship assistance with the added criterion of financial need) to all needy students who are admitted to study at Northwestern. We must decide which students from among the admitted financial aid applicants will receive grant assistance. Grant aid is distributed to only the most talented students.

Your Financial Aid Counseling Responsibility

In the beginning, the prospective student should be made aware of the costs at Northwestern for one academic year. For the 1979–80 year, the budget will be approximately:

Tuition and fees	$5,415
Room and board	2,100
Books and supplies	200
Miscellaneous	500
Total	$8,215

Travel expenses should be added to this figure—assume $0 to $200 from the Midwest, $380 from the East and South, $420 from the Mountain States, $680 from the West Coast.

Once a student knows our costs and indicates that the family cannot afford to pay these expenses in their entirety, he should be urged to apply for financial aid. Because of our planning, limited enrollment, and financial strength, the chances are very great (95 out of 100) that a student in financial need, regardless of whether the need is modest or very substantial, will receive adequate assistance to permit attendance.

Freshman Financial Aid Application Procedure

To be considered for all Northwestern scholarships (including National Merit and National Achievement Scholarships), grants, loans, part-time work opportunities, as well as the federally funded National Direct Student Loans (NDSL), Supplemental Educational Opportunity Grants (SEOG), and College Work-Study (CWS), *the student's family completes a single, omnibus form, the Financial Aid Form* (FAF). The student need only:

1. Have his parents, step-parents, or legal guardians complete the Financial Aid Form (FAF) according to the instructions printed on the FAF.
2. If parents are divorced, a Financial Aid Form must be completed by the parent with whom the student is living and the parent who takes the student as a tax deduction. If the student has been living with one parent who has taken the student as a tax deduction for the previous three years, the other parent does not have to file the FAF. In cases where the parents are separated, both parents must complete the FAF.
3. Mail the FAF to the College Scholarship Service before the deadline for applying for admission.
4. Complete an application for admission to undergraduate study at Northwestern before the deadline.

Only students who have applied for and been granted admission will be considered for financial aid. No other application papers need be completed for university or federal financial aid programs, *except* residents of states with state scholarship/grant programs (for example, Illinois, Massachusetts, Pennsylvania, New Jersey, Rhode Island) must apply to the state source.

Because of the month-long processing period at CSS, *families are urged to forward the FAF to CSS at least one month before the application deadline,* and even sooner if possible. Deadline for submission of the FAF to CSS is the same as the deadline for submission of the undergraduate application for admission—i.e., January 1 for Early Notification and February 15 for Regular Notification. *Last-minute submission of the FAF may substantially decrease the student's chances of receiving financial aid.* Early submission of the FAF has never hurt anyone, though the FAF should not be submitted prior to the beginning of the last year of high school.

Students granted admission, for whom FAFs have been received, will automatically be considered for financial aid from all sources listed above. Freshmen receiving financial aid in September 1979 shared approximately $2.6 million in scholarship/grant, $1.0

million in no-interest or low-interest loans, and $0.7 million in part-time work income from sources listed above. In addition, they received approximately $1.5 million additional assistance from state and local scholarship/grant agencies and competitions.

Decisions on the amount and types of financial aid offered a student are usually sent in the same envelope as the offer of admission, if the FAF is on file at the deadline.

Please read the information on financial aid for Northwestern University students, forwarded with each application for admission, in order to be completely informed.

Address all correspondence and questions regarding financial aid to the Assistant Director of Admission and Financial Aid, Northwestern University.

The student who is interested in applying for financial assistance will have questions. To aid your understanding of the financial aid process, these concepts should be kept in mind.

Need Analysis. Northwestern subscribes to the College Scholarship Service, which requires parents, step-parents, or guardians of the applicant to submit a Financial Aid Form (FAF). This statement provides the university with financial information that is necessary to objectively determine the amount of aid a student needs.

Parental Responsibility. The university believes the family is the party primarily responsible for the education of its children. Information filed on the Financial Aid Form is used to determine how much the family can contribute toward educational costs for the next school year. In estimating the amount the parents can provide, many factors are taken into consideration, among them size of family and associated typical living expenses, current income, added expenses due to employment of both parents, taxes, other educational expenses, predictable and nondiscretionary expenses (such as unreimbursed medical expenses), indebtedness due to nondiscretionary expenses, assets, and retirement needs.

Student Responsibility. A student who needs financial assistance should be willing to provide a reasonable part of the total amount of money required to meet college expenses through summer employment. Our studies have shown that the average freshman can apply $500 from summer earnings. In order to "stretch" the university's grant resources, a number of students are offered, in addition to or instead of a scholarship/grant, part-time employment during the school year, moderate loans, or both as a portion of their financial aid.

Packaging Concept. The "packaging concept" used by the financial aid program combines a scholarship/grant and/or loan and/or employment as the financial assistance offered to a student. The grant is strictly a gift scholarship. University *loans* average approximately $860, and repayment begins only when the student has ceased full-time degree candidacy. (For example, a student receiving a bachelor's degree and immediately proceeding to graduate or professional school would not begin repayment until he completed graduate or professional school.) No interest is paid and no interest accumulates while the student is in school because the interest is paid by the government while the student is in school. Once repayment of principal begins, the student has ten years in which to repay principal. Interest is 3-7 percent per year on the unpaid balance once repayment begins. Through *part-time work*, approximately 12-15 hours a week, the student earns approximately $1,100 in the process of the academic year. Although the student is not required to accept a loan or job if offered, the dollar value of the loan and job are considered financial aid and believed by the university to be necessary, in combination with all other assistance granted, to meet the student's financial aid.

Renewals. Once a student receives financial aid from the university, a new Financial Aid Form is submitted each year to document the family's continuing inability to meet expenses. The statement is reviewed in light of new financial circumstances which may have occurred in the form of educational costs and family circumstances. There are no grade requirements for continuation of financial assistance, but financial need must continue to be evident. It is the responsibility of the faculty (the Academic Standing Committee of the school in which the student is enrolled), not the Financial Aid Office, to exclude from the university students whose academic progress is considered inadequate.

Example of Financial Aid Calculations—Comparing Northwestern with Other Types of Colleges, 1979–80 Academic Year (All Figures in Dollars)

	Representative Community College	Representative Prestigious State University	Northwestern University
Costs			
Tuition and fees	300	1,100	5,415
Room and board	900	1,950	2,100
Books and supplies	200	200	200
Miscellaneous	500	500	500
Transporation	1,000–1,400	Varies[c]	Varies[c]
Total costs	3,100	3,750	8,215
Resources			
Contribution from:			
Parents	3,800	3,800	3,800
Student summer earnings	500	500	500
Nonfamily and nonuniversity funds (local, national, and state scholarships, and so on)[a]	000	000	000
Student personal assets[b]	000	000	000
Total resources	4,300	4,300	4,300
Financial Need			
Total costs less total resources (resources exceed costs)	None	None	3,915

[a]Example presumes student is not the recipient of nonfamily and nonuniversity funds—receipt of such funds increases resources and hence decreases financial need and financial aid received from the university.

[b]Example presumes student has no personal assets—contribution is expected from student assets when such assets exist.

[c]Assumes student lives on campus and therefore no automobile is needed.

Notes on the Financial Aid Example

Basic presumptions regarding the financial aid example:

- Family size: two parents and three dependent children, one of college age and the others younger
- Adjusted gross income: $30,800, mother not employed
- Taxes: itemizing federal and state income taxes; real estate, personal property, and other taxes at 8 percent of adjusted gross income
- Educational expenses (other than applicant's college): none; presumes children in public schools
- Nonpredictable nondiscretionary expenses (for example, unusual and/or emergency medical expenses not reimbursed by insurance): none; example presumes family in average health
- Debts: small and short-term only (for example, one month of gasoline on credit card)
- Assets: student, none; parental, $23,000 equity in house and $5,000 in savings account; no other assets
- Retirement: father 49; Social Security withholding only retirement provision (that is, no annuity, pension, and so on) other than home equity and savings

Two points should become apparent from an inspection of the accompanying example.

1. The factor most directly linked to financial need (amount of aid) is the cost of education at any given school. This is due to the fact that a family's maximum expected contribution to educational expenses is a constant dollar amount. This amount is constant inasmuch as it is the same family in terms of size, income, and noneducational expenses, regardless of where the student goes to college. This sample family is well off by community college standards, marginally well off by public standards, and distinctly in financial need by Northwestern standards, as witnessed by the increasing financial need, even though family contribution remains a constant $4,300 in all instances.
2. Most families are not good at predicting the savings they will realize at home if the student lives at college. Research by the

U.S. Department of Agriculture, the Department of Commerce, home-economics extensions of several universities, the College Scholarship Service, and other sources indicates that $900 can be realized in the typical American family when the student leaves home. Although it is a hidden cost, the cost of room and board and other expenses of basic maintenance, such as moderate clothing, sundries, and recreation, is a factor the typical family will usually misgauge to the detriment of consideration of educational choice for the student.

Questions Asked Frequently

Financial Aid

1. How do I get an application for financial aid?

As can be seen from the table below, the FAF (Financial Aid Form) serves most needs. The wise student will have the family complete the FAF as soon as it becomes available in the fall of the final year of high school.

Program	Application and Where to Get Application
Northwestern National Merit Scholarships	FAF High School Guidance Office
Northwestern National Achievement Scholarships	FAF High School Guidance Office
Northwestern Scholarships	FAF High School Guidance Office
Northwestern Loans	FAF High School Guidance Office
Northwestern Part-time Work	FAF High School Guidance Office
Federal National Direct Student Loan (NDSL)	FAF High School Guidance Office
Federal College Work-Study Program (CWSP)	FAF High School Guidance Office

Federal Supplemental Educational Opportunity Grant (SEOG)	FAF High School Guidance Office
Federal Basic Educational Opportunity Grant (BEOG)	FAF High School Guidance Office
Your State's Scholarship/Grant Program	Varies High School Guidance Office
Your State's Guaranteed Loan Program (GLP)	State Loan Application Your local bank
Federally Insured Student Loan (FISL)	FISL Application Your local commercial lender (bank, savings and loan, or credit union)
"No Need" Federally Insured Student Loans from Northwestern University	FAF High School Guidance Office

2. How is financial aid awarded?

At Northwestern, grant aid (scholarships with the added criterion of financial need) is *based on the need of the student in addition to academic and extracurricular aptitude and performance*. No scholarships are based solely on merit, and no scholarships are based solely on need. Scholarship/grant requires *both merit and need*. Loans are available to many students who are not in financial need but do merit admission. Part-time work is readily available for many non-financial aid recipients. The amount of assistance the student receives from the Financial Aid Office is determined by use of information appearing on the Financial Aid Form.

3. What is the package concept of financial aid?

The financial aid "package" consists of parts of financial aid that make up the total amount of money offered to a student. At Northwestern, this may include grant (which carries no obligation to repay) and/or loan (which may be a university loan or government loan) and/or work. A student may accept or turn down any part of the aid offered by the university. For example, he may accept a grant and work program but turn down a loan offered to him.

4. What work opportunities are available on the campus and within the area?

There are many different types of jobs available on campus —dormitory work, secretarial help, library work. Within the Evanston area there are innumerable jobs available to students.

5. If I receive a job through the Financial Aid Office, how many hours a week do I have to work?

Generally, 12–15 hours a week is expected of students who receive work through the Financial Aid Office.

6. Does having a job negatively affect the academic achievement of a student?

Generally, it is the reverse. Students are not expected to work a large number of hours a week, and thus we do not find that working has a detrimental effect on the academic part of the student's life. Students who work seem to adjust to their new academic and nonacademic experience more quickly than those who do not work.

7. Are there any restrictions put on students by the university as to the number of hours they may work during a week?

No. There are no restrictions put on a student, but it should be kept in mind that the primary purpose at the university is academic and all other activities, including part-time work, should be in support of this purpose, rather than in conflict with it.

8. Is there a grade-point average that has to be maintained to retain financial aid?

No. As long as a student is enrolled as a full-time student in the university, he may retain his financial aid. The Academic Standing

Committee of the school in which the student is enrolled, not the Financial Aid Office, is responsible for academic discipline and dismissal.

9. May a student receive financial aid if, after he is enrolled in the university, financial need should develop?

Yes. Financial aid may be reviewed at any time if there is a major change in circumstances of the family. The university feels a commitment to students who are on campus to see that they are able to finish their work here. All aid is reviewed each year.

10. What number of students received gift aid from the university last year?

Out of 1,776 freshmen, 897 received assistance in the form of scholarship/grant.

11. What percentage of students who applied for financial assistance received financial aid?

97 percent of those students who showed need received scholarship/grant assistance. Many received work and/or loan offers in addition to scholarship/grant assistance. *Most of those who did not receive assistance failed to meet the application deadline.*

12. Should an applicant apply for specific scholarships?

Generally speaking, no. Assignment of the student to a specific scholarship fund is done by the university and does not call for action on the part of the student. All students will automatically be considered for each of several hundred scholarship funds the university administers. To achieve this consideration the directions above are to be followed. See also 13 below for the only exceptions.

13. What special steps are necessary for what specific scholarships?

    a. Athletics. If a student feels that he has the ability to compete athletically, contact should be established with our

Athletic Office through the student's coach. A student may
also write to the appropriate coach—that is, swimming
coach, track coach, and so on—c/o Athletic Department,
Northwestern University, Evanston, Illinois 60201.

b. Debate. The student must address a request for debate-
scholarship consideration and at the same time send a
vita directly to Director of Forensics, c/o School of Speech,
Northwestern University, Evanston, Illinois 60201. *In addition*, the regular procedure for applying for all scholarships above must be followed (that is, file the FAF).

c. Music. The School of Music will automatically notify all
music applicants of the procedure to compete for Eckstein
awards, which are awarded only on the basis of performance. Only applicants for admission to the School of
Music may compete for these awards. Detailed information
regarding Eckstein awards may be obtained from the School
of Music, Northwestern University, Evanston, Illinois 60201.

d. Naval Reserve Officer Training Corps (NROTC). Deadline for submission of the NROTC application is November of the last year of high school. The student applies
locally rather than through Northwestern. The high
school guidance office or principal is usually familiar with
the procedure.

Applying for Admission

1. Who should apply for Early Notification (January 1) from
Northwestern?

A student who declares Northwestern as his first choice or who
is applying to universities which also notify early (that is, most state
universities) should request Early Notification. He must apply by
January 1 and submit all information: SAT *or* ACT scores, Achievement scores, transcripts, counselor's recommendation, and FAF
when requesting aid. He will receive admission notification by February 15 and must respond by March 1. A student must choose *either*
Early *or* Regular Notification.

2. Should I apply to a specific school within the university or simply to Northwestern?

You apply for admission to Northwestern *and* to a specific school within the university. Each of the schools has its own requirements for admission.

3. Is it possible for me to transfer from one school within the university to another while I am on campus?

Yes, you may transfer from one school to the other with approval of the appropriate deans. Exception: The School of Journalism cannot admit transfers at the present time.

4. May I take courses within any school of the university, or am I limited only to the school in which I am enrolled?

You may take a certain number of courses as electives in any of the schools in the university. There is a limit, depending on the school in which you are enrolled and in which school you are planning to take courses.

5. Is an interview required for admission?

No, it is not required for admission. However, it is recommended that every prospective student, if possible, have a personal interview. Communication between the Admission Office and the applicant is of vital importance, and the personal interview is one of the best means for this communication.

6. If a student is accepted to Northwestern and decides to defer his enrollment for a year, what should he do?

He should send in his $200 tuition deposit by the March 1 or May 1 deadline with a letter stating that he plans to defer his admission for one year. If he does not attend another college full-time, his admission and financial aid offers will be fully reinstated for the following year.

Deadlines

Dec. 15	Requests for Honors Program in Medical Education applications must be received at the Undergraduate Admission Office
Jan. 1	Early Notification applications have to be filed
Jan. 1	Financial Aid Form should be filed with the College Scholarship Service
Jan. 15	The application for admission to the Honors Program in Medical Education is due at the Medical School
Feb. 15	Early Notification candidates will be notified of the decisions regarding their applications for admission and financial aid
Feb. 15	Application for Regular Notification should be filed
Feb. 15 to Apr. 15	Admission and financial aid decisions will be sent to Regular Notification candidates on a "rolling admission" basis
Mar. 1	Early Notification candidates accepted must confirm their intention to enroll by submitting a nonrefundable $200 tuition deposit or the offer of admission is withdrawn
May 1	Regular Notification candidates accepted must confirm their intention to enroll by submitting a nonrefundable $200 tuition deposit or the offer of admission is withdrawn; among many colleges, May 1 is known as the "Candidate's Reply Date"

Testing

1. What tests are required for admission to Northwestern?

Tests required for general admission are either the SAT *or* ACT (Scholastic Aptitude Test *or* American College Test). They must be taken by the *December* testing date of the senior year. Students who plan to matriculate, excluding those in the School of Music, must take three Achievement Tests by the *May* testing date of their senior year. Earlier testing is encouraged, however.

2. When and where are these tests offered?

They are offered at most high schools throughout the country beginning in October.

3. How does a student register for these tests?

A student secures a form from his high school counselor and should register for the test approximately six weeks before the scheduled testing date.

4. Are the College Entrance Examination Board Achievement Tests required for admission or for Advanced Placement?

Candidates interested in *special programs*, such as the Honors Program in Medical Education, the Three-Year B.A. Program in the College of Arts and Sciences, the Integrated Science Program, or the Honors Program in Mathematical Methods in the Social Sciences, must submit three Achievement Tests both for admission and for Advanced Placement consideration.

5. If a student takes the same test twice, which score will be used?

Northwestern will accept the highest scores presented by the student.

6. Are junior-year tests acceptable to the university?

Yes.

7. Which is more important, the test scores or the high school records, regarding admission to the university?

Generally, the high school record is more important than test scores. The best indicator of future college success is a successful high school career. Test scores indicate the aptitude of the student. The high school record indicates actual performance.

Course Programs

1. What courses would a student take in his freshman year?

This depends greatly on what school a student enrolls in and what program he takes in this individual school. On this question and the question regarding graduation requirements, refer to the catalogue. All College of Arts and Sciences (CAS) students must complete a minimum of three quarter-courses in each of the following areas: (1) fine arts, literature, and music, (2) natural sciences and mathematics, (3) social sciences, and (4) history, philosophy, and religion. The list of courses that may be used to satisfy these requirements is available at the CAS Office of Studies. In addition, at least six quarter-courses outside the department of a student's major must be at the B or C level. Two one-quarter freshman seminars are required, as well as a two-year foreign or classical language proficiency. Please check the catalogue for requirements in education, journalism, music, speech, and engineering.

2. What is the average size of the classes?

They vary greatly, ranging from seminars as small as ten to lectures of 200 or more. In a four-year period approximately 50 percent of a student's courses are classes of fifty or fewer.

3. Are seminars available to students?

Yes, they are, on the advanced level (with the exception of the Introductory Studies courses in the freshman year). They are quite small, individual discussion-type of classroom situations, usually enrolling twenty students. Independent study is also available to advanced students. This is on an individual basis between professor and student, and the work is accredited.

4. Does Northwestern have a junior-year-abroad program?

With the dean's approval, a student may study during the junior year through any accredited American college program and receive credit for the work he does. It is generally felt by the university that in studying abroad, studies should be appropriate to the specific major (that is, language, history, and so on). Study abroad is an honors program. Tuition and fees are paid to Northwestern, and financial aid is administered in the usual way.

5. Do graduate students teach classes?

In a few cases, but most of their work is in quiz sections, as laboratory assistants, advising students, and tutoring.

6. Describe the "premed" and "prelaw" programs at Northwestern.

These are not specific programs but are general programs preparing a student for entrance into law school or medical school. There are traditional majors associated with premedicine, such as chemistry and biology, as there are with law, such as political science, history, and English. However, a specific major is not required for either premed or prelaw.

7. Is it an advantage for a student to do his undergraduate work at Northwestern if he wishes to go to Northwestern's medical or law school?

A great deal of emphasis is placed on recommendations for entrance to the medical or law school; thus it is natural these schools tend to rely on the recommendations of people they know well. In this sense only, it might be advantageous for a student to attend undergraduate school at Northwestern. However, the number of Northwestern undergraduates who are admitted to Northwestern's law and medical schools is limited.

8. What is the percentage of graduates who continue on to graduate school?

In the class of 1977, almost 52 percent of those graduating planned to continue their education. This includes 52 percent of the men and 40 percent of the women. For the College of Arts and Sciences, 66 percent of the men and 46 percent of the women planned to continue their education. This is approximately 56 percent of the graduates of the college.

9. What percentage of Northwestern graduates applying to medical and law schools are accepted?

In the past five years the medical school percentage has been as low as 60 percent and as high as 75 percent. The law school percentage has ranged from 83 percent to 95 percent in the past five years.

10. What is the national average?

Medical schools—35 percent; law schools—60 percent.

Special Programs

Integrated Science Program (ISP)
1. What is the Integrated Science Program?

ISP leads to a three-year bachelor's degree, which is designed for students with superior high school records and strong motivation in science and mathematics. Its special curriculum provides a thorough and rigorous background in all major scientific disciplines but attempts to integrate them into a unified whole and to diminish the sharp but artificial boundaries that traditionally separate them.

2. How many students enroll each year?

Thirty.

3. What are the requirements?

See question 3 under the "Honors Program in Medical Education," below.

4. Is a separate application, in addition to the regular undergraduate admission application, required?

Yes.

5. What does a bachelor's degree in ISP lead to?

There are several options: (a) Graduate school at the doctoral level. (b) Professional schools: for example, medicine, law, dentistry. (c) Employment in industry or government.

The 3-2 Program in Management
1. What is the 3-2 Program?

This program in management offers the talented student, planning a career in business, an opportunity to complete degree requirements for both the Bachelor of Arts and the Master of Management in five years instead of the usual six.

2. In what areas does a student specialize?

There are several options: (a) Business management. (b) Public management. (c) Hospital and health services management. (d) Education management. (e) Transportation management. In addition to one of these industry concentrations, each student is required to have a concentration in one of the traditional functional areas of business, such as accounting and information systems, banking and finance, or marketing.

3. How does a student apply?

Students enrolled in the College of Arts and Sciences submit an application for admission and an additional form for the 3-2 Program after September 1 of their junior year at Northwestern.

4. Are there any required tests?

The Admission Test for Graduate Study in Business (ATGSB) should be taken no later than January of the candidate's junior year at Northwestern.

5. What are the opportunities for placement?

More than 250 firms and organizations from across the nation interview on campus annually; many others are in regular contact with the Placement Office. Graduates hold a wide range of responsible positions in small and large business organizations, government agencies, community organizations, educational institutions, hospitals and health care organizations, labor unions, churches, and foundations.

6. Can students from other colleges and universities transfer into this program?

   No.

The National High School Institute (NHSI)
1. What is the National High School Institute?

   NHSI is a five-week program for high school students which is offered in the summer between their junior and senior years (in some cases between their sophomore and junior years).

2. What areas of interest are included?

   Speech: forensics, theater arts, radio-TV-film. Music: three weeks only—audition is required. Journalism. Engineering-science.

3. What are the requirements?

   Students who apply must be recommended by their high school teachers. They usually rank in the top quarter of their class and have some experience in their interest areas. They also should submit SAT scores.

4. How long is the program and how much does it cost?

   Five weeks—$720, which includes room, board, and tuition. (Music is three weeks and is $375.)

5. What else should a student know about NHSI?

   It is called "The Cherub Program." Most students find this title ridiculous when they enter the program. (Historically, the nickname was given by a professor who thought the NHSI students looked like "cherubs.") However, if you ask a student from the program why he is attending Northwestern, he will say proudly, "I am a Cherub!"

Honors Program in Medical Education (HPME)
1. What is the Honors Medical Program?

A six-year program which includes two years of undergraduate work and four years of medical school, culminating in the M.D. The student is admitted to the undergraduate school and N.U.'s medical school simultaneously.

2. How many freshmen are accepted each year?

Sixty freshmen are accepted to the program. Thirty come from the state of Illinois.

3. What are the requirements for admission?

Most students who are accepted rank in the top 3 percent of their high school graduating classes with SATs in the high 600s or 700s. They have completed four years of science and four years of math in high school. They must have taken three Achievement Tests: English Composition, Chemistry, and Math Level II. Personal interviews are required.

4. Is a separate application required?

Yes.

5. Are students required to attend college during the summer?

No.

6. Are an Honors Medical Student's first two years in undergraduate school restricted to math and science?

No. One-half of his courses (two out of four per quarter) are requirements in math and science. The other half of his courses are electives. With no specific requirements in other academic areas, he has the flexibility to take whatever he chooses in areas such as social sciences, political science, history, economics, foreign languages, speech, and music.

Three-Year Bachelor of Arts Program
1. What is the Three-Year Program?

An opportunity for exceptional students in the freshman class to complete the work required for a bachelor's degree in three years instead of four.

2. How does a student apply for this program?

He does not apply specifically. All candidates who apply to the College of Arts and Sciences as freshmen are considered for this program if they have taken their SATs and Achievement Tests. From the accepted candidates, a faculty committee chooses approximately 300 students who will be offered the Three-Year Program.

3. Does the Three-Year Program require extra work during the summer?

No. It limits the bachelor of arts degree requirements to thirty-six units of credit instead of the usual forty-five. The student must complete the course requirements in general education and an approved program in his field of major interest. This can be accomplished in three academic years.

Four-Year Master's Program
1. What departments at Northwestern offer four-year master's degrees?

Biology, Chemistry, Economics, Mathematics, Communication Studies, and all foreign languages. Other departments may make similar arrangements for individual students. If students are interested in any of these programs, they should write to the Admission Office for further information.

Advanced Placement
1. When and where should a student take the Advanced Placement Program examinations?

These are offered at individual high schools in May. A student should check with his adviser as to whether he should plan on taking the Advanced Placement Program examinations.

2. How does a student receive advanced placement and/or credit at Northwestern for work he has done in high school?

Advanced *placement* is granted on the basis of Advanced Placement Program examinations, CEEB Achievement Tests and high school record, and placement tests given on our campus during New Student Week. *Credit* is granted *only* for high performance on the Advanced Placement examinations.

3. When will a student be notified of what advanced placement and/or credit he will be receiving on the basis of the Advanced Placement Program examinations?

Early in August.

4. How may credits be received for work done in the Advanced Placement Program?

Through high performance on the Advanced Placement exams offered in May. Of the class entering in the fall of 1977, 620 submitted tests; 50 percent received credit and advanced placement.

5. What scores are necessary on the Advanced Placement examinations for a student to receive advanced placement credit?

Generally, if a student scores 4 or 5 on the Advanced Placement Test, he will receive full credit. A score of 3 will result in advanced placement in Art, Art History, Chemistry, Mathematics, and Calculus AB/AC.

6. Will a student receive credit for college courses taken while in high school?

If the college where he took the courses will offer him credit for the work completed and if the college is accredited by the regional accrediting association, Northwestern will offer credit for that work. Credit will not be offered if the course is being used to fulfill a high school graduation requirement.

7. In the languages, will a student receive credit if he has completed three or four years of the same language in high school?

No. He may place out of the first year or two of a language, by scoring 650 or above on the language Achievement Test, although he will not receive college credit for work completed in three or four years of high school *unless* he takes the Advanced Placement examination and achieves a high score.

Campus Life

1. Where do freshman students live?

Most freshmen who are not within commuting distance or living with relatives in the area live in residence halls provided by the university. Approximately 87 percent of the freshmen live on campus. However, residence on campus is not a requirement.

2. Generally, how many students are there to a room?

Two to a room is the most common arrangement. There are some suites, but this is not the common facility. The newest dormitory has 600 single rooms—four rooms sharing a bath.

3. Are eating facilities within the residence halls?

There are eating facilities in the large residence halls. Students in the small halls can have their meals in one of the larger dormitories.

4. Where do sophomore men live?

There are three options available to sophomore men. They may stay in university residence halls. If they pledge fraternities, they may move into the fraternity houses. Or they may live off campus. Approximately 70 percent of all men live on campus.

5. Where do sophomore women live?

Almost all sophomore women live in the residence halls provided by the university. Starting in the sophomore year, women who have pledged sororities may live in the sorority houses. Approximately 71 percent of all women live on campus.

6. May a student have a car on campus?

In his freshman year, if he lives on campus, he may not have a car or a motorcycle unless he rents off-campus parking. Following this first year, he may have one.

7. Must students be in at certain hours if they live in residence halls or fraternity houses?

No. A student who comes to Northwestern must be mature, self-disciplined, and able to manage both his academic and social life independently.

8. What counseling program exists?

The university provides a full-time staff of academic, resident, and personal counselors to assist students.

9. How important are fraternities and sororities on the campus?

Approximately one-third of the students pledge and belong to sororities and fraternities at Northwestern. With the diversity of activities provided by the university, there are alternatives to pledging a fraternity or sorority at Northwestern. Pledging a social organization is a decision which has to be made by the individual, relative to what he personally feels about social organizations.

10. What kind of input do students have in policy making?

There are student representatives on the Northwestern Community Council, which is a university policy-making body. The Associated Student Government is the major student organization. However, students are represented on all policy-making committees at Northwestern.

11. What is a residential college?

A living unit which incorporates into the living arrangement the features of the classroom, seminar, and faculty counseling. A faculty member is master of the house.

12. Is the residential college a substitute for the classroom experience?

No. It is an additional experience. Students will continue to take classes within their major departments. They will be able to take extra classes for credit in their living units.

13. Are the residential units different in curricular orientation?

The three general, or nonthematic, colleges are characterized not so much by their curricular orientation as by their programs of activity, their nonrequired seminars, and the forms they choose for self-government. The three thematic colleges are established with specialized interdisciplinary programs in the areas of community studies, women's studies, and humanities.

Athletics

1. What athletic programs are open to Northwestern students?

   a. Big Ten Conference: This includes Illinois, Indiana, Iowa, Michigan, Minnesota, Northwestern, Ohio State, Purdue, and Wisconsin.
      Men can compete in the National Collegiate Athletic Association (NCAA) and the Big Ten spectator sports, including baseball, basketball, cross-country, football, golf, swimming, tennis, track, and wrestling.

Women can compete in basketball, cross-country, field hockey, gymnastics, indoor and outdoor track, softball, swimming, tennis, and volleyball, all under the auspices of the Association of Intercollegiate Athletics for Women (AIAW).

b. Intramural Conference on Campus: For men: Basketball, three-man basketball, bowling, floor hockey, football, indoor soccer, softball (12″), softball (16″), swimming, tennis, track, volleyball, and wrestling. For women: Basketball, "powder-puff" football, softball (12″), swimming, tennis, and volleyball. Coed: Basketball, bowling, track, and volleyball.

2. Are there athletic scholarships offered by the university?

Yes, in Big Ten sports (the largest number is in football). These are not based on financial need. If a student is interested in an athletic scholarship, he or she should contact the coach of the sport concerned, c/o Athletic Department, Northwestern University, Evanston, Illinois 60201.

Northwestern University—Information Frequently Requested 1979-80

Population:

	Full-Time	Part-Time
Evanston campus		
Number of undergraduates	6500	133
Number of graduate students	2800	407
Total	9300	540
Chicago campus		
Medical-Dental-Law and Evening Division	2500	3385
Grand Total	15725	

By Schools:

	(freshmen)
Arts and Sciences	1029
Engineering	276
Speech	221
Journalism	169
Education	11
Music	100
Total	1806

New Campus (1970s):

Library
Astronomical Research Center
Computer Center
Biological Research Center
Student Center
Communicative Disorders Center
Education Center
Graduate Business School
Concert Hall
Science-Engineering Library
Theater Facility
GSM Conference Center

Special Programs:

Six-year Honors Medical
Afro-American Studies
Urban Development
Biomedical Engineering
Three-Year Bachelor's Degree
Four-Year Master's Degree
Integrated Science Program
New Careers in Education
Mathematical Methods in the Social Sciences
National High School Institute (summers)

Requirements for Admission

SAT or ACT
Three Achievement Tests
High school grade and rank
Counselor recommendation
Interview (recommended)
Transfers may submit CLEP or ACT as a substitute for SATs—they do not need Achievement Tests

Credit Options

Independent Study
Pass/no credit courses
Student-organized seminars
Advanced Placement credit (from A.P. test scores)

Cost (from September to June):

Tuition:	$5415
Room and Board:	2000

Dates:

	Early Notification	Regular Notification
Application deadlines	January 1	February 15
Notification of Admission Decision	by February 15	April 15
Acceptance of Admission by Applicant	March 1	May 1

Miscellaneous

Faculty-student ratio: 1 to 9; 82 percent of faculty members in College of Arts and Sciences have Ph.D.s; 66 percent of men and 45 percent of women (CAS) and 52 percent of all undergraduates continue on to graduate school.

Appendix C

Worksheet Information to Help Choose a College

The information that follows provides prospective college students and their families with a method of measuring their impressions of various colleges and with a device to determine their eligibility for financial assistance.

What Factors Should You Consider in Your College Choice?

The following questions have proved to be those most commonly asked by prospective college students and their families. As you begin your investigation, you can quantitatively assess on each question each institution you consider. For this purpose, a scale is provided, ranking 1 as low and 5 as high. As you ask yourself each question, assign a numerical value to your answer. Then consider applying to those institutions with the highest totals.

These criteria should help you make an intelligent choice about your college education. Each institution has a "personality." The more closely you match your personality with that of the institution, the more likely you are to be both successful and happy in your college experience.

Scale

1 = Poor
2 = Below average
3 = Average
4 = Above average
5 = Superior

Colleges

Question

Will the various programs meet
my intellectual needs?

___ ___ ___ ___ ___

Will the various programs meet
my personal needs?

___ ___ ___ ___ ___

Are the various programs being well
maintained and/or expanded?

___ ___ ___ ___ ___

Are the various facilities (libraries,
laboratories, classrooms, living
units, and recreational areas) being
well maintained and/or
expanded?

___ ___ ___ ___ ___

Is there a tradition of academic
innovation and intellectual
excitement?

___ ___ ___ ___ ___

Is the faculty distinguished for
research as well as teaching?

___ ___ ___ ___ ___

Will I have access to the faculty
(student-faculty ratio, class size,
percentage of classes taught by
professors versus teaching assistants, extracurricular faculty
programs)?

___ ___ ___ ___ ___

Is the nature of the student body
consistent with my own intellectual capability and academic
interests?

___ ___ ___ ___ ___

Is the student body sufficiently
diverse to stimulate my personal
growth?

___ ___ ___ ___ ___

Will the location of the university
enhance my learning experience?

___ ___ ___ ___ ___

Will the size of the institution be
an advantage?

___ ___ ___ ___ ___

Will I fit in?   ____ ____ ____ ____ ____

Will a degree from this institution
assist me in achieving my future
goals?   ____ ____ ____ ____ ____

                    Total   ____ ____ ____ ____ ____

How Will You Pay for Your College Education?

Contrary to the facts, many students believe that you cannot meet the cost of attending an out-of-state public institution or a private college or university. What most families do not understand is that 90 percent of the college-age population is eligible for grant assistance from government and/or institutional sources at higher-priced private institutions. In addition, there are in-school, interest-free loans and job opportunities for all students. However, you will want to know what your family will be expected to pay for your education. The financial aid information that follows will provide you with an estimate of your parents' contribution, which is derived by adding together the expectation from income and from assets. The parents' contribution is a fixed amount that remains the same regardless of the variation in cost among the institutions that you might attend. Therefore, if you attend one of the higher-priced institutions and demonstrate greater need, you will qualify for additional financial aid.

In order to estimate what you will pay for your college education at any given institution, divide the estimated total parents' contribution by the number of family members attending college full-time, and subtract that amount from the total cost of attendance. This figure is the estimated total need. Institutions that award need-based grants also calculate as a part of the total financial assistance a student's contribution from self-help. The amount for self-help varies from approximately $1,000 to $2,500 ($500 for summer earnings + $500 to $2,000 for college work and/or loans). Your estimated total need minus your estimated total self-help is your estimated total grant eligibility.

Although the following information will provide a rough estimate of what you will pay for your college education, every family's financial situation is unique. Therefore, exact financial aid figures will depend on a full need analysis, including some aspects that are open to interpretation at the discretion of officers administering financial aid for the individual colleges and universities.

Table C-1 shows the 1979–80 estimates of the expected parents' contribution from gross income as determined by the College Scholarship Service (CSS). This table is based on a two-parent family with one parent employed and with one child in college, but no other unusual expenses. Adjustments have been made for median living and medical expenses and for local, state, and federal taxes paid. The parents' contribution would be lower when additional adjustments are made for two working parents, for more than one child in college, or for any other unusual expenses.

Table C-1. Expected Parental Contribution from Gross Income, in Dollars, by Gross Income and Number of Children

	Number of Children					
Gross Income ($)	1	2	3	4	5	6
5,000	0	0	0	0	0	0
10,000	280	0	0	0	0	0
15,000	1,030	720	430	100	0	0
20,000	1,950	1,510	1,170	840	600	360
25,000	3,330	2,690	2,170	1,680	1,380	1,110
30,000	4,740	4,130	3,540	2,900	2,440	2,050
35,000	6,040	5,440	4,880	4,240	3,780	3,320
40,000	7,250	6,660	6,110	5,490	5,050	4,590
45,000	8,370	7,790	7,250	6,650	6,220	5,790

Source: Reprinted with permission from *CSS Need Analysis Theory and Computation Procedures for the 1979–80 FAF.* Copyright © 1979 by College Entrance Examination Board, New York.

Because of the many factors involved, a standard expectation from assets cannot be reduced to a general table like Table C-1 here. However, as a guideline, the parents' contribution from assets will not exceed, and is generally much lower than, 5 percent of net assets (gross assets minus related indebtedness, such as the unpaid mortgage on a home).

A Financial Aid Example

Table C-2 shows the 1979–80 standard estimates of the parents' contribution from net assets for a typical middle-income family:

a two-parent family with one parent employed, with three children but only one in college, and having a gross income of $25,000. Given these factors, the contribution from assets, to be added to the amount in Table C-1 will vary with the amount of net assets and the age of the wage earner.

Table C-2. Expected Contribution from Net Assets, in Dollars, by Net Assets and Age of Wage Earner, for Family with Three Children and $25,000 Gross Income

	Age of Wage Earner				
Net Assets ($)	40	45	50	55	60+
20,000	420	270	80	0	0
30,000	980	810	580	300	0
40,000	1,540	1,370	1,150	850	440
50,000	2,110	1,940	1,710	1,410	1,000
60,000	2,670	2,500	2,280	1,970	1,560
70,000	3,240	3,060	2,840	2,540	2,130

Source: Reprinted with permission from CSS Need Analysis Theory and Computation Procedures for the 1979–80 FAF. Copyright © 1979 by College Entrance Examination Board, New York.

In this example—the family with a gross income of $25,000 and other particulars as described above—if the net assets were $30,000 and the age of the wage earner 45, the contribution from net assets would be $810. Since the contribution for this family would be $2,170 (see Table C-1), the estimated total parents' contribution would be $2,980 ($810 + $2,170).

If this student were from Washington, D.C., and attending Northwestern, the 1979–80 estimated cost of attendance, including the cost of two round-trip plane fares, would be $8,530. This amount minus the estimated parents' contribution leaves an estimated need of $5,550. This sum minus the average amount for self-help ($1,750) leaves a grant eligibility of $3,800. Further adjustments are possible. For example, if both parents are working full-time and earning a combined gross income of $25,000, the adjustment for two working parents would reduce the contribution from income to $1,380. Therefore, since the contribution from assets would remain $810, the estimated total parents' contribution would be $2,190 ($810 + $1,380).

Family Contribution Worksheet

Estimated Parents' Contribution	*NU Example*	*Your Own*
Parents' contribution from income (see Table C–1)	$2,170	_____
Parents' contribution from net assets (see Table C–2)	810	_____
Total	$2,980	_____

Estimated Costs for 1979–80		
Tuition	$5,415	$5,415
Room and board	2,100	2,100
Books	200	200
Personal expenses	500	500
Transportation	315	(Two round-trip air coach fares)
Total	$8,530	_____

Estimated Financial Need		
Estimated cost	$8,530	_____
Less: estimated parents' contribution	- 2,980	_____
Financial Need	$5,550	_____
Less: student self-help (summer earnings, work-study, loans)	- 1,750	- 1,750
Total Grant Eligibility	$3,800	_____

Significant References

~~~~~~

To those new to the field of higher education, selected works by Alexander W. Astin should be required reading. All the works by Astin in the list of references that follows will be helpful in developing an understanding of the college decision-making process and of the impact of colleges on students. Papers on marketing by Kotler and by Geltzer and Ries are recommended and can be found in a collection published by the College Entrance Examination Board. In this same collection, an article by Doermann provides an assessment of the ability of the market to pay for higher education. Sandage and Fryburger's book on advertising is most useful if the promotional budget of the admission office is to be used efficiently. Monographs by Henderson and by Henderson and Plummer identify market trends, including student migration patterns.

In addition to the above references, those who have been involved in higher education for some time, including presidents, should be interested in the following: references on attrition by Astin (1975) and Noel (1978), the monograph on the relation among tuition, student aid, and enrollment by Corwin and Kent (1978), and the three works on marketing in the nonprofit sector by Kotler.

References

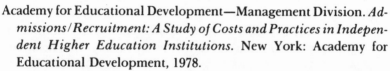

Academy for Educational Development—Management Division. *Admissions/Recruitment: A Study of Costs and Practices in Independent Higher Education Institutions.* New York: Academy for Educational Development, 1978.

American Assembly. "The Integrity of Higher Education." *Final Report of the Fifty-Sixth American Assembly.* New York: Columbia University, 1979.

Andersen, C. (Ed.). *A Fact Book on Higher Education: First and Second Issues.* Washington, D.C.: American Council on Education, 1976.

Anderson, R. E. "Private Public Higher Education and the Competition for High Ability Students." *Journal of Human Resources,* 1975, *10* (4), 500–511.

Anderson, R. E. "Determinants of Institutional Attractiveness to Bright, Prospective College Students." *Research in Higher Education,* 1976, *4*, 361–371.

Anderson, R. E., assisted by Haar, J. N. *Strategic Policy Changes at Private Colleges: Educational and Fiscal Implications.* New York: New York Teachers Press, 1977.

Arbeiter, S., and others. *40 Million Americans in Career Transition.* New York: College Entrance Examination Board and Policy Studies in Education, 1978.

Astin, A. W. "College Preferences of Very Able Students." *College and University,* 1965, *40* (3), 282–297.

Astin, A. W. *Preventing Students from Dropping Out.* San Francisco: Jossey-Bass, 1975.

Astin, A. W. *Four Critical Years: Effects of College on Beliefs, Attitudes, and Knowledge.* San Francisco: Jossey-Bass, 1977.

Astin, A. W., King, M. R., and Richardson, G. T. *The American Freshman: National Norms for Fall 1977.* Los Angeles: Laboratory for Research in Higher Education, Graduate School of Education, University of California, and the Cooperative Institutional Research Program, American Council on Education, 1977.

Astin, A. W., King, M. R., and Richardson, G. T. *The American Freshman: National Norms for Fall 1978.* Los Angeles: Laboratory for Research in Higher Education, Graduate School of Education, University of California, and the Cooperative Institutional Research Program, American Council on Education, 1978.

Beck, N., and Park, E. *Institutional Functioning Questionnaire.* (Rev. ed.) Princeton, N.J.: Educational Testing Service, 1978.

Boyd, J. D., and Pennell, K. L. *National Association of State Scholarship and Grant Programs.* 10th Annual Survey. Deerfield, Ill.: National Association of State Scholarship and Grant Programs Survey, 1978–79.

Boyd, J. E., Fenske, R. J., and Maxey, E. J. "Trends in Meeting College Costs over the Past Ten Years." *Journal of Student Financial Aid,* 1978, *8* (3), 5–17.

Bracken, T. *Enrolling the Class of 1978: An Analysis of the 1974 Student Market at Twenty-Three Private Institutions.* Hanover, N.H.: Consortium on Financing Higher Education, 1975.

Bracken, T. *Enrolling the Class of 1979: Second Annual Report on the Student Market at Twenty-Three Private Institutions.* Hanover, N.H.: Consortium on Financing Higher Education, 1976.

Bracken, T. *Enrolling the Class of 1980: Third Annual Report on the Student Market at the Consortium Institutions.* Hanover, N.H.: Consortium on Financing Higher Education, 1977.

Carnegie Commission on Higher Education. *Less Time, More Options.* New York: McGraw-Hill, 1971.

Carnegie Council on Policy Studies in Higher Education. *Fair Practices in Higher Education: Rights and Responsibilities of Students and Their Colleges in a Period of Intensified Competition for Enrollments.* San Francisco: Jossey-Bass, 1979.

Carnegie Foundation for the Advancement of Teaching. *More than Survival: Prospects for Higher Education in a Period of Uncertainty.* San Francisco: Jossey-Bass, 1975.

Cartter, A. M. *Ph.D.s and the Academic Labor Market.* New York: McGraw-Hill, 1976.

Centra, J. A. *College Enrollment in the 1980s: Projections and Possibilities.* New York: College Entrance Examination Board, 1978.

Clark, B. R., and Trow, M. "The Organizational Context." In T. M. Newcomb and E. K. Wilson (Eds.), *College Peer Groups.* Chicago: Aldine, 1966.

Clark, B., and others. *Students and Colleges: Interactions and Change.* Berkeley: University of California, 1972.

Claudy, J. G. "Educational Outcomes Five Years After High School." Paper presented at annual meeting of the American Educational Research Association, New York City, 1971.

College Entrance Examination Board. *National Report: College Bound Seniors, 1978.* New York: Admission Testing Program of the College Board, College Entrance Examination Board, 1978.

Corwin, T. M., and Kent, L. (Eds.). *Tuition and Student Aid: Their Relation to College Enrollment Decisions.* Washington, D.C.: Policy Analysis Service, American Council on Education, 1978.

Doermann, H. "The Future Market for College Education." In *A Role for Marketing in College Admission: Papers Presented at the Colloquium on College Admissions, May 16–18, 1976, at the Abbey on Lake Geneva, Fontana, Wisconsin.* New York: College Entrance Examination Board, 1976.

Eddy, M. S. "Part-Time Students." In *Research Currents.* Vol. 30. Washington, D.C.: American Association for Higher Education, 1978.

Esenwein, G. A., and Karr, J. *A Report from the Library of Congress on the Tax Burden and the Increasing Cost of Higher Education.* Unpublished report requested by the House of Representatives

Subcommittee on Postsecondary Education. Washington, D.C., May 1978.

Feldman, K. A., and Newcomb, T. M. *The Impact of College on Students.* (2 Vols.) San Francisco: Jossey-Bass, 1969.

Fox, K. F. A. "Attracting a New Market to Northwestern's Undergraduate Programs: Older Women on the North Shore." Report to William Ihlanfeldt, Vice-President for Institutional Relations, Northwestern University, May 1979.

Geltzer, H., and Ries, A. "The Positioning Era: A Marketing Strategy for College Admission in the 1980s." In *A Role for Marketing in College Admission: Papers Presented at the Colloquium on College Admissions, May 16–18, 1976, at the Abbey on Lake Geneva, Fontana, Wisconsin.* New York: College Entrance Examination Board, 1976.

Golladay, M. A. *The Condition of Education: 1976 Edition.* Washington, D.C.: U.S. Government Printing Office, 1976.

Golladay, M. A., and Noel, J. *The Condition of Education: 1978 Edition.* Washington, D.C.: National Center for Education Statistics, 1978.

Gould, S. B., and Cross, K. P. (Eds.). *Explorations in Non-Traditional Study.* San Francisco: Jossey-Bass, 1972.

Grant, W. V., and Lind, C. G. *Digest of Education Statistics: 1976 Edition.* Washington, D.C.: U.S. Government Printing Office, 1977.

Gwinn, D. "Report on the 1975 Pre-Freshman Questionnaire." Unpublished report, Northwestern University, May 1976.

Hansen, J. S., Gladieux, L. E. *Middle-Income Students: A New Target for Federal Aid? Tax Credits and Student Assistance Programs.* New York: College Entrance Examination Board, 1978.

Henderson, C. *Changes in Enrollment by 1985.* Policy Analysis Service Reports, Vol. 3, No. 1. Washington, D.C.: American Council on Education, 1977.

Henderson, C., and Plummer, J. C. *Adapting to Changes in the Characteristics of College-Age Youth.* Policy Analysis Service Reports, Vol. 4, No. 2. Washington, D.C.: American Council on Education, 1978.

Ihlanfeldt, W. "A Management Approach to the Buyer's Market." *Liberal Education,* May, 1975, *41* (2), 133–148.

Illinois Board of Higher Education. Minutes of the board meeting. Springfield: Illinois Board of Higher Education, June 6, 1978.

Institute of International Education. *Open Doors.* Task Force Report. New York: Information and Counseling Division, Institute of International Education, 1978.

Institute for Services to Education, Inc. *Profile of Enrollment in the Historically Black Colleges.* Washington, D.C.: Institute for Services to Education, 1978.

Kotler, P. *Marketing for Nonprofit Organizations.* Englewood Cliffs, N.J.: Prentice-Hall, 1975.

Kotler, P. "Applying Marketing Theory to College Admission." In *A Role for Marketing in College Admission: Papers Presented at the Colloquium on College Admissions, May 16–18, 1976, at the Abbey on Lake Geneva, Fontana, Wisconsin.* New York: College Entrance Examination Board, 1976.

Kotler, P. "Strategies for Introducing Marketing into Nonprofit Organizations." *Journal of Marketing,* 1979, *43,* 37–44.

Lavin, D. E. *The Prediction of Academic Performance: A Theoretical Analysis and Review of Research.* New York: Russell Sage Foundation, 1965.

Life Insurance Marketing and Research Association. *College Costs.* Hartford, Conn.: Life Insurance Marketing and Research Association, 1979.

Luxenberg, S. "Education at A.T.&T." *Change Magazine.* December–January, 1978/79, *10* (11), 26–35.

Marquand, J. R. Letter to Dean Edgar F. Becham, North College, Wesleyan University, February 11, 1974.

Minter, W. J., and Bowen, H. R. *Independent Higher Education: Fourth Annual Report on Financial and Educational Trends in the Independent Sector of American Higher Education.* Washington, D.C.: National Association of Independent Colleges and Universities, 1978.

Nichols, R. *College Preferences of Eleventh Grade Students.* Vol. 2, No. 9. Research report. Evanston, Ill.: National Merit Scholarship Corporation, 1966.

"The 1980s: New Challenges, New Responsibilities." *College Board Review,* 1979, *112,* 16–17.

Noel, L. (Ed.). *New Directions for Student Services: Reducing the Dropout Rate*, no. 3. San Francisco: Jossey-Bass, 1978.

O'Neill, J. *Resource Use of Higher Education: Trends in Output and Inputs, 1930 to 1967*. Berkeley, Calif.: Carnegie Foundation for the Advancement of Teaching, 1971.

Pace, C. R. *College and University Environment and Experiences*. Los Angeles: Laboratory for Research on Higher Education, University of California, 1977.

Pantages, T. J., and Creedon, C. F. "Studies of College Attrition: 1960-1975." *Review of Educational Research*, 1978, *48* (1), 93-96.

Peng, S. S., and Fetter, W. B. "Variables Involved in Withdrawal During the First Two Years of College: Preliminary Findings from the National Longitudinal Study of the High School Class of 1972." *American Educational Research Journal*, 1978, *15* (3), 3-7.

Pepin, A. J. *1977 Fall Enrollment in Higher Education—Final Count*. Unpublished report. Washington, D.C.: University and College Surveys and Studies Branch, U.S. Department of Health, Education, and Welfare, 1978.

Pyke, D. L. "The Future of Higher Education: Will Private Institutions Disappear in the U.S.?" *The Futuristic Magazine*, December, 1977, *11* (6), 371-374.

Rivchun, S. "Motivation: The Art of Building a Winning Team." *Leadership Magazine*, May, 1979, pp. 25-30.

Roark, A. C. "Federal Student Aid and How It Grew." *Chronicle of Higher Education*, 1977, *15*, (6), p. 6

Sandage, D. H., and Fryburger, R. V. *Advertising Theory and Practice*. (9th ed.) Homewood, Ill.: Irwin, 1975.

Sidar, A. G., and Potter, D. A. *No-Need/Merit Awards*. New York: College Entrance Examination Board, 1978.

Spies, R. R. *The Effect of Rising Costs on College Choice*. New York: College Entrance Examination Board, 1978.

Spies, R. R. *The Future of Private Colleges: The Effect of Rising Costs on College Choice*. Princeton, N.J.: Industrial Relations Section Princeton University, 1973.

Tierney, M. L. "The Impact of Financial Aid on Student Demand for Public/Private Higher Education." Unpublished paper, Center for the Study of Higher Education, Pennsylvania State University, 1978.

"Trade Schools May Be 'Bargain.'" *Chicago Tribune,* July 29, 1979, p. 65.

Trent, J. W., and Medsker, L. L. *Beyond High School: A Psycho-sociological Study of 10,000 High School Graduates.* San Francisco: Jossey-Bass, 1968.

University of California, Berkeley, Academic Senate. *Education at Berkeley: Report of the Select Committee on Education.* Berkeley: University of California, 1966.

U.S. Bureau of the Census. "Projections of the Population of the United States, 1977 to 2050." Current Population Reports, Series P-25, No. 704. Washington, D.C.: U.S. Government Printing Office, 1977.

U.S. Congress, Congressional Budget Office. *Federal Aid To Post-secondary Students: Tax Allowances and Alternative Subsidies.* Washington, D.C.: Congressional Budget Office, 1978.

Vermilye, D. W. (Ed.). *Lifelong Learners—A New Clientele for Higher Education: Current Issues in Higher Education 1974.* San Francisco: Jossey-Bass, 1974.

Wayland, F. *Report to the Corporation of Brown University on Changes in the System of Collegiate Education, Read March 28, 1850.* Providence, R.I.: George H. Whitney, 1850.

"Why Business Takes Education into Their Own Hands." *U.S. News & World Report,* July 16, 1979, p. 70.

Index